JESUS CHRIST AND THE CHRISTIAN CHARACTER

AN EXAMINATION OF THE TEACHING OF JESUS IN
ITS RELATION TO SOME OF THE MORAL
PROBLEMS OF PERSONAL LIFE

BY

FRANCIS GREENWOOD PEABODY

PLUMMER PROFESSOR OF CHRISTIAN MORALS
IN HARVARD UNIVERSITY

*THE LYMAN BEECHER LECTURES
AT YALE UNIVERSITY
1904*

New York
THE MACMILLAN COMPANY
LONDON: MACMILLAN & CO., Ltd.

1905

Norwood Press
J. S. Cushing & Co. — Berwick & Smith Co.
Norwood, Mass., U.S.A.

MY DARLING BOY, SO EARLY SNATCHED AWAY
   FROM ARMS STILL SEEKING THEE IN EMPTY AIR,
THAT THOU SHOULDST COME TO ME I DO NOT PRAY,
   LEST, BY THY COMING, HEAVEN SHOULD BE LESS FAIR.

STAY, RATHER, IN PERENNIAL FLOWER OF YOUTH,
   SUCH AS THE MASTER, LOOKING ON, MUST LOVE;
AND SEND TO ME THE SPIRIT OF THE TRUTH,
   TO TEACH ME OF THE WISDOM FROM ABOVE.

BECKON TO GUIDE MY THOUGHTS, AS STUMBLINGLY
   THEY SEEK THE KINGDOM OF THE UNDEFILED;
AND MEET ME AT ITS GATEWAY WITH THY KEY, —
   THE UNSTAINED SPIRIT OF A LITTLE CHILD.

CONTENTS

vii

JESUS CHRIST AND THE CHRISTIAN CHARACTER

CHAPTER I

THE MODERN WORLD AND THE CHRISTIAN CHARACTER

In another volume[1] the teaching of Jesus has been considered in its relation to some of the problems of modern social life. It is an inquiry which, in one form or another, forces itself upon every mind which has, on the one hand, any reverence for the teaching of Jesus, and, on the other, any understanding of the present age. This is the age of the Social Question. Never before were so many people concerned with problems of social amelioration and programmes of social transformation; never before were social solutions so freely proposed or social panaceas so confidently prescribed. Social institutions which for centuries have been assumed to be rooted in human nature or ordained of God are frankly discussed as social expedients or experiments, to be reformed, transformed, or abolished. Is the institution of the family to survive the present movement toward

---

[1] "Jesus Christ and the Social Question," Macmillan, 1900.

disruption ?   Is the institution of private property
to be maintained among the economic changes of
the future ?   Is the new social order to arrive by
peaceful processes of evolution, or must the pain
and travail of social revolution attend the birth
of a better world? — such are the questions which
confront all thoughtful persons who observe the
signs of the times.

A similar change in the centre of gravity is
to be observed within the Christian Church.
Where the mind of the Church was once absorbed
by questions of doctrine, it is now devoted to
questions of practice ; and instead of a survival of controversies concerning God, there is a
revival of devotion to the service of man.   Christian convocations which were once preoccupied
with definitions of orthodoxy and refutations of
heresy are now discussing the relation of the
Church to the family, the duty of the Church to
the hand-workers, the application of the Church
to philanthropy, the missionary opportunity of the
Church.   A distinguished preacher of the last
generation, being asked whether Christianity was
outgrown, answered that, on the contrary, it had
never been tried.   The present age is making this
trial of Christianity.   The mighty wind of the
Social Question has swept through the Church, as
through the world, with cleansing and refreshing
force, and has swept away the barriers which once
divided worship from work, the single life from
the social order, the love of God from the love of

man, the salvation of the soul from the salvation of the world. It is the age of the Social Question.[1]

At such a time one is inevitably led to examine afresh the teaching of Jesus, and to consider the applicability of that teaching to modern social life. Has a teacher so remote from the circumstances of the modern world any message to give which that world should hear? Is there in the Gospels, besides their personal and religious inspiration, a social teaching which is still timely and significant? Many a modern mind which had almost abandoned interest in the Christian religion is drawn back to it by such questions as these. The theology of Christianity has lost its grasp on great numbers of such lives; the ecclesiastical claims of the various sects have become simply uninteresting; the piety of the Christian mystic has retreated before the demands of the busy world; but the world itself, with its unredeemed masses, its unsolved problems, its cry for help, is of unprecedented and dramatic concern; and those who stand, as it were, on the shore of the present age and watch the social life of the time, drifting like a rudderless vessel without course or helmsman, turn with a pathetic eager-

[1] So, Kidd, "Social Evolution," 1894, pp. 13, 14: "We are beginning to hear from many quarters that the social question is at bottom a religious question, and that to its solution it behoves the Churches in the interests of society to address themselves. . . . We have the note sounded in various keys, that, after all, Christianity was intended to save not only men but man, and that its mission should be to teach us not only how to die as individuals but how to live as members of society."

ness to Jesus Christ, as to a pilot who is at home in this uncharted and perilous sea.

When one turns with this new problem to the Gospels, he discovers with fresh surprise the extraordinary richness and variety of the teaching of Jesus. Each period in history goes with its question to the simple record, and finds an answer which seems written to meet the special problem of the time. In an age of theology the Gospels were a source of theological doctrine; in an age of ecclesiasticism they fortified the Church; in an age of emotionalism they kindled the flame of piety. The same adaptability is now discovered once more by the age of the Social Question. As others have found in the teaching of Jesus the key of doctrine or organization or religious experience, so there is now delivered by the same teaching to the mind of the present age a key of the Social Question. Remote from the condition of the modern world as was the life of Jesus, and primarily directed as was his teaching, not to social but to spiritual ends, he has much to say of social duty. His ethics are not individualist, atomic, a doctrine of the single soul; but organic, social, a doctrine of the common life.

This characteristic gives, indeed, to the whole Bible its freshness, contemporaneousness, and applicability. The Bible is not only a book of life, but a book of life in common. "The Bible," said John Wesley, "knows nothing of a solitary religion." The stream of the Bible story flows not only through quiet places of personal experience, but also through a world of social relationships, as a great river runs through changing scenes of town and country, society and solitude, light and shade. One who embarks on its current finds himself floating down through political changes, national problems, social reforms, the sins and repentances of Israel, the needs and hopes of the Gentile world, until at last this social teaching issues into the broad, calm current of the message of Jesus Christ. It was not an accident, therefore, that when Jesus announced the purpose of his mission, he defined it in the language of the ancient but still effective Law;[1] still less was it an accident that this law was social as well as religious, the love of one's neighbor as well as the love of God; least of all was it an accident that Jesus said of these two laws, one religious, and one social, that the second was like the first. The social teaching of Jesus was the corollary from his religious faith. The love of God involved the love of one's neighbor as one's self.

In one of the most striking of his parables Jesus commits himself unreservedly to this social mission. Standing among the grain fields of Palestine, which had often seemed to him the symbol of his work, he speaks not only of the grain, the soil, and the sower, but of the scope and horizon of his hope. The field, he says, is not restricted, fenced in, local, national; the

[1] Deut. vi. 5; and Lev. xix. 18.

field is the world.[1]   His message is not personal
only, as in the parable of the soil and the seed,
but comprehensive, expansive, universal.   Beyond
the Palestinian valleys, beyond the mountains that
shut in the North, and the strip of sea touched
with the Western light, stretched the field of his
social dream.   " Neither pray I for these alone,"
says the fourth Gospel in the same spirit, "but
for them also which shall believe on me through
their word.   For their sakes I sanctify myself."[2]   It
was the comprehensive, generous dream of a consecrated society.   The field is the world.[3]

It may be not unreasonably urged that, in this
transfer of interest, there is grave danger of mis-
interpreting the teaching of Jesus.   He was, we
are reminded, not a social agitator, but a religious
teacher; not a reformer, but a Revealer; not primarily concerned with social conditions, but with the
life of God in the soul of man.   His social ideal was
not of an industrial order, but of a Kingdom of
God.   Whatever his social teaching may have been,
it was but a by-product of his religious mission.
All this is obviously true; and no misinterpretation of the Gospels is more superficial than that
which describes the work of Jesus as essentially that
of a labor leader, an anarchist, or a social revolutionist.[4]   It must be remembered, however, that a

[1] Matt. xiii. 38.   [2] John xvii. 19, 20.
[3] Compare also *Homiletic Review*, May, 1904, pp. 330 ff.   F. G.
Peabody, " The Social Teaching of Jesus Christ."
[4] Renan, " Marc-Aurèle," 1882, p. 598 : " Le christianisme

by-product, though in itself subordinate, may have peculiar adaptability to certain conditions and needs; and even though the social teaching of Jesus be not his supreme concern, it may be an aspect of his message which for the moment claims attention. There are many paths which lead to the understanding of Jesus; but the path of his social teaching is, for the present age, the path which is most open. Here is where the thought of the time happens to be. The foreground of human interest is for the present occupied by social problems, and the way to any contemporary interpretation of the Christian religion is not to be found by going round the Social Question, but by going through it. It is, therefore, quite superfluous to consider whether there may not be other ways which might lead more directly to the truth of the Gospels. What must be frankly recognized is the fact that a new way of approach is

fut, avant tout, une immense révolution économique." "Vie de Jésus," 13th edition, 1867, p. 133: "Une immense révolution sociale, ou les rangs seront intervertis, . . . voilà son rêve." So, Nitti, "Catholic Socialism," 1895, pp. 58 ff.: "Poverty was an indispensable condition for gaining admission to the kingdom of heaven." Rade, "Die sittlich-religiöse Gedankenwelt unsrer Industrie-Arbeiter," 9th Evang. Soz. Kongress, 1898, ss. 103 ff.: "Christ was a revolutionist, like thousands now living." "A true friend of working people, not with lips alone, like his followers, but with deeds." "He was persecuted as the Social Democrats are persecuted now." "To-day he would have been the greatest of socialists." Compare H. Köhler, "Sozialistische Irrlehren von der Entstehung des Christentums," 1899, ss. 9–16; and F. G. Peabody, "Jesus Christ and the Social Question," p. 26, note; p. 65.

prescribed by the conditions of the time. Other paths open before the thought of other generations ; but straight before the age of the Social Question lies the social teaching of Jesus Christ. The modern mind must start from the point where it is, and must proceed by its own path to its own form of Christian loyalty and service.

When, however, one frankly commits himself to this recognition of social redemption as the immediate problem, both of the world and of the Church, a further question presents itself to which the age of the Social Question is now called to reply. Though it be true, as the title of a book, which is itself a sign of the times, affirms, that the world is the subject of redemption,[1] it is still left to inquire what shall be the means of that redemption, and what instrument of social service can be permanently effective. Here is a question which must be answered before a campaign of social service can be wisely undertaken. It is in vain to enter upon a modern war until one is . equipped with modern weapons. It is impossible to redeem the world without a well-considered plan of redemption. What, then, is the weapon of social amelioration which must be antecedently provided before the age of the Social Question can fulfil its task ?

No sooner does one ask this question than he is confronted by two theories of social progress,

[1] Fremantle, " The World as the Subject of Redemption," 2d edition, 1895.

which are often regarded as irreconcilable competitors. Social amelioration may be sought, on the one hand, through external, mechanical, and economic change; or, on the other hand, through spiritual, ethical, personal renewal. It is the perennial issue between environment and personality, the world and the individual. Does the world make the person, or does the person make his world? Is personality the product of circumstances or are circumstances the instrument of personality? Is the secret of social progress to be found in better social conditions, or are such conditions unredemptive unless met by better men?

The first answer now offered to this question is the answer of externalism. The Social Question has been interpreted as a consequence of external maladjustments, and relief has been sought by revolutionizing the conditions which are dehumanizing and unjust. How can people, it is asked, become better in character, if they are not better fed and housed and clad? How can the soul be saved if the body is starved? The Social Question, it is urged, is a "Stomach Question." "*Man ist was er isst.*" Conditions create character. Change the conditions of industrial life, establish a living wage, supplant the rule of the capitalist by the rule of the hand-worker, create circumstances fit for a human life, and the better human life will spring out of the better soil.

This answer of externalism was soon fortified

by the philosophy of socialism. The spiritual
condition of any civilization, it was taught, is
the corollary of its economic system. Given the
industrial order of a land or time, and one may
prophesy what shall be its ethics or art or
domestic life or religion. Character is the product
of circumstances. Social revolution must precede
ethical progress. "Religion is a mirror in which
is reflected the prevailing social condition. As
society develops religion is transformed. . . .
Both religious and moral conceptions spring from
the contemporary circumstances of human life." [1]
"The bourgeois moralist . . . holds fast to the
old fallacious standpoint, according to which individual good men make healthy social conditions, rather than acknowledge the truth that it is
healthy social conditions which make good men." [2]
Abolish, therefore, the institution of private property, transform the machinery of society, emanci-
pate women from domestic bondage; and from
the new circumstances thus created will emerge
new moral capacity, as surely as the moral degradation and social discontent of the present time
have been the consequences of the competitive
system.[3]

[1] Bebel, "Die Frau und der Sozialismus," 1891, ss. 314, 315.

[2] Bax, "The Religion of Socialism," 1886, p. x: "Socialism breaks
through these shams in protesting that no amount of determination
on the part of the individual to regenerate himself . . . will of
itself affect in aught the welfare of Society."

[3] Marx, "Zur Kritik der polit. Oekonomie," 1859, Vorwort,
s. xi: "The form of material production is the general cause of

There is unquestionably much in the modern world which appears to justify this application to society of the philosophy of materialism. Many conditions of modern life are almost prohibitive of morality. Precepts of chastity are mocking words to dwellers in one-room tenements; exhortations to patience find few listeners when children are hungry and work is slack. Many processes of modern industry convert the worker into a de-humanized fragment of the machine at which he works. The moralization of industry is an essential part of the Social Question. It does not, however, follow from these solemn facts that the only key of social progress must be found in external changes, or that favoring conditions are sure to make good men. On the contrary, most great transitions in social welfare have occurred, not through mechanical, external, or economic changes,

social, political, and spiritual processes. It is not consciousness which determines conditions, but, on the contrary, social conditions which determine consciousness." Compare Bernstein, " Die Voraussetzungen des Sozialismus," 1899, s. 5; and Masaryk, " Die phil. und sociol. Grundlagen des Marxismus," 1899, s. 93. So also J. A. Hobson, " The Social Problem," 1901, p. 140: " To preach that each individual can, by his own private conduct, contribute to the solution of a social problem is a barren gospel." C. H. Kerr, " The Central Thing in Socialism," p. 1 : " Tell me *how you get* what you eat and I will tell you what you are. In other words, the laws and customs of a people in any stage whatever, . . . grow out of the way in which the people get their food, clothing, and shelter." The issue is clearly described by Arndt, " Die Religion der Sozialde-mokratie," 1892, ss. 9 ff., with many references. See also " Jesus Christ and the Social Question," p. 18, with references.

but through personal initiative, moral or intellectual leadership, mastery of circumstances by force of character. The story of Christianity, of Protestantism, of Greece, of Germany, of New England, is not one of favoring conditions accepted, but of hostile conditions conquered, the victory of the mind or will or conscience over the flesh or the world.

If this be true of history, it is still more obviously true of the social movement which characterizes the present age. The social ferment of the time is most inadequately described when it is regarded as the sheer consequence of evil conditions, or as proceeding altogether from material desires; and it is one of the most unfortunate accidents of history that a philosophy derived from Neo-Hegelian materialism should have filtered down into the popular creed and have obscured the real nature of the working-class movement.[1] What gives pathos and power to the modern Social Question is not the economic programme which it proposes, but the human note which it utters, of sympathy, pity, justice, brotherhood, unity. The sense of discontent is most conspicuous, not where

[1] F. Engels, " Ludwig Feuerbach u. der Ausgang der deutschen klassischen Philosophie," 1888, s. 68: "The German workingmen's movement is the heir of the German classic philosophy." Schäffle, "The Impossibility of Social Democracy," tr. 1892, pp. 32, 33: "Its philosophy is in reality the offspring of the subjective speculation of Hegel. Three important Socialists were followers of this philosopher's school, Marx, Lassalle, and Proudhon. . . . But the grass has long grown upon the grave of Hegelianism."

social conditions are at their worst, but where they are at their best; not in Turkey and Egypt, but in Western Europe and the United States. It is not an evidence that people have less, but an evidence that they think and feel more. It proceeds, not from the decrease of possessions, but from the increase of desires. The Social Question is the demand of human beings for a more humanized life, a "*Menschenwürdiges Dasein.*" It is the protest of character against conditions, rather than the pressure of conditions on character. Within the Social Question, that is to say, mechanical and material though it may seem to be, lie ethical questions of duty, compassion, humanity, service, which are the signs, not of a degenerating social order, but of a regenerated social conscience. The truth of history is precisely reversed when it is affirmed that economic changes must invariably precede moral progress. Ethical education, personal character, and intellectual initiative are much more likely to create the demand for social change. The Social Question meets civilization, not on its way down but on its way up.

There is a further aspect of the modern situation which is equally significant. The special attention which has been for two generations devoted to external and mechanical progress, whether in industry or politics, philanthropy or religion, has had as its result a disproportionate development of machinery and of men. "This faith in mechanism," said Carlyle, in 1829, "has now struck

its roots deep into men's most intimate, primary
sources of conviction. . . . By arguing on the
force of circumstances we have argued all force
from ourselves and stand leashed together, uniform
in dress and movement, like the rowers of some
boundless galley." [1] Organizations, consolidations,
combinations, federations, we have in prodigal
abundance, and the wheels of the social world
revolve with a speed and smoothness never before
attained; but the age of machinery has brought
with it a new demand for persons competent to
control the intricate mechanism of a new world.
Civilization has had the skill to harness social
forces which it has not had the time to tame; and
it is by no means certain whether the present age
can control the runaway steeds which it is com-
pelled to drive. The pace of modern life demands
at every point new alertness, new sobriety, new
integrity, in those who administer its affairs; and
the need of the time is not so much for better
social machinery as for competent social engineers.
A science of poor-relief has been devised, but where
are the persons equipped with the sagacity and
sympathy to utilize that science? Vast aggrega-
tions of capital are created, but where are the dis-
interestedness and integrity to convert new forms
of industry into new instruments of social peace?
An army of hand-workers is organized for war, but
where is the incorruptible leadership without which
an army becomes a mob?

[1] "Signs of the Times," Miscellaneous Essays, II, 162, 168.

In Plato's famous parable[1] of spiritual experience, two horses, one "noble and of noble origin," the other "ignoble and of ignoble origin," draw the chariot of the soul. One steed is ever eager to mount, the other wishes to descend, and the charioteer who guides these divergent passions keeps his course by fixing his eye on the "colorless, formless, and intangible essence . . . which is the only lord of the soul." Looking up to his ideal, the driver controls his errant steeds; and "feeding on the sight of truth is replenished." It is a picture of the conflicting forces which threaten disaster to the hurrying life of the modern world, if the soul of the time shall fail to master the forces which it is called upon to drive. The Social Question is not one of alternative theories of progress, as though one must choose between horses without reins or a driver without steeds. It is a question of controlling the mechanism of the age by strength of the spirit. In its form it is an economic question, a question of chariots and harness; but in its essence it is ethical, a question of personal capacity and idealism. Circumstances wait on character. Machinery is the instrument of power. Social progress has for its charioteer the conscience of the age. Better methods may simplify the Social Question, it can be solved by nothing less than better men. "We are idealists," wrote Schiller to von Humboldt, "and should be ashamed to have it

[1] "Phædrus," tr. Jowett, 1871, I, 580 ff.

said of us that we did not form things, but that things formed us." [1]   The whole creation of modern society, as the Apostle Paul said of the world of nature, groaneth and travaileth in pain, waiting for the revealing of the sons of God.

At this point, where the Social Question opens into the question of character, we meet, once more, the teaching of Jesus Christ.   Concerning the machinery of the world he has little instruction to give.   His teaching is misapplied when utilized as a manual of social mechanics.   Even his own social ideal of the Kingdom of God, is not for him, in form or method, to define.   " Of that day and hour knoweth no man, no, not the angels of heaven, but my Father only." [2]   When, however, we inquire for the instrument of social redemption, the teaching of Jesus becomes explicit and undisguised. His care is for the person.   He has what has been called a passion for personality.   He is concerned, not with devising ways of social redemption, but with creating people applicable to social redemption.   The Kingdom is the end of his desire, but the person is a means to that end.   First character, then usefulness ; first persons fit for the Kingdom, then the better world,— that is the method of Jesus. The field of his purpose, according to his parable, is the world ; but the good seed which is to possess and fertilize that world, are the children of the Kingdom.   These are they who shall take com-

---

[1] Sime, " Schiller," 1882, p. 212.
[2] Matt. xxiv. 36; Mark xiii. 32.

mand of circumstances and, like strong, productive seed, crowd down the tares by their superior vitality.

The teaching of Jesus, therefore, even when its form is social, is fundamentally personal. Out from behind the Social Question emerges the antecedent problem of the Christian character. It is for others to plough and harrow the field of the world, to arrange its schemes of work and wages, of politics and reform; the mission of Jesus is to create a type of character which shall be sown like good seed in the waiting field and possess it as children of the Kingdom. The more commanding the Social Question grows, the more essential becomes this demand for people fit to meet that question. The more intricate is the machinery of the world, the more competent must be its engineers. At every point the Social Question drives one back to the antecedent question of character; from the acquisition of goods to the need of goodness; from the problem of cheapening the product of labor to the problem of raising the standard of men; from things to life; from the thought of the world as a factory to the thought of the world as a field, where the good seed are the children of the Kingdom. The problem of other centuries was that of saving people from the world; the problem of the present century is that of making people fit to save the world.[1]

[1] E. Grimm, "Die Ethik Jesu," 1903, ss. 1, 2, 3: "Out of the Social Question rises more and more distinctly a new and ethical

If, then, the study of the Social Question opens as by an inner door into the interior problem of the Christian character, it becomes of peculiar interest to follow the teaching of Jesus as it thus enters the region of personal morality. What are the traits which he is most concerned to inculcate? By what kind of persons is the service of the world to be effectively undertaken? What is the way of growth, and what are the consequences of the Christian character? Is the character trained in the way of Jesus Christ fit to meet the demands of the present age?·

Such an inquiry would seem to be peculiarly free from difficulty. It appears to lie on the very surface of history and to require no venture into the depths of criticism or speculation. Nothing would seem to be more easily determined than the kind of character which is inspired and exemplified by Jesus Christ. The type is derived directly from the Master's principles and practice, and these are reported to us with vivid and unconscious picturesqueness in the plain narratives of the first three Gospels. Whatever other material offers itself for such an inquiry must be regarded as of subordinate importance. The fourth Gospel

question . . . What did Jesus desire and what did he teach?" George Harris, "Moral Evolution," 1896, p. 244: "Another characteristic of the personal ideal of Christian ethics remains to be noticed. It proceeds from the individual to society rather than from society to the individual. . . . Christianity deals directly with individuals rather than with institutions and tendencies."

moves in a region of exalted speculation which
lies for the most part quite above the zone of
ethics, and the reader, as he enters it, feels a
climatic change of environment and intention.
One may believe that he hears at certain points
the echo of an independent tradition, but this
impression is trustworthy only as it is confirmed
by the Synoptic record.[1] The Book of Acts is
primarily concerned with the expansion of the
new faith, and the ethical enthusiasms and sacrifices of the little company of believers are but
incidents along the way. In the Epistles of Paul,
it is true, a series of precepts concerning practical
morality appear as corollaries of his speculative
theology. "Therefore," he says, "Wherefore,"
as though the logic of his dialectics brought him
to the maxims of his ethics; yet here also the

[1] O. Holtzmann, "Leben Jesu," 1901, ss. 34, 35: "So remote an
interpretation and working over of tradition should, preferably, not
be used as a historical source. . . . Yet the stream of Apostolic
report might bring with it much which the Synoptists had not
appreciated." Stevens, "Teaching of Jesus," 1901, p. 30: "Unlike
the Synoptic tradition, it is not so much a report of Jesus' words
and deeds, as a reproduction of the meaning which his person and
work had assumed for one who had long lived in the mystic contemplation . . . of his saving power." "Encyclopædia Britannica,"
E. A. Abbott, Art., Gospels: "Independently, therefore, of its intrin-
sic value, John is important as being in effect the earliest commentary
on the Synoptics." Warschauer, "The Problem of the Fourth Gospel," 1903: "The Jesus of the Synoptics is chiefly a great teacher
of applied religion, the Jesus of the Fourth Gospel is a theological
figure, expanding himself under a variety of thought-allegories, as
bread, the door, the vine, etc., all of which are without parallel
in the first three Gospels."

ethical teaching is subordinated to the main intention of clarifying and universalizing the revelation
of God in Christ.   When we turn back to the first
three Gospels the scene changes.   The atmosphere
is ethical.   Instead of the mystic heights of the
fourth Gospel, or the obscure depths of Pauline
theology, one enters, as it were, a region of homes
and fields, of natural and familiar experiences, and
through this rolling country, with its varied vocations, its joys and pains, its happiness and temptations, among old and young, rich and poor, good
and bad, walks the Teacher of the higher righteousness, showing by words of blessing and deeds of
mercy the way that men should go.   The Synoptic
Gospels are in their primary intention not the ex-
position of a doctrine, but the narrative of a life.
Whatever further disclosures they may make of
the relation of that life to God are inferences from
the narrative rather than its conscious aim.   Whatever else may be in debate concerning the life of
Jesus, the character which he illustrates and commends seems to be beyond dispute.   Profounder
problems may be left to the learned to explore,
but the Beatitudes, the Parables, the grave, compelling, gracious Master, bidding men of imperfect
faith and halting decision follow him — these
aspects of the record are for the unlearned to
appreciate and obey.   It seems a simple task to
detach from other questions of interpretation the
ethical teaching of Jesus, and to contemplate the
Master as he unfolds the principles of the Christian

character. The first three Gospels are like a sea-beach, where one may note the ebb and flow of the tides of the spirit and the many fragmentary reminiscences which are thrown up by the unconscious waves; but where, along the shore, runs a high-water mark, indicating by its indisputable evidence how far into the continent of truth the flood-tide has at least once made its way.[1]

This plain inquiry into the ethics of the Gospels is, however, met by unexpected obstacles. The approach to the message of Jesus by way of his ethical teaching is not, as might be anticipated, the path habitually followed by the most competent guides; but is, on the contrary, a comparatively untravelled way. Instead of finding one's self on the main road of Biblical study, one is surprised

---

[1] So, W. Knight, "The Christian Ethic," 1893, p. ix: "There can be no doubt that the teaching of the Founder of Christianity was primarily moral teaching." Bruce, "With Open Face," 1896, p. 184: "Note the first general thesis: ethics before religion. This was fundamentally in our Lord's teaching enforced with much emphasis and due reiteration." A. Thoma, "Gesch. der christl. Sittenlehre," 1879, ss. 134, 136: "The teaching of Jesus is specifically ethics, not religion, . . . yet the ethics of Jesus are penetrated by his religion." Wernle, "Die Anfänge unserer Religion," 1901, s. 58: "In the first three Gospels we hear nothing of great words like redemption, atonement, justification, regeneration; yet every reader realizes that the companions of Jesus were lifted into a life of supreme, spiritual joy." Fairbairn, "Philosophy of the Christian Religion," 1902, p. 565: "Would it not have been to the infinite advantage of the religion if these Councils had concerned themselves as much with the ethics as with the metaphysics of the person of Christ?"

to observe that he has left the path pursued by the great majority of New Testament scholars, and must proceed in large part alone. This meagre travel along the road of ethics is not difficult to explain. It is a striking evidence of the overmastering interest which through all the centuries of Christian thought has been felt in the theology of the New Testament. Practical morality, the conduct of life, the traits of the Christian character, have seemed too elementary and obvious subjects of inquiry to command the attention of scholars. What they have sought is a background for morality, a metaphysics of religion, the satisfaction of the thirst of the mind for the living God. To define the place of Jesus in God's plan for humanity, and the place of humanity in God's plan for eternity, has been the absorbing passion of the theological habit of mind. From this habit of mind has issued what may be called a dramatic rather than an ethical conception of the Christian religion. A vast world-drama appears to unfold its plan, from the first act of creation to the climax of redemption, and when the spectator of this scheme of universal love is called to consider the details of personal character, it may well seem a trifling, if not a sacrilegious interruption. It is that sense of deprivation and regret which the disciples felt when they were bidden to go down from the mount of transfiguration; a descent to the valley of commonplace, when one has seen the vision on the heights. The theology of the New Testament invites us to the large horizon of God; the ethics of the New Testament calls us down to the common people and the demoniac boy.

Even the science of Christian ethics, which by its very name would appear to be a study of the Christian character, has been generally regarded, not as a plain, inductive inquiry concerning the ethics of Jesus Christ, but as a chapter in the history of dogma. Christian ethics, it has been remarked, was treated by the earlier theology as the step-child of Christian dogma; a Cinderella whom the proud sisters, theology and philosophy, might patronize or neglect.[1] It would be more just to say that Christian ethics has itself undertaken the part of a proud sister and has sought the gay company of the speculative theologians, instead of remaining contentedly at the fireside of fact. Nothing could be more remote from the form of teaching which prevails in the first three Gospels than the erudite discussions of many a

[1] A. Thoma, "Geschichte der christl. Sittenlehre," 1879, s. 1: "Die christliche Sittenlehre wurde von den alten Theologen in Verbindung mit der Glaubenslehre als deren Gefolge behandelt; und begreiflicherweise sehr stiefmütterlich; aber dies nachgeborene und vernachlässigte Stiefkind, das Aschenbrödel der christlichen Lehrwissenschaft, wurde nachgerade auch mündig, und erweist sich wohl als das dankbarste für eine aufmerksame Pflege. Ja, es wäre kein Schade wenn es die Stelle der vorgezogenen Schwester einnähme und das Lieblingskind der Mutter Theologie würde, ist es doch das echteste Geisteskind des Christentums, wie dessen Urgeschichte nachweist."

treatise on Christian ethics. Instead of concrete problems of experience, we are confronted by elaborate discussions of the being of God, the nature of evil, and the doctrine of the Highest Good, which approach the facts of conduct from so distant a point, and with such leisureliness of movement, that the modern world cannot wait for their tardy arrival. A revival of simplicity, a discarding of the fine attire of theology, and a return to the teaching of Jesus, seem essential if Christian ethics is to have a hearing from the present age. Meantime, the monumental works which were the pride of one generation are for the most part consigned by the following generation to those upper shelves where, like the early Christians in the catacombs, repose the honored remains of our dead literature.[1]

[1] It is instructive to observe the various relations which have been proposed between Christian ethics and Christian theology. I. Ethics a corollary of dogmatics. Dorner, " System of Christian Ethics," tr. Mead, 1887, begins with Creation. Division I: "The order of the world as fixed by God at creation, antecedent to the moral process." So, p. 5: " Ethics cannot be called the foundation of dogmatics, but stands to dogmatics in a relation of dependence." So, Martensen, " Christian Ethics," tr. Spence, 1873, of which Gass (Geschichte d. Ch. Ethik, 1887, III, 304) remarks: " Martensen's method is like a three-arched hall approached through a row of columns." (" Martensen konnte daher nicht ohne Propyläen in den dreifach gewölbten Saal seiner Wissenschaft eintreten.") Section I: " Postulates of Christian Ethics, theological, anthropological, cosmopological, eschatological," pp. 61–140: " Dogmatics is the firstborn and thus enjoys the higher dignity." So, Wuttke, " Christian Ethics," tr. Lacroix, 1873, p. 21: " Ethics forms a part of systematic theology, . . . and has dogmatics as its immediate presupposi-

It should not be hastily concluded that this absorbing interest in the theology of Christianity

tion." Newman Smyth, "Christian Ethics," 1892, p. 13: "Christian ethics naturally follows Christian theology."

2. A second alternative is proposed by approaching Christian ethics, not through dogmatic theology, but through ethical philosophy. Hermann Weiss, "Einleitung in die christl. Ethik," 1889, § 6, I, "Of ideas in general"; II, "Of the idea of goodness," § 7, I, "Goodness and the good in general"; II, "The relation of goodness to the world of man and nature." (Earlier literature of various tendencies is indicated, s. 40, note.)

3. A third adjustment is made by fusing ethics with theology, in a "System of Christian Doctrine," as in Rothe, "Theologische Ethik," 1845, § 5: "It will always be an impracticable venture to discriminate theological ethics from theology."

4. All these academic undertakings overlook the modest path which begins in an inductive inquiry concerning the moral type commended and illustrated in the New Testament. Such an examination presupposes no preliminary speculation concerning the nature of God, or the Highest Good, but begins with the obvious facts of duty-doing, and proceeds to the implications which these facts suggest. A foreshadowing of such a method is made in the "Moral Proof" of Kant ("Critique of Practical Reason," tr. Abbott, 1883, p. 360: "We may divide all religions into two classes — favour-seeking religion (mere worship), and moral religion, that is, the religion of a good life "); in the "Theology of experience" of Schleiermacher, "Die Christliche Sitte," 1843, ss. 12, 13: "To expound the idea of the Kingdom of God is to expound the law of Christian conduct, and this is nothing else than Christian ethics." s. 17: "If we assume that the original characteristic of Christianity is a way of life, we must present the doctrine of Christianity as a unit, of which ethics is the foundation and dogma is the corollary "; and again in Ritschl's "Theology without metaphysics " ("Lehre der Rechtfertigung und Versöhnung," 1888, III, 415): "A scientific understanding of the relations of Jesus as expressed in his religious conception appears attainable only by assuming that we have understood his historical and human manifestations ; that is, have perceived its ethical con-

has been misdirected or superfluous.   On the contrary, it may be more justly described as inevitable.

sistency and law." So also, Kaftan, " Wahrheit der christl. Religion,"
1888, s. 383 : " The question is whether the will or the intellect naturally takes the lead (von Haus aus das Regiment führt).   It is no
difficult question.   The primacy of the will is so obvious that it can
hardly be proved."   So, Pfleiderer, " Moral und Religion," 1872,
s. 214 : "Ethics, in its manifestations in a moral world, is independent
of religion and antecedent to the religious expressions of the
Church."   Baur, " Christenthum der ersten drei Jahrhunderte,"
1860, s. 35 : " This ethical note which is heard in the simple phrases
of the Sermon on the Mount is the purest and most unmistakable
element in the teaching of Jesus and the essential core of Chris-
tendom."   Ehrhardt, " Der Grundcharakter der Ethik Jesu," 1895,
s. 106: "The essence of the character of Jesus is not in his vision
of the Eternal, but the loving sacrifice of his devotion to the humblest human needs."

The systematic acceptance of this inductive procedure is, however, a modern incident in the history of Christian ethics.   Thus
Jacoby (" Neutestamentliche Ethik," 1899) remarks (s. VI), that
but one book, that of Thoma (cited above), is known to him as
anticipating his treatment.   "The present work may claim to be
the first to present the ethics of the New Testament in scientific
form."   So, A. Thoma, s. 3 : " A specific treatment of the history of
Christian morality in its original expression does not, to my knowledge, exist."   Of special significance is the address at the 14th
Evang.-soz. Kong., 1903, W. Herrmann, " Die sittlichen Gedanken
Jesu in ihrem Verhältnis zu der sittlich-sozialen Lebensbewegung
der Gegenwart" (reprinted and expanded in "Die sittlichen
Weisungen Jesu," 1904), s. 12: " We can continue to be Christians only by recognizing in our contemporary and inevitable condition of morals and manners the fulfilment of the purpose of
Jesus Christ."   s. 29 : " The ethical ideas of Jesus are incontestably
the essential element of the spiritual experiences of the modern
world."   The discussion was continued in 1904 (15ter Evang.-soz.
Kong., 1904) by Troeltsch, " Die christl. Ethik und die heutige Ge-
sellschaft" (supplementing, as Rade points out (s. 51), the Paper

Nothing, after all, is of such permanent worth as a rational interpretation of the universe. The mind

of Herrmann). To the same effect, E. Grimm, "Die Ethik Jesu," 1903, s. 4: "There was a time when ethics was almost devoured by dogmatics. . . . All this has radically changed. . . . The more the dogmatic element recedes in interest the more the ethical element is emphasized." Gallwitz, "Das Problem der Ethik," 1891, s. 272, "The moral significance and uniqueness of the person of Christ is discerned in his illuminating the dark problems of morality which confront the present and the future, and which find their solution only in the light proceeding from his person." Wellhausen, "Israel. und Jüd. Gesch.," 5te Ausg., 1904, s. 386: "Christianity has a wholly different root from Judaism. The contrast of Jew and Gentile withers and the moral contrast takes its place. . . . Good and evil are two distinct worlds. . . . Moral responsibility gets the chief emphasis." See also, O. Holtzmann, "Leben Jesu," 1901, Kap. IX, X; Bonhoff, "Christentum und sittl.-soz. Lebensfragen," 1900, Kap. IV, "Die Religion Jesu Christi als Kraftquelle der Sittlichkeit"; Feddersen, "Jesus und die sozialen Dinge," 1902 (a protest against excessive emphasis on the social teaching, ss. 107 ff.); Otto, "Leben und Wirken Jesu," 1902, ss. 47 ff.

Of literature to the same purpose in English may be mentioned: "Ecce Homo," 1866, Ch. IX, "Reflections on the Nature of Christ's Society," p. 100: "The object of the Divine Society is that God's will may be done on earth as it is done in heaven. In the language of our own day, its object was the improvement of morality." Phillips Brooks, "The Influence of Jesus," 1879, Lect. I, "The Influence of Jesus on the Moral Life of Man," p. 14: "To tell men that they were, and to make them actually be, the sons of God, — that was the purpose of the coming of Jesus, and the shaping power of His life." Martineau, "A Study of Religion," 1888, I, 16 ff.: "Why Ethics before Religion." See also his "Faith and Self-Surrender," 1897. W. S. Bruce, "The Formation of Christian Character," 1902, p. ix: "The chief contribution of Jesus Christ to the Social Problem is the production of spiritual personality. In the Christian Character He provides that element of social progress of which the world stands most in need." Harris, "Moral Evolution," 1896,

of man is unsatisfied until it contemplates the thought of God. " Thou hast formed us for Thyself," said Augustine, "and our hearts are restless till they find rest in Thee."[1] The criticism which the present age has to make on the ages of theology is not that they have gone too far, but that they have gone too fast. They have scaled

p. 392 : " In the order of time Christian doctrine followed Christian ethics. Jesus was a moral teacher." G. B. Stevens, " The Teaching of Jesus," 1901, Ch. XI, p. 130: "The religion which Jesus taught . . . was moral to the core, that is, was wholly concerned with righteousness of life." Harnack, " What is Christianity? " tr. Saunders, 1901, pp. 153 ff.: " The Gospel is no theoretical system of doctrine or philosophy of the universe. . . . It is a glad message assuring us of life eternal. . . . By treating of life eternal it teaches us how to lead our lives aright. . . . How great a departure from what he thought and enjoined is involved in putting a Christological creed in the forefront of the Gospel. . . . He takes the publican in the temple, the widow and her mite, the lost son, as his examples; none of them know anything about ' Christology.' " So also, F. P. Cobbe, " Studies New and Old," 1865, p. 1 : " Christian Ethics and the Ethics of Christ "; George Matheson, " Landmarks of New Testament Morality," 1889 ; G. H. Gilbert, "The Revelation of Jesus," 1899; C. A. Briggs, " The Ethical Teaching of Jesus," 1904, Pref., p. x: " Jesus' principle of voluntary love is the great transforming principle of Christianity." W. deW. Hyde, " Jesus' Way," 1902 ; R. F. Horton, "The Teaching of Jesus," 1895, Part I, The Synoptics ; Broadus, " Jesus of Nazareth," 1890, Lect. I, " His Personal Character "; Lect. II, " His Ethical Teachings "; A. L. Bruce, " With Open Face," 1896, Ch. X, "The Moral Ideal " ; J. Drummond, "Via, Veritas, Vita," Hibbert Lectures, 1894 ; Lect. VI, VII, " Ethics "; VIII. "The Motive Power of Christianity "; G. Jackson, "The Teaching of Jesus," 1903, IX ; " Concerning Righteousness."

[1] "Confessions," I, 1 : " Fecisti nos ad te et inquietum est cor nostrum, donec requiescat in te."

the heights of heaven without providing themselves with the necessities of earth. "Give me
the luxuries of existence," said a distinguished
historian, when describing his personal tastes, "and
I can dispense with the necessities." That is what
one is tempted to say of a theology which substitutes
a dramatic redemption for an ethical revival. A
theology which does not begin by establishing the
foundations of morals may be subtle and lofty as the
clouds, but to the modern mind appears, like
the clouds, remote and intangible. Whatever else
the City of God may have, it must have a foundation. Whatever else theology may be, it must be
first of all a moral theology. Whatever other attributes may be ascribed to God, the first must be his
goodness. The theologians are obeying the call of
the highest when they press upward to the heights
of the knowledge of God, but it is by no means
certain that they have chosen the only practicable
way. It is not always the straightest line, said
Lessing, which is the shortest.[1] The steep ascent
of theological reasoning seems reserved for the
few, while for the many the modest footpath
of ethics is less arduous and obstructed. Vistas
into reality may open along the way of simple
duty-doing, which are hid from the highway of
theological learning; and though one may not
ascend by this path to the summit of vision, he
may see clearly the lower landscape instead of
being lost in the fog.

[1] "Education of the Human Race," § 91: "Es ist nicht wahr
dass die kürzeste Linie immer die grade ist."

In a lecture of Cardinal Newman's, concerning the nature of Christian faith, he describes, with astonishing candor, the effect of a theology which begins in something else than ethics.[1] " A feeble old woman," he says, " first genuflects before the Blessed Sacrament and then steals her neighbor's handkerchief. She kneels because she believes, she steals because she does not love. . . . How merciful a Providence it has been that faith and love are separable, as the Catholic creed teaches." It is not too much to say that this divorce of faith from love, of religion from ethics, of prayer from pocket-picking, appears to the modern mind unthinkable. It seems to propose a religion with an end but without a beginning, with a top but with no bottom, in the air but not on the ground, a separation not alone of faith from works, but of religion from common sense, of the character of God from the character of man ; and one turns with a sigh of relief from a system of theology which is consistent with larceny, to a code of ethics which begins with honesty.

[1] "Lectures on Certain Difficulties felt by Anglicans on submitting to the Catholic Faith," 1857, pp. 225–229. Compare Lecky, "History of European Morals," 1869, I, 359: "That the greatest religious change in the history of mankind should have taken place under the eyes of a brilliant galaxy of philosophers and historians . . . that, during the space of three centuries, they should have treated as simply contemptible an agency which all men must now admit to have been . . . the most powerful moral lever that has ever been applied to the affairs of man, are facts well worthy of meditation. . . . The explanation is to be found in that broad separation between the spheres of morals and of positive religion."

Such considerations restore in some degree the self-respect of those who turn from the steep way of theology and enter the Gospels by the wicket-gate of ethics. It is a modest way of approach, unfrequented by the learned, but the gate swings easily open and the path is plain. One may perhaps not hear the highest message of the Gospel, but he is not likely to miss its most obvious lessons. His contemplation of a cosmic drama will not hide from him the elementary demands of duty. His theology, such as it is, will at least be inconsistent with moral delinquency; his God will at least be good; his creed will not encourage the suspicion that loose business ethics are compatible with firm Christian discipleship. It must be frankly admitted that theology is viewed by many modern minds with scepticism, if not with complete indifference. Theological speculation seems to many persons to deal with much that lies quite beyond the horizon of knowledge, and with little that concerns the ordinary life of man. Even if such scepticism be unjustified, the lesson for theology is plain. It must establish connection with the world of conduct; it must reconsider the ethical basis of theology; it must restate the doctrine of the Christian character. If there is to be a restoration of confidence in theology, it must be secured, not by annexing new fields of speculation, but by exploring more thoroughly the familiar field of morality. If theology is to remain the queen of the sciences, righteousness and judgment must be the foundations of her throne.

For the moment, therefore, it is of no great importance to consider whether ethics or metaphysics offers the most direct road to truth. It is only necessary to observe that one of these roads lies straight before our feet, and that to reach the other we must transfer ourselves to the mind of another age. To pass from the temper of the present time to the method of dogmatic theology is to go a long way round. The ideals of the modern world express themselves in the desire for practical effectiveness; the intellectual speculations of other ages are supplanted by the passion for usefulness, leadership, and service. Does such a transfer of interest dry up the sources of idealism? On the contrary, it simply creates a new channel for idealism, and directs its refreshing stream to social instead of to speculative ends. Does it, on the other hand, detach the modern mind from the influence of Jesus? On the contrary, it calls attention to an aspect of that influence which theology has often overlooked. Never was there a time when plain people were less concerned with the metaphysics or ecclesiasticism of Christianity. The constructions of systems and the contentions of creeds, which once appeared the central themes of human interest, are now regarded by millions of busy men and women as mere echoes of ancient controversies, if not mere mockeries of the problems of the present age. Even the convocations of the Churches manifest little appetite for discussions which were once the bread of their life and the wine of their exhilaration, and one of the leaders of a great Christian communion has been led of late to say: "I do not know what conclusions they arrived at, nor do I think that it is of any particular consequence that they arrived at any conclusion. The most desirable thing was that they should come to an end." [1]

Under these very conditions of theological satiety, however, the mind of the age returns with fresh interest to the contemplation of the character of Jesus Christ. "Back to Jesus;" "In his Name;" "What would Jesus do?" "Jesus' Way" — phrases like these, caught up by multitudes of unsophisticated readers, indicate the force and scope of the modern imitation of Christ. To follow Jesus even though one does not fully understand him; to do the will even if one has not learned the doctrine; to perceive through much darkness that the Life is the light of men; — these are the marks of the new obedience. The character of Jesus Christ speaks with its own convincing authority to the mind of the present age.

A striking example of this new discipleship may be observed in the prevailing temper of the modern labor-movement. To the great mass of hand-workers nothing could seem more unreal or uninteresting than the ordinary methods and concerns of the Christian Church. Priests and par-

[1] Henry van Dyke, "Straight Sermons," 1893, X, "The Horizon," p. 229.

sons, formal worship and conflicting creeds, appear
to deal with matters that have no vital relation
with the work of the world. On the day when
Christians meet for prayer, trade-unionists and
socialists meet to consider what they believe the
not less sacred themes of human fraternity and
industrial peace; and by great numbers of hand-
workers the Christian Church is frankly regarded
as a mere club of the prosperous, if not a mere
symbol of the capitalistic system. Yet hostile or
contemptuous as may be their attitude toward institutional Christianity, at one point their sense of
alienation is supplanted by sympathy. It is when
they recall the character of Jesus Christ. Nothing,
indeed, is left of a supernatural halo round his person. "He would have accomplished more," it is
urged, "if he had worked for economics and
science rather than religion."[1] He was a plain
working-man, a friend of the poor, a social reformer,
"who if he were now living would give himself to the labor-movement." "The ancient forms
and symbols in which Christian faith has been
hitherto expressed are," says an observant inquirer
among German working-people, "for the great
majority of hand-workers irretrievably shattered.
. . . One thing alone is left to them all, — respect
and reverence for Jesus Christ."[2] Imperfect and

[1] Rade, 9te Evang.-soz. Kong., 1898, s. 104: "Die sittlichrel.
Gedankenwelt unsrer Industriearbeiter."

[2] P. Göhre, "Drei Monate Fabrikarbeiter," 1891, s. 190; compare
"Jesus Christ and the Social Question," 1900, p. 71 ; *American*

superficial as this judgment of Jesus may be, it at least makes a point of contact between the Christian faith and the modern working-man. The Church, it was once said, hears none but Christ. The labor-movement, it may now be said, hears not the Church of Christ, but gladly listens to the voice which says: "Come unto me, all ye that labor;" "I will give unto this last even as unto thee." At this point — and probably at this point only — it is possible to bridge the chasm which divides the ideals of Christianity from the ideals of the hand-workers. From a common reverence it may be possible to cross to a common understanding; and the times are waiting for the great teacher, the Pontifex Maximus of his generation, who shall build this bridge from the daily concerns of the working masses to the teaching of Jesus Christ.

Nor is this ethical susceptibility a mark of the present age alone. It is quite as conspicuously a mark of the age of Jesus himself. The same sense of unreality and remoteness then affected many minds as they surveyed the formalism of Hebrew worship. They were ready for an ethical revival; they looked for a teacher who should say, "Seek

Journal of Sociology, March, 1899, pp. 621 ff.; H. F. Perry, "The Working-man's Alienation from the Church" (evidence of American hand-workers, collected), p. 622: " Working-men understand that Christianity is only another name for justice, love, and truth, and that 'Churchianity' is only another name for wrong, injustice, oppression, misery, and want. Then they take the two apart and cheer the name of Jesus Christ and hiss the Church . . . honoring the one, scouting the other."

first the Kingdom of God and His righteousness."
Jesus met his age where it was. He did not begin
with a philosophy like that of the fourth Gospel,
or a theology like that of Paul, but with the personal problems of fisherfolk and publicans, of the
doubting and sinning, the good and bad. His
first blessings were offered to the humble, the
merciful, the peace-makers; his first discriminations
were between conformity, externalism, legalism,
and brotherhood, chastity, moderation, sincerity,
love. His first rebukes were pronounced against
worldliness, anxiety, and hypocrisy; his first tests
of discipleship were those of practical ethics. "By
their fruits ye shall know them."

In short, the teaching of Jesus was primarily
a teaching of character. Further intimacy with
him might give to his followers deeper insight into
his purposes and hopes; but the way to this com-
prehension lay through the path of personal loyalty
and obedience. Seeking first the Kingdom of God
and His righteousness, other things would be added
unto them. Character was the gate of conviction.
Purity in heart would have as its consequence
the capacity to see God. Obedience, as Robertson said, was to be the organ of spiritual knowledge. If any man willeth to do the will, says
the fourth Gospel, he shall know the doctrine.[1]

[1] Wernle, "Die Anfänge unserer Religion," 1901, s. 47: "The
central desire of Jesus is to awaken the conscience and set before
it the thought of Eternity. . . . One can understand Jesus only
when one recognizes this desire in him." So also, s. 54: "The

The ethical teaching of Jesus is, therefore, not only
the way which leads most directly from the mind
of the present age to the interpretation of the
Gospels, but it is also the way by which the men
of the Gospels actually approached their Master.
It presents the sequence of experiences, the chronology of conviction, which— though it be by no
means universal — is none the less that which the
first three Gospels, as a rule, present.

If, then, it be the truth of history that the first
disciples were led on from moral attachment to
spiritual insight, from reverence for the character
of Jesus to confession of the faith of Jesus, it may
be reasonably believed that the same path of
spiritual development may be followed to the same

demands of Jesus are so thoroughly simple and positive, that they
may be completely set forth without involving them in questions
of the Law, the Pharisees, or Jewish ethics." So, von Dobschütz,
"Die ur-christlichen Gemeinden," 1902, VI : "It is an ancient and
approved method of apologetics, to begin with the moral proofs
of Christianity. Πρᾶξις ἐπίβασις θεωρίας, says Gregory of Nazian-
zen; and a preacher of the Primitive Church teaches: 'Neither
life without knowledge, nor safe knowledge without true life;'"
Epist. ad Diogn., XII, 4. Harnack, "What is Christianity ?" tr.
Saunders, 1901, p. 76 : "To represent the Gospel as an ethical
message is no depreciation of its value. . . . There is a sphere of
ethical thought which is peculiarly expressive of Jesus' Gospel."
R. Otto, "Leben und Wirken Jesu," 1902, s. 52 : "The first work
of Jesus is to set free the moral life." George Harris, "Moral
Evolution," 1896, p. 404 : "Theology starts now with the historical
human person." So, Channing: "The sense of duty is the greatest
gift of God ; the idea of right is the primary and highest revelation
of God to the human mind ; and all outward revelations are
founded on and addressed to it."

end by the mind of the present age. Other times have first been taught of the nature of God and then have turned to the service of man. It may be the distinction of the present age to reverse this order of religious experience and to rediscover the knowledge of God through the doing of duty. It may be that beyond the ethical renaissance of the present time there is waiting a revival of religion. As philanthropy reconsiders its foundations, it may find that the word which it obeys: "Thou shalt love thy neighbor as thyself," prepares the mind to receive that other command which is like to it: "Thou shalt love the Lord thy God." Christian ethics may come to be recognized, not as a step-child of the faith of the past, but as a parent of the faith of the future. An ethical revival may be the prophecy of a new theology, in which the goodness of God will be supreme. The call to social service may be a new utterance of the voice of God. Perhaps the very life of Christianity is being borne through the troubled waters of the present time by the faithful servants of its human needs, as the giant Christopher found that it was the Christ-child whom he had carried stumblingly to the shore. It may happen again, as with the first disciples, that those who are at first drawn by the character of Jesus to ethical obedience, will be finally led by him toward the Source of his ethical authority. The Christian theology of the future may be a corollary from the character of Jesus Christ.

CHAPTER II

THE conditions of the modern world give new significance to the problem of the Christian character. The Christian character is, however, a consequence of the imitation of Christ; the reproduction, under the varying conditions of different ages, of the characteristic aspects of the conduct of Jesus. A study of the Christian character must, therefore, begin by contemplating the moral type which the Teacher himself illustrates.

The imitation of Christ may be misdirected in many ways. He may be imitated literally, fragmentarily, capriciously, as though each act or saying expressed his total purpose and had no relation to time, place, race, or occasion. He may be imitated, on the other hand, overconfidently or arrogantly, as though the saying: "Greater things than these shall ye do," emancipated his disciples from the limitations of science or civilization or common sense. A rational imitation of Christ is not the conduct of a mimic or a puppet. It means what the imitation of other characters means, — an influence of leadership, power, authority, example, applied to the conditions of one's own life. The traits in him which command appreciation are applied.

not to suppress one's own character, but to enrich and ennoble it.   Jesus comes not to destroy, but to fulfil.   If any man will come after me, he says, let him take up his own cross, his own burden, his own experience, and follow.

What, then, was the character of Jesus Christ? What kind of person is this from whom so rich and persuasive a teaching proceeds?   Detaching ourselves, so far as practicable, from the traditions and presuppositions which thrust themselves between the Gospels and their readers; setting ourselves in imagination, if we may, on a hillside in Galilee or in a street in Jerusalem in the days of Jesus, what, we ask ourselves, is the impression we receive from this new teacher who arrests our attention and compels our obedience?

It would be of extraordinary interest if we might, in the first place, picture to ourselves the external appearance and physical traits of Jesus.   The simple record, however, offers practically no material for the reproduction of his face or form.   It is indeed reported, not without great suggestiveness, that the first impression of his teaching was for the moment created, not so much by its contents, striking as these were, as by the demeanor and personality of the Teacher.   "He taught as one having authority," is the first comment of the narrator.   There was a calmness and mastery, a force and restraint, an originality and reverence, which dominated the scene.   As Jesus proceeded in his ministry, this effect of his personal bearing is often evident. To a soldier he seemed like a commander who was born to be obeyed; to many a hearer he had but to say, " Follow me," and busy men left all and followed; to minds possessed by devils he had but to speak and they grew self-controlled and calm; to those who would seize him at the last his very presence seemed to strike a blow, so that, as the fourth Gospel says, "they went backward, and fell to the ground."[1] Little children, on the other hand, came when he called, and nestled in his arms; women followed him and ministered unto him gladly. Command and sympathy, power and charm, must have been singularly blended in a person who drew to himself these varied types of loyalty. Authority and affection, playfulness and gravity, the light of love and the shadow of rebuke, must have touched in quick succession the face of Jesus. He smiles at the sport of children; he perceives with sympathetic imagination the symbolism of the woman's costly gift; he stands before the representative of Cæsar and asserts himself a king; and all these moods, childlike, poetic, kingly, are genuine and consistent expressions of his many-sided character.

These suggestions of external demeanor are, however, far from establishing any trustworthy tradition of the physical appearance of Jesus. Pious imagination soon pictured him as fulfilling in form and face what had been prophesied of the

[1] John xviii. 6.

Messiah, and later history has perpetuated in the
portraiture of Jesus the various ideals of physical
manhood which have prevailed in successive ages
of the Church.   The Gospels, on the other hand,
preserve to us no portrait of the Teacher.   They
were not written to satisfy the curiosity of future
ages; they were the artless and incidental summary of an oral tradition, designed to perpetuate
the record of the Master's deeds and words.   The
same unconsciousness and spontaneity appear in
Jesus himself.   He is not posing before the glass of
the future.   He is indifferent to great occasions or
striking effects.   He lavishes his care on single,
obscure and unresponsive lives.   He is marked by
what has been called accessibility,[1] the unassuming
candor of the unconstrained and unaffected life.
He is occupied in doing not his own will, but the
will of the Father who sends him, and in accom-
plishing the work which is given him to do.   Thus
it happens that we are more familiar with the
spiritual traits of Jesus than with his outward
form.   His profoundest utterances and even his
private thoughts are preserved to us by the reten-
tiveness of love, while his physical appearance can
be at the best only inferred from the impression
created by his acts and words.   His face was once

---

[1] Fairbairn, "Philosophy of the Christian Religion," 1902,
p. 361 : "There are multitudes of the saintly less accessible than He,
. . . so remote from all weakness and so severe to self-indulgence
that we dare not confess our sins in their presence. . . . But we
can do this before Him."

a key to his character; his character must now
suggest his face.[1]

What, then, one asks again, were the special
traits of the character of Jesus Christ? Dismiss-
ing for the moment the inquiries which concern themselves with the interior nature of the
person of Jesus, and approaching him as one
might have done when he taught the people by
the lake, or faced the Governor in his palace,
what is the main impression which his character
creates? The question seems as simple and un-
embarrassed as any historical question can be. It
demands neither theological subtlety nor critical
erudition. On every page of the first three Gospels stands this character of singular positiveness
and consistency, whose most conspicuous traits it
would appear difficult to mistake.[2]

---

[1] The history of the portraiture of Jesus is told with abundant
learning by von Dobschütz, "Christusbilder," 1899, p. viii ("Texte
und Untersuchungen," Gebhardt und Harnack, Bd. XVIII) : "In its
legends a people often registers the best of its religious feeling."
See also, Keim, "Jesus of Nazara," tr. Ransom, 1876, II, 190 ff.;
Wünsche, "Der lebensfreudige Jesus," 1876, ss. 65 ff., with the
descriptive summaries of Strauss, König, Renan, and Keim; H.
Schell (R. C. Professor in Würzburg), "Christus," 1903 (89 illustrations) ; Farrar, "Life of Christ as represented in Art," 1894
(with many illustrations); Sir W. Bayliss, "Rex Regum, a Painter's
Study of the Likeness of Christ," 1898 (a somewhat emotional
defence of the catacomb frescoes, but with many illustrations from
the masters); H. D. M. Spence (Dean of Gloucester), "Early
Christianity and Paganism," 1902 (with interesting illustrations,
pp. 284 ff.).

[2] W. Boyd Carpenter (Lord Bishop of Ripon), "Introduction to

The impressions made by the character of Jesus have been, however, as various as the temperaments and needs of different times and men.   Jesus has been called the light of the world, but this light has been broken as though passing through a prism, and each color of its spectrum has seemed to some minds the complete radiation.   He had, it has been variously urged, the character of a fanatic, an anarchist, a socialist, a dreamer, a mystic, an Essene. It is one of the evidences of the moral greatness of Jesus that each period in Christian history, each social or political change, has brought to view some new aspect of his character and given him a new claim to reverence.[1]   From these various conceptions there have emerged two, of exceptional permanence, each of which represents to many minds the special traits of his moral personality.   One view interprets his character in terms of asceticism, the other in terms of æstheticism.   One contem-

the Study of the Scriptures," 1903, pp. 131, 132: " It is this character, apart from any miraculous or supernatural accessories, which has profoundly impressed mankind : it is this character which still holds up, as it were, its own ideal to humanity. . . .   Our belief in Jesus Christ must be based upon moral conviction : not upon physical wonder. . . .   In other words, we must invert the process. . . . You can never compel moral admiration by physical power, but you can understand that the lower ranges of life may be subservient to one whose greatness lies in the higher, *i.e.* in the moral order of life."

[1] The most noteworthy of modern interpretations of the character of Jesus, from Strauss to Naumann, are analyzed in the interesting volume of Weinel, " Jesus im neunzehnten Jahrhundert," 6te Aufl., 1904.

plates the suffering of Jesus, the other his joy.
One is the view of ecclesiasticism, the other is
the view of humanism. Tradition perpetuates the
first, imagination welcomes the second.

On the one hand is the prevailing tradition which
associates Jesus with the Messianic prophecies.
When the Second Isaiah writes of the servant of
God : " He is despised and rejected of men, a man
of sorrows and acquainted with grief ; he hath no
form or comeliness, we did esteem him smitten of
God and afflicted " ; whom, it is asked, could these
passages prefigure if it was not him who expressly
claimed to fulfil the Messianic promise ? Thus
the character of Jesus becomes a historical necessity. The Teacher of the New Testament is the
answer to the hope of the Old Testament. He
was the Lamb of God, the patient victim, the willing sacrifice. The ethical type, therefore, which
shall reproduce his character can be none other
than a resigned, self-mortifying, ascetic type. The
Hellenic character of harmony, symmetry, virility,
is supplanted by the Hebraic type of patience,
pathos, pain. The Christian character, un-Hellenic
and other-worldly, utters the poignant note of suffering Israel.

This tradition of the character of Jesus was
early accepted by the Church. The Christian life,
it was taught, could be indeed attained in a certain degree under the conditions of the secular
world ; but the *Vita Religiosa* was a product of the
asceticism of the monastic cell. It was intended,

as Strauss has said, " to depict as strikingly as possible the contrast between the μορφὴ θεοῦ and the
μορφὴ δούλου." [1]   Here, also, is the dominant ideal
of mediæval Christian art.   With but few exceptions
the Christ of the masters is the Man of Sorrows,
whom it hath pleased the Lord to bruise, and who
is stricken for the transgressions of his people.
One of the most eminent of German philosophers [2]
has set forth in detail this conception of the character of Jesus.   The Christian character, says
Professor Paulsen, is marked by abnegation (*Welt-
verleugnung*), the Greek character by appreciation
(*Weltbejahung*); the one represents the scorn of
the natural, the other the development of the
natural.   The Greeks prized intellectual development, the Christians distrusted it.   To the Greeks
courage was a cardinal virtue ; the Christians were
taught to resist not evil.   All Greek virtues were,
therefore, in the light of Christianity "splendid
vices."   All that was of worth in Greece was
worthless in Christianity.   For a Greek to become
a Christian it was necessary that the old man should
die and a new man be born.   Thus the Christian
character, self-effacing, ascetic, contrary to nature,
admirable though it may have once appeared, be-

[1] "Life of Jesus," tr. Marian Evans, 1856, p. 202.

[2] Friedrich Paulsen, "System der Ethik," 1889, ss. 50 ff., "Die
Lebensanschauung des Christentums."   Rejoinders to Paulsen are
made, among others, by Jacoby, "Neutest. Ethik," 1899, ss. 464 ff.;
Gallwitz, "Das Problem der Ethik," 1891, ss. 271 ff. ; E. Grimm, "Die
Ethik Jesu," 1903, Kap. 18, "Lebensbejahung und Lebensver-
neinung."

comes impracticable for a healthy-minded man in the modern world.[1]

On the other hand is the interpretation of the character of Jesus in terms of æstheticism, as the type of gladness, graciousness, spiritual peace, and joy. According to Renan, a young Galilean peasant, " sprung from the ranks of the people," of parents " of humble station living by their toil," is entranced by the vision of the Divine life, and gives himself with delight to its expression. "An exquisite perception of nature furnished him with expressive images." " A remarkable penetration, which we call genius, set off his aphorisms." "Tenderness of heart was in him transformed into infinite sweetness, vague poetry, universal charm." " His lovely character, and doubtless one of those transporting countenances which sometimes appear in the Hebrew race, created round him a circle of fascination." In the same spirit Strauss remarked : " Jesus appears as a naturally lovely character (*eine schöne Natur von Hause aus*), which needed but to unfold and to become conscious of itself." [2]

---

[1] The same conclusion was reached by Augustine (L. Stein, "Die sociale Frage im Lichte der Philosophie," 1897, s. 244): "His doctrine . . . has a dark and monastic quality (etwas mönchisch Finsteres) which is hostile to social and philosophical inquiries based on confidence in human nature." So many modern philosophers; *e.g.* F. H. Bradley (*International Journal of Ethics*, October, 1894, p. 25) : " We have lived a long time now the professors of a creed which no one consistently can practise, and which, if practised, would be as immoral as it is unreal."

[2] Renan, "Vie de Jésus," 13me ed., 1867, pp. 74 ff.; Strauss,

It is interesting to recall the many incidents in the life of Jesus which tend to confirm each of these impressions of his character. On the one hand, there is a quality of self-sacrifice in his experience

" Das Leben Jesu, für das deutsche Volk bearbeitet," 2te Aufl., 1864, s. 208. So, Hase, " Geschichte Jesu," 1876, § 53: " Jesus defends human life from the asceticism which so often allies itself with religious earnestness. . . . He shares freely in the good things of this life. . . . He is as a bridegroom among his companions. Never did a religious hero shun so little the joys of life." So also, though in less unmeasured words, Keim, " Geschichte Jesu von Nazara," 1867, I, 458: " Is not the primitive description of him as being gentle and joyous (seine Herzlichkeit und die milde Heiterkeit) — the character which Strauss assigns to him — justified by the record ?" One of the most curious illustrations of scholarly candor is the somersault of conviction performed by A. Wünsche in his " Der lebensfreudige Jesu," 1876. In 1870 he published his " Leiden des Messias," describing with much erudition the Messianic ideal of lowly suffering in its fulfilment through Christ. Six years later Jesus appears to him in a wholly opposite character, joyous, triumphant, with a delight in life in which the Talmudic teachers could find no satisfaction. s. 24: " My problem is to deliver the figure of Jesus from the unhistorical shadows in which it has laid, and set it in the sunshine where it belongs." See also the essay of I. Zangwill, " Dreamers of the Ghetto," 1899, pp. 491, 492: " I give the Jews a Christ they can now accept, the Christians a Christ they have forgotten . . . Christ, not the tortured God, but the joyous comrade, the friend of all simple souls . . . not the theologian spinning barren subtleties, but the man of genius protesting against all forms and dogmas that would replace the direct vision and the living ecstasy, . . . the lover of warm life, and warm sunlight, and all that is fresh and simple and pure and beautiful." So in many popular studies of the Gospels, *e.g.* the fresh and thoughtful narrative by W. J. Dawson, " The Life of Christ," 1901, pp. 87 ff. : " He became the incarnation of the spirit of joy, the symbol of the bliss of life. . . . Christ's gracious gayety of heart proved contagious."

which removes him from all positive relation with Hellenism.[1]   A whole series of virtues — humility, self-forgetfulness, the bearing of burdens not one's own — appear in Jesus, for which no room is found in the Greek ideals of σοφροσύνη and μεγαλοψυχία. Such a saying as "He that will be chiefest among you shall be the servant of all," would have seemed, as St. Paul said of the crucified Christ, "unto the Greeks foolishness."[2]   On the other hand, there is heard throughout the ministry of Jesus an underlying note of tranquil and lofty joy.   He is quick to note the beautiful in nature and in character.   He detects qualities worthy of love even in unlovely lives.   In his teaching the instinct for spiritual principles is met by the instinct for artistic expression. The universe is picturesque and eloquent to his sensitive mind, and at the end of a short career, abounding in misinterpretations and disappointments, there still lingers the happy tradition of his spiritual joy.[3]   "These things have I spoken unto

[1] A. Harnack, " What is Christianity ? " tr. Saunders, 1901, p. 37 : " The picture of Jesus' life and his discourses stand in no relation with the Greek spirit. . . .   That he was ever in touch with the thoughts of Plato or the Porch . . . it is absolutely impossible to maintain."   [2] 1 Cor. i. 23.

[3] Ehrhardt, " Der Grundcharakter der Ethik Jesu," 1895, s. 110 : " In Jesus the Messianic idea is rather a means than an end (mehr ein instrumentaler Begriff als ein Zweckbegriff).   He used its form for the expression of his ideal.   The ascetic element in the ethics of Jesus is its transient, the service of God its permanent, element." See also, Strauss, " Leben Jesu," 2te Aufl., 1864, s. 34 : " This joyous, continuous conduct of a lovely soul . . . may be described as the Hellenic quality in Jesus."

E

you," says the fourth Gospel, "that my joy might
remain in you, and that your joy might be full." [1]

[1] John xv. 11. In a voluminous work (H. S. Chamberlain, "Die
Grundlagen des neunzehnten Jahrhunderts," 2 Bd., 5te Aufl.,
1904, I, ss. 219 ff.) which, though written by an Englishman,
has attracted attention chiefly in Germany, the author raises the
question whether this fusion of the Hellenic and Hebraic spirit
in Jesus may not be referred to the conditions of his birth. Galilee, he remarks, lay on the main track of Greek migration toward
the East, and its population must have been one of mixed blood
and descent. It may well have happened, he concludes, that
Jesus was thus a child of two races, and that the Hellenic traits
which are so marked in him were his, not by supernatural gift, but
by inherited right. "One who asserts that Jesus was a Jew is
either ignorant or insincere." The probability "that Jesus was
not a Jew and had not a drop of pure Jewish blood in his veins is
so great that it approaches nearly to certainty." "By religion and
education he was unquestionably a Jew, but in race in all probability not." "I have felt obliged to enter in some detail into this
question, because I do not find in any other work that the facts in
the case are clearly brought together."

This venturesome hypothesis of mixed descent, though it is not
without plausibility, is not only unsupported by positive tradition,
but is altogether in conflict with the earliest tradition of Jesus. If
among the first disciples there had been the least intimation of extra-
Jewish descent in him, — and the facts of his birth must have been
familiarly reported by the companions of his childhood, — it could
but have happened that as the new religion expanded into the
Hellenic world, its claim to authority through an origin partially
Greek must have been repeatedly emphasized. The Epistle to the
Romans is in large part devoted to commending the Gospel of Christ
to the extra-Jewish world, and its second chapter, devoted to the
distinction between Jew and Gentile, must have called attention
to the fact that Jesus represented in himself both Gentile and
Jew. The fourth Gospel, deliberately appropriating Greek philosophy as the witness to Christ, must have recalled the natural
right of Jesus to a place in Greek philosophy. The hypothesis of

Striking, however, as are both these traits of the character of Jesus, it is far from probable that they touch its deepest note. The asceticism of Jesus, however un-Hellenic it may be, and his delight in life, however un-Messianic it may be, are obviously not ends in his teaching, but incidents along his way. They are the by-products thrown off in the development of his career. The problem of the character of Jesus first comes into view when behind his sufferings and his joy there is observed a quality of spiritual life which makes these various experiences so subordinate and contributory that they become the mere rhythm of his step as he moves steadily toward his supreme desire.[1] The

Chamberlain, though ingenious and at its first statement striking, is in reality a superfluous and unverified interpretation of a character which is simply larger than the limits of national traits, and in which Hebraism and Hellenism are but formal names for piety and joy.

[1] So Keim, " Geschichte Jesu von Nazara," 1867, I, 445 : " . . . a Galilean in the freshness and susceptibility of his sense of nature in all her forms, a Hebrew in his contemplative seriousness and the depth of power of his life with God. . . . Let us at the same time confess that humanity can elsewhere hardly exhibit the even balance of centrifugal and centripetal forces."   O. Holtzmann, " War Jesus Ekstatiker ? " 1903, s. 139: " It is the quality of paradox and contradiction of traits which often makes a person attractive. The contrasts of tranquillity and enthusiasm in Jesus attached his followers to him, and the union of these opposite qualities was not the least part of the secret of his first results."   The contrast and union of types is admirably stated by Hugh Black, " Culture and Restraint," 1901, p. 349: " He preserves the Hellenic spirit from degradation and selfishness. . . . He saves the Hebraic spirit from formalism."

explorer in a rugged country does not seek for hardships. He expects them as the cost of success. He accepts the solitude, the fatigue, the perils, as incidents along his way. He is no more an ascetic than he is a Sybarite; he is bent on his errand and takes the risk of his road. Something like this is the attitude of Jesus toward asceticism. He neither courts nor shuns suffering. He is not consciously imitating the sorrows foretold of the Messiah; but he is doing the Messiah's work, and, as the Prophet had anticipated, he is despised and rejected of men. His asceticism is real, but it is incidental. The pains and pleasures of the body and the soul are the rough places and fair prospects which meet him as he goes. He is neither a mediæval saint nor a Galilean dreamer, but a Teacher whose pains and pleasures are but the scenery and environment of the soul.

What, then, was the first impression of this Teacher, which seized upon his hearers with such extraordinary compulsion, that when he said, "Follow me," men left all to follow? The answer to this question concerning the original and general impression of the teaching of Jesus seems beyond dispute. The immediate effect of the teaching of Jesus was an effect of power, of authority and mastery, the commanding impressiveness of a leader of men. It is striking to notice how often this word "power" is applied in the New Testament to the influence of Jesus. "The multitude glorified God," says Matthew, "who had given such power unto men."

"The Kingdom of God comes with power," says
Mark.   "His word was with power," says Luke.
" Thou hast given him power over all flesh," says
John.   "God anointed Jesus of Nazareth with
power," says the Book of Acts.   "The power of
our Lord Jesus Christ," says Paul.   His ministry,
that is to say, was, first of all, dynamic, commanding,
authoritative.   When he announced the principles
of his teaching, he did not prove or argue or
threaten like the Scribes; he swayed the multitude
by personal power.   It was the same throughout his
ministry.   He called men from their boats, their
tax-booths, their homes; and they looked up into
his face and obeyed.   He commends the instinct
of the soldier who gives orders to those below him
because he has received orders from above.

What is the note of character which is touched in
such incidents as these ?   It is the note of strength.
This is no ascetic, abandoning the world; no
"joyous comrade," delighting in the world; here
is the quiet consciousness of mastery, the authority of the leader, the confidence which makes him
able to declare that a life built on his sayings is
built on a rock.   Jesus is no gentle visionary, no
contemplative saint, no Lamb of God, except in the
experience of suffering; he is a Person whose
dominating trait is force, the scourger of the
traders, the defier of the Pharisees, the commanding Personality whose words are with the authority
of power.   Women, it is true, were drawn with
peculiar loyalty to the service of Jesus, and it has

been inferred from such feminine devotion that the character of Jesus must have had in it more of the womanly than the masculine. Quite the contrary inference would be indicated by the ordinary relationships between women and men. It is not feminine traits in men which attract women, but masculine qualities of force, initiative, and leadership. Gracious consideration for women marked indeed the thought of Jesus, from the time when he went down to Nazareth and was subject to his mother, to the day when he commended his mother to the disciple whom he loved; but for softness and sentimentality, such as characterizes the feminine man, there was no room in his rugged, nomadic, homeless life.

From whatever side we approach the life of Jesus this impression of mastery confronts us. On the one hand is the ethical aspect of strength, to which our later inquiries must repeatedly return. Solemn exaltations of mood, experiences of prolonged temptation, moments of mystic rapture, occur, indeed, in his career; but when we consider what a part these emotional agitations have played in the history of religion, one is profoundly impressed by the sanity, reserve, composure, and steadiness of the character of Jesus. He is no example of the "twice-born" conception of piety, which has been of late presented to us with such vigor and charm. His "Religion of Healthy-mindedness" is not a psychopathic emotionalism, but a normal, rational, ethical growth. His method is not that of ecstasy, vision, nervous agitation, issuing in neurological saintliness; it is educative, sane, consistent with wise service of the world, capable of being likened in an infinite variety of ways to the decisions and obligations which every honest man must meet.[1]

---

[1] The captivating lectures of my distinguished and beloved colleague, William James ("The Varieties of Religious Experience," 1902), abound, it is needless to say, in illuminating suggestions concerning the expansion of life through religious emotion ; and, in spite of his startling pluralistic theism, the conclusion that "the conscious person is continuous with a wider self through which saving experiences come" makes an epoch in psychology. The sweep and charm of the discussion cannot, however, obscure the fact that among the varieties of religious experience which come under consideration, no place is found for a character like that of Jesus Christ. The "once-born" are dismissed as an imperfect type, in whom "optimism may be quasi-pathological," — a type which culminates in Walt Whitman, and in which the great names of constructive and rational religion hardly appear. St. Theresa is, to Professor James, an important "document," and St. John of the cross, and Mr. Ratisbonne, and Mr. Dresser ; but Luther is interesting only when he is recalling his spiritual tortures while a monk ; and Schleiermacher's "Discourses on Religion" are unaccounted for ; and while the coldness of Channing's bedroom gets attention, the warmth of his religious life is unexplained. One of the most curious of the copious footnotes in this monumental study of human documents is the allusion to an evangelical estimate of Channing (p. 488). He was, it is reported, "excluded from the highest form of religious life by the extraordinary rectitude of his character." No wonder that Professor James remarks, in comment, that "the twice-born look down upon the rectilinear consciousness of life . . . as not properly religion." A religion rendered imperfect by perfectness of character seems to present a paradox which American slang would describe as "the limit." This sense of lack reaches its climax when we observe the almost complete absence

On the other hand is the intellectual aspect of the same quality of power, — a strength of reasoning, a sagacity, insight, and alertness of mind, which give him authority over the mind not less than the will. It has often been assumed that Jesus was an untutored peasant, an inspired working-man, whose intuitions were his only guide; and it is undoubtedly true that his intellectual gifts had not been trained in Rabbinical schools of academic legalism. "How knoweth this man letters," asked the Pharisees, "having never learned?" — learned, as they probably meant to say, as a student from the

of reference to the character of Jesus Christ. Among the "varieties of religious experience," here, it would seem, was one which deserved consideration; yet it is noticed in a single footnote, where Harnack is cited as suggesting that "Jesus felt about evil and disease much as our mind-curers do." It is open to some question whether Harnack would regard this as a just inference from a passage where he says: "He [Jesus] calls sickness sickness, and health health," — which is precisely what many mind-curers do not admit. However this may be, it is evident that the character of Jesus is not a document to Professor James's immediate purpose. What Strauss ("Leben Jesu für das deutsche Volk bearbeitet," 1864, s. 208) has said is too obviously true to give Jesus a place among the "twice-born" saints. "In all those natures which have been purified through struggle and violent revolution of nature, — as in Paul, Augustine, Luther, — there remains something hard and bitter throughout life; but of this quality there is in Jesus not a trace. . . . He does not have to be converted and to begin a new and different life." Many a cordial admirer of Professor James's genius is eagerly hoping that his promise "to return to the same subject in another book" may be happily fulfilled, and that he may be led from this fascinating discussion of the pathology of religion to the interpretation of its normal, heroic, rational, dynamic types.

masters of the law.[1] Yet, on almost every page of the Gospels there are indications that the new master was neither unlettered nor untrained, but equipped with intellectual as well as spiritual authority.

When, at the beginning of his work, Jesus is solicited by the temptations of a misused ministry, he meets them all with the weapons of the scholar; confronting his adversary with the testimony of the Scriptures, and quoting to him, "It is written; it is written." When the time arrives to set forth the principles of his teaching, he expounds them through their contrast with the teachings of the past: "Ye have heard that it hath been said, but I say unto you." When he returns to Nazareth, where he had been brought up, there is delivered unto him the Book to read. He is habitually addressed as Teacher or Master. When his enemies would entangle him, they assume his familiarity with the literature which they cite, and he in his turn does not hesitate to use against them their own weapons of dialectic, so that they dare ask him no more questions.

Yet, sufficiently equipped as Jesus was to adapt his teaching to the learning of his age, it was not his scholastic wisdom which most impressed his hearers. There was perceived in him a

[1] Weinel (op. cit.), s. 59: "To see how far Jesus stood from Pharisaism, not only in his public teaching but before it, we need only compare his figures of speech with those of Paul." Compare H. Holtzmann (op. cit.), I, ss. 119, 120.

quality of insight which, instead of being akin to the learning of scholars, was distinct from it, and was seen to be an original endowment, a spiritual gift. When the boy Jesus met the wise men of Jerusalem, it was this untaught wisdom which startled them. He lingered among the doctors, eager to hear and to ask them questions; and when his parents sought their child, he turned to them with one of those deep, strange sayings with which other children sometimes perplex their parents, as though they were listening to another voice and heard a command their parents had not given. From that time on, as it is written, Jesus increased, not in stature only and in charm, but in wisdom. He was a Teacher, but the authority of his teaching was not that of the scribes. His wisdom was not erudition. It left, not an impression of academic acquisition, but of penetration, discernment, grasp. It was one aspect of his central quality of power.

It has been said that the distinction between the best modern practitioners of the law and men of the second order lies in the capacity to discriminate between the essential point on which the issue should be determined, and the multitude of interesting but subordinate issues which the case may suggest; and a Justice of the Supreme Court of the United States has remarked, concerning a leader of the bar, that the point urged by him had never failed to be the point which finally determined the mind of the court. A similar statement might be made of the teaching of

Jesus. It proceeds directly to the fundamental issue. Many aspects of life which might appear to others of importance are touched by him with surprising lightness, but without preamble or amplification he touches the dominant note of each situation and discerns the permanent principle which it involves.

His principle of selection from the earlier tradition is marked both by reverence and by audacity. It was written: "Do that to no man which thou hatest."[1] Jesus rests on this authority, but the saying gets new significance when he restates it in the positive form of the Golden Rule: "Whatsoever ye would that men should do to you, do ye even so to them."[2] He confirms the law of the Sabbath, but chooses as his authority the ethics of Hosea: "I will have mercy, and not sacrifice,"[3] rather than the theology of Exodus: "In six days the Lord made heaven and earth."[4] He does not hesitate to discriminate between the law of Moses and the law of God,[5] with something of that distinction between form and spirit, the accidental and the essential, which is now described as the critical spirit. Jesus, however, was not a critic, but a seer. He did not balance and weigh the various traditions; he saw the truth which these traditions, with different degrees of completeness, had desired to express.

[1] Tobit iv. 15.
[2] Matt. vii. 12.
[3] Hos. vi. 6 ; Matt. xii. 7.
[4] Ex. xx. 11.
[5] Matt. xix. 8 ff.

An interesting witness of this untaught wisdom is to be found in the attitude of Jesus to the world of nature. It would be misleading to speak of his mind as scientific, for there is in him no trace of the special discipline in which students of science are trained. His attitude toward nature, however, is the prerequisite of the scientific mind. Nature in every phase and form is his instructor, his companion, his consolation, and each incident of nature is observed by him with sympathetic insight and keen delight. He is a poet rather than a naturalist; but with him, as with all great interpreters of nature, poetic insight gives significance to the simplest facts. The hen and her chickens, the gnat in the cup, the camel in the narrow street, the fig-tree and its fruit, the fishermen sorting their catch, — all these and many other of the slightest incidents which meet his observant eye become eloquent with the great message of the Kingdom.

The contrast at this point between the mind of Jesus and the mind of Paul is striking. In the Epistles of Paul one finds hardly an allusion to the familiar and homely aspects of the world of nature. We hear the distant sound of cosmic tragedies, the groaning and travailing of creation; but of the birds and lilies, the seed and harvest, the lake and the fish, the vines and the cattle, Paul takes no account. He is a man of the city. His figures of speech are of the market-place, the athletic contests, the military career. The mind of Jesus, on the other hand, is most at home in the country. When he seeks the companionship of God in prayer, he goes, not into his closet, but into the comforting and quickening solitude of the hills. Each process of nature, the growth of the grain, the working of the leaven, the blossoming of the trees, the flight of the birds, is observed by him with an accuracy which never falters and is reported with a precision which gives us, as has been said, "a compact, coherent, living world, which we can rearticulate, revivify, and visualize." [1] From the day when Jesus pointed to the lilies and the crops, the mountain and the lake, as symbols of the Kingdom, the messages of nature have been, for millions of minds, spoken in his words and interpreted in his spirit. As Shelley wrote of Keats : —

> " He is made one with Nature. There is heard
> His voice in all her names. . . .
> He is a presence to be felt and known,
> In darkness and in light, from herb and stone."

[1] Fairbairn, "Philosophy of the Christian Religion," 1902, pp. 383 ff. The whole paragraph, concerning the responsiveness of the mind of Jesus to the suggestions of nature, is singularly beautiful. So also, H. Holtzmann, "Lehrbuch der Neutest. Theol.," 1897, s. 112: "One could not thus have spoken whose soul had first awakened in the narrow alleys of Jerusalem and been brought too soon into contact with the spirit of the Schools." H. Weinel, in the "Festgruss für Bernhard Stade," 1900 ("Die Bildersprache Jesu in ihrer Bedeutung für die Erforschung seines inneren Lebens "), s. 57: "This use of figures is the best evidence for the genuineness of the tradition concerning Jesus. For since the Christian religion through its great apostle became a faith of the lower classes

A further and still more striking evidence of this intellectual mastery was a certain lightness of touch which Jesus often employed in controversy, and which sometimes approaches the play of humor, and sometimes the thrust of irony.   His enemies attack him with bludgeons, and he defends himself with a rapier.   No test of mastery is more complete than this capacity to make of playfulness a weapon of reasoning.   The method of Jesus pierces through the subtlety and obscurity of his opponents with such refinement and dexterity that the assailant sometimes hardly knows that he is hit.[1]   Instead of a direct reply, the immediate question is parried and turned aside, and the motive which lies behind it is laid bare.   People come to him with an inquiry about the division of prop-

in Greek cities, and since — on the other hand — it was soon touched in Palestine with Pharisaism, these figures and parables, in their original freshness and homeliness, could not have been a later invention."   So, W. M. Ramsay, "The Education of Christ," 1902, Ch. I, "On a Mountain Top"; Renan, tr. Allen, 1896, pp. 122 ff. : "The region round about Jerusalem is perhaps the dreariest country in the world; Galilee, on the contrary, was extremely verdant, well shaded, smiling. . . .   In no country in the world do the mountains spread themselves out with more harmony or inspire loftier thoughts. . . .   The entire history of infant Christianity has in this way become a delightful pastoral."

[1] So, Renan, "Life of Jesus," tr. Allen, 1896, p. 143 : "Sometimes a wonderful keenness, like what we call wit, put his aphorisms in sharp relief. . . .   'Let me pull out the mote out of thine eye; and, behold, a beam is in thine own eye.' "   So, Jacoby, "Neutest. Ethik," s. 138.   The trait has been traced with perhaps excessive ingenuity by G. W. Buckley, "The Wit and Wisdom of Jesus," 1901.

erty, and Jesus at first seems to decline jurisdiction in the matter. "Who made me," he says, "a judge or a divider over you?" Then, however, looking round at the faces of the crowd who are seeking his guarantee for their greed, he penetrates to the thought which the economic problem has disguised, and answers, not their inquiry, but their hearts: "I say unto you all, keep yourselves from covetousness." His disciples ask for the reward of their loyalty: "Lo, we have left all and have followed thee"; and Jesus answers: "Ye shall receive an hundredfold, houses and brethren, sisters and mothers, and children and lands"; and then, as if with a playful sense of the little that all this tells them of that which is to happen, he goes on: "Yes, houses and lands indeed, with persecutions." He opens the Book in the synagogue, and with the familiarity of one versed in the Scriptures, selects that passage which is fulfilled by him: "He hath anointed me to preach the acceptable year of the Lord"; but while the minds of his hearers run on into the next phrase of the Prophet's saying, Jesus abruptly closes the Book in the middle of a sentence, and gives it back to the attendant, leaving it for the congregation to perceive that he declines to appropriate the ancient threat: "And the day of vengeance of our God." [1]

Here is intellectual insight matching spiritual

---

[1] This incident is noted by S. M. Crothers in a "Sermon on the Simplification of Life," 1901.

authority. This is no recluse or peasant or passive saint, but an intellectual as well as moral leader, who may be rejected indeed, but who cannot be despised. The picture of the historic Jesus which would reproduce this type of character, and which is still left for Christian art to paint, is not of the pallid sufferer, stricken by the sins of the world, but of the wise, grave Master, whom to meet was to reverence, if not to obey. Tempted he may be, but his are the temptations which come to power. Confronted by learning he must be, but the weapons of scholarship are his also. Thwarted by the kingdoms of this world he will be, but he remains a king in the empire of the truth. Suffer he must, but it is the suffering of the strong. He dies as if defeated, but his power asserts itself commandingly even when he is gone; and the very memory of it brings to his cause men who could resist his teaching. Nicodemus, the scholar, returns to care for the body of Jesus; and Judas, the betrayer, hangs himself for shame.

This central quality of moral and intellectual power becomes still more impressive when one proceeds to notice the habit of life and way of conduct which are its natural expressions. There are two ways in which the conduct of Jesus discloses a character whose dominant note is strength, and both of these habits of life increase the pathos and impressiveness of his character. The first is the prodigality of his sympathy; the second is his solitude of soul.

The first mark of power is its self-impartation. It gives itself lavishly because there is so much to give. It feels no need of thrift. This is what impresses one in the conduct of Jesus. He is extravagant and unthrifty in his teaching. On one occasion only does he seem to gather an audience about him and address to them any formal announcement of his mission. For the most part he lavishes his teaching on a few, and sometimes charges even these to tell no man what he has taught. He takes three friends apart from their companions and shows them his glory. His parables are flung out into the world with little care for their interpretation. Those who have ears to hear may hear them; but many shall hear and not understand. His favorite symbolism is that of the sower's work, with its broad, free sweep of arm and its widely scattered seed. What matter was it if much seed be wasted, if that which falls on good ground has such reproductive power? There is the same prodigality in his relation with the diverse types of people who came to him. It is often asked whether Jesus should be classified with reformers or with working-men, with the proletariat or the poor. The fact is, however, that the ordinary social classifications are inapplicable to him. He is equally at home with the most varied types. He moves with the same sense of familiarity among rich and poor, learned and ignorant, the happy and the sad.

What does this range of sympathy, this prodi-

F

gality of distribution, mean? It has been sometimes regarded as the sheer manifestation of an
appreciative and responsive mind. This is the
trait which has encouraged the æsthetic interpretation of the character of Jesus. This lavish offering is, it is said, a mark of his delight in life. But
delight in life is robbed of its significance when it
has no background of rational justification. Sympathy to be effective must be the expression of
power. To give, one must have. To give one's
life a ransom for many is of no avail if the ransom
be insufficient. To say that the Son of Man comes
not to be ministered unto, but to minister, is to
utter no great truth, unless the Son of Man has the
capacity for ministering. To dig a channel for the
water-power of one's mill is no wise investment if
the stream has run low. The sympathy of Jesus
is the channel through which his power flows, and
the abundance of the stream testifies to the reserve
of power at the source.

The second mark of the conduct of Jesus is his
spiritual solitude. Give himself as he may to
others in lavish word and deed, there remains
within the circle of these relationships a sphere
of isolation and reserve. Eager as he is to communicate his message, there are aspects of it which,
he is forced to see, are incommunicable, so that his
language has at times a note of helplessness. Men
see, but they do not perceive; they hear, but they
do not understand. "No man knoweth the Son, but
the Father; neither knoweth any man the Father,

save the Son." [1]   In the fourth Gospel this sense
of solitude is expressed with solemn reiteration.
"I have yet many things to say unto you, but ye
cannot bear them now." [2]   "It is expedient for
you that I go away: for if I go not away, the Comforter will not come unto you." [3]   Behind the region of communication, Jesus recognizes in the life
of the spirit a realm of reticence, where the heart
knows its own secret and the life must make its
way alone.   Instead of intruding, as many a teacher
has done, into the solitude of personality, Jesus
says: "Let not your heart be troubled. . . .   If it
were not so, I would have told you." [4]   He
respects the reserve of others, as he maintains
his own.   It is the confident silence which is the
assurance of love.

> "I count that friendship little worth,"

says a Christian poet,

> "Which has not many things untold,
>   Sweet longings, that no words can hold,
>   And passion-secrets, waiting birth." [5]

The reserve of Jesus is the background and the
support of his sympathy.   The throng that presses
about him seems to drain his strength, and he
seeks the solitude of the hills or of the lake to
recover poise and peace.   Here is the meaning of
those passive virtues which appear to give the note

[1] Matt. xi. 27.   [4] John xiv. 1, 2.
[2] John xvi. 12.   [5] Henry van Dyke, "The Builders."
[3] John xvi. 7.

of asceticism to the Gospels. Meekness, patience, forbearance, silence, — these are not the signs of mere self-mortification, they are the signs of power in reserve. They are the marks of one who can afford to wait, who expects to suffer, who need not contend; and all this, not because he is simply meek and lowly, but because he is also strong and calm.

A touching evidence of this sense of solitude is offered by the relation of Jesus to his family. Christian art has here again misled the sentiment of the devout, and has pictured the mother of Jesus as continuously aware of his profoundest hopes, from the time of his boyhood, when she "pondered these things in her heart," to the time of the Cross, when she stood near by, leaning on the disciple whom Jesus loved. The fact is, how-ever, that in many glimpses of the domestic relations of Jesus we see him separated from an undiscern-ing, if not an alienated, home. When his parents find their boy in the Temple, they keep his sayings indeed in their hearts, but they do not open their minds to those sayings. On the contrary, it is written that "they understood not the saying which he spake unto them." Even when his teach-ing had gained many other followers, his own kin had no ears for his message. What infinite pathos is in that scene at Capernaum, when the people crowd upon him so that he and his friends cannot find time to eat, and his mother and his brethren cannot "come at him for the press"! They come, it is plain, to take him from the dangers which be-

set him.   Perhaps they see the political peril that
threatens him ; perhaps they lament his break with
the sacred law ; perhaps they even doubt his sanity.   At any rate, they come, not to listen, but to
deter, and Jesus is smitten with the poignant realization that a man's foes are of his own household.
If he is to go on, it is to be alone.   Those who
should know him best are the last to comprehend
him.   With a look of profound sorrow, yet of un-
deterred resolution, he turns from those who are
dearest to him and gives himself to that larger sympathy, which is at the same time personal solitude.
" And he looked round on them which sat about
him and said : ' Behold my mother and my brother ;
for whosoever shall do the will of God, the same is
my mother and my brother and my sister.' "

Here, indeed, is the pathos of the character of
Jesus ; yet here also we approach the source of his
strength.   It was in this detachment of nature, this
isolation of the inner life, that Jesus found his communion with the life of God.   At this point his
ethics melt into his religion.   The crowd press
round him and he serves them gladly, and then it
seems as if his nature demanded solitude for the re-
freshment of his faith.   The tide of the spirit ebbs
from him in the throng, and when he goes apart
he is least alone, because the Father is with him.
Thus, from utterance to silence, from giving to
receiving, from society to solitude, the rhythm of his
nature moves ; and the power which is spent in
service is renewed in isolation.   He is able to bear

the crosses of others because he bears his own.
He can be of use to men because he can do
without men. He is ethically effective because he
is spiritually free. He is able to save because he
is strong to suffer. His sympathy and his solitude
are both alike the instruments of his strength.

How, then, shall one approach the type of character which is derived from him? It must be
approached, not as a survival of monastic or sentimental ideals, inapplicable to the conditions of
the modern world, but as a form of power, expressing itself in sympathy and fortifying itself in solitude. Its evidence is its effectiveness. It is able
to serve the world, as an unstinted river flows
down among the utilities of life because it is replenished from the eternal hills. It has its abundance and its reserves, its stream of service and its
peace in solitude; and the power which moves the
busy wheels of the life of man is fed from the
high places of the life of God.

CHAPTER III

WE turn from the Teacher to the teaching. If the character of Jesus Christ was, in any degree, such as has been indicated, it must have stamped itself upon his message, and have prescribed the moral type which should reproduce the spirit of his life. The creation of such a type was his fundamental desire. The Christian character was his chosen instrument for the establishing of the Kingdom of God.

What, then, is the nature of the character which thus proceeds from the teaching of Jesus Christ? From what roots does its growth begin, and into what foliage does its growth expand? What were the moral traits which Jesus most immediately welcomed, and the moral defects which he most unqualifiedly condemned? What was his hierarchy of ethical judgments, his classification of the supreme virtues and of the nethermost sins? By what steps of growth, according to his teaching, does the good life expand, from root to flower and from flower to fruit? What are the enemies without and the weaknesses within which threaten its vitality? Is the moral type which represents his influence fit to survive among the conditions of the modern world?

These questions appear to lead one directly to the most obvious aspect of the Gospels. Jesus was a teacher. More than forty times in the New Testament he is thus addressed. The immediate subject of his teaching is equally unmistakable. It is conduct, life, practical morality, character. Other aspects of his message, indeed, lead one beyond the sphere of ethics; but his first teaching is of duty, conscience, humanity, love, the conduct of life. "Whosoever heareth these sayings of mine, and doeth them, I will liken him unto a wise man, which built his house upon a rock."[1]   "Come, ye blessed of my Father; . . . inasmuch as ye have done it unto one of the least of these my brethren, ye have done it unto me."[2]   If, therefore, Jesus, the Teacher, is primarily a teacher of character, it would seem as if nothing could be simpler than to determine what that character is which he desires, and how it comes to be.

When, however, one turns to this elementary inquiry, he is at once confronted by two uses of the New Testament which gravely obscure this ethical teaching. They are the two chief heresies of Biblical interpretation. The first is the heresy of the casuist; the second is the heresy of the dogmatist.

The casuist turns to the Gospels to find ethical prescriptions applicable to specific ills.   He looks

[1] Matt. vii. 24.   [2] Matt. xxv. 34, 40.

for a code of maxims.   Conduct presents itself to him as a piecemeal, incidental, fragmentary series of decisions.   God says, Thou shalt, and, Thou shalt not, as each problem of duty stands in the way. The Gospels, however, when thus approached, are among the most baffling of documents.   They deal, it is true, with cases of conduct, and record specific moral judgments; but these detached instructions give, in themselves, no consistent law of life.   On the contrary, they are often perplexing and sometimes contradictory in their teaching, and the casuist, having determined his conduct by one precept, is surprised to find himself reproved by another teaching from the same lips.   "Resist not evil," says Jesus, and the casuist erects this precept into the essence of the Gospels,[1] only to find the teaching of non-resistance refuted by Jesus himself as he scourges the traders from the Temple or says to his friends: "I came not to send peace, but a sword"; "He that hath no sword, let him sell his garment, and buy one."[2]   "Swear not at all," says Jesus again, and the casuist proceeds to prohibit

---

[1] Tolstoi, "My Confession," tr. 1887, p. 190: "Whoever shall not utterly renounce all the cares and advantages of the life of the body, cannot fulfil the will of the Father."   "My Religion," tr. 1887, p. 94: "This simple, clear, and practical fourth commandment (Matt. i. 33–37), 'Never resent evil by force, never return violence for violence; if any one beat you, bear it; if any one would deprive you of anything, yield to his wishes; if any one would force you to labor, labor; if any one would take any of your property, abandon it at his demand.'"

[2] Matt. x. 34; Luke xxii. 36.

judicial oaths as an offence to Christ, only to find Jesus himself, when "adjured by the living God," ready to make solemn reply.[1] "I will give unto this last, even as unto thee,"[2] says Jesus, and the casuist justifies by this teaching a doctrine of social equality; but no sooner does he turn a few more pages of the Gospels than he hears Jesus say: "For he that hath to him shall be given: and he that hath not, from him shall be taken even that which he hath," as though nothing were more obvious than the truth of essential inequality.[3]

These paradoxes in which Christian casuistry finds itself involved indicate that the Gospels should be approached in quite another frame of mind. They are not collections of maxims, or utterances of oracles, or text-books of rules to be learned by rote. They are, on the contrary, the simple record of unstudied discourse as it was applied to varied incidents and needs. It is the occasionalism of the teaching which gives it the appearance of para-dox. Jesus is not weighing his utterances as though the world were listening; he is dealing with the immediate problem of the individual soul. "What he taught," said Robert Louis Stevenson, "was not a code of rules, but a loving spirit; not truths, but a spirit of truth; not views, but a view." The task of the modern student is not to detach his aphorisms from their circumstances and give to each a universal validity, but to discern through these occa-

[1] Matt. xxvi. 63.   [2] Matt. xx. 14.
[3] Mark iv. 25.

sional utterances the principles which control the Master's mind. It is easy enough, as has been wittily said, to die for an idea, if you have but one idea. It is easy enough, one might add, to define the Christian character, if you reduce that character to a single virtue. The casuist's trouble begins when he is confronted by the richness and many-sidedness of the teaching of Jesus. Idolatry of a single saying may be as misdirected as indifference to it. The nature of the Christian character is not comprehended by an incident or an aphorism, though the incident or aphorism may disclose some aspect of the teacher's comprehensive plan. The prescription of a physician in a given case may not be a remedy which is universally applicable, but the physician's dealing with the single case may disclose the prevailing habit of his mind. Here is the difference between the teaching of Jesus and that of the Pharisees. They were expounding precepts of casuistry; Jesus was teaching principles of morality. Instead of washings and tithings, he set forth the comprehensive commandments upon which the whole law and prophets hung. Christian casuistry tabulates the precepts of the Gospels; Christian ethics seeks the mind of Christ.[1]

[1] Herrmann, "Die sittl. Weisungen Jesu," 1904, ss. 48, 65 : "The most common and most pernicious misconception of the interpretation of these sayings is their acceptance as invariable laws. . . . Such an interpretation is possible for those only who care more for his words than for himself. . . . The teachings of Jesus are to be accepted, not as exhibitions of an arbitrary power, or flashes of inspiration, but as rays of light from his consciousness. They are not cords to bind us, but signs to point out the way to liberty."

On the other hand is the heresy — or more accurately, perhaps, the orthodoxy — of the dogmatist. To this habit of mind the Gospels offer, first of all, a body of doctrine, and the Christian character is a consequence of the Christian creed.   "Give me," a distinguished theologian has remarked, "the Incarnation and Resurrection of Christ, then Sin, the Atonement and Justification follow. . . .   In the defence of Supernatural Christianity everything is at stake. . . .   The great battle of the twentieth century . . . is a struggle between a Dogmatic Christianity, on the one hand, and an out-and-out naturalistic philosophy, on the other."[1]

Much there certainly is, both in the New Testament and in religious experience, which justifies this view of the Christian religion.   Righteousness, says Paul, "shall be imputed, if we believe on him that raised up Jesus our Lord from the dead."[2] Is it not rash, however, to maintain that in the defence of Dogmatic Christianity "everything is at stake"?   Much, no doubt, that is precious is involved; but is there no path leading to the Christian life except through consent to Christian dogma?   Does not this demand for doctrinal assurance as antecedent to the sense of sin reverse the natural order of Christian experience, and bar the door of discipleship to many who are trying to find their way to Jesus Christ? A different spiritual chronology meets one in

[1] F. L. Patton, "Princeton Theological Review," January, 1904, pp. 135, 136.   [2] Rom. iv. 24.

the first three Gospels. To the Apostle Paul,
as in the prevailing tradition of the later Church,
intellectual apprehension of Christ was antecedent to obedience; in the teaching of Jesus
himself, obedience is, as a rule, the path to intellectual apprehension. Jesus accepts as a disciple
many a hearer whose confession of faith would
satisfy few modern churches; he commends the
centurion's faith as greater than that of Israel; he
says to responsive and receptive lives: "Great is
thy faith"; "Thy faith hath saved thee"; even
though these lives are uninstructed in dogma and
untried in loyalty. In short, his teaching is not of
a logic of doctrine, but of a way of life. "Follow
me," he says, "Take up thy cross, and follow me";
and along the way of the Christian character may
be discovered the articles of the Christian creed.
The dogmatist overloads the teaching of Jesus with
theology, while the casuist strips that teaching
of its comprehensiveness and wealth. Casuistry
obscures the Gospels with legalism; dogmatism
complicates the Gospels with intellectualism. One
reduces Christian ethics to a meagre conformity;
the other involves Christian ethics in a superfluous
complexity. Between the two stands the teaching of
Jesus, — not casuistical or theological, but vital, personal, creative, — the recognition and development
of the capacity to follow him, the creation of the
Christian character.

How does he approach this ethical enterprise?
What was the process of moral growth which he

desired to quicken? From what root of spiritual
vitality does it proceed? What is to be its issue
for oneself and for the world? These are questions, not of Christian casuistry or of Christian
dogmatics, but of what a distinguished scholar has
called " psychological hermeneutics," [1] — the discovery of the spiritual intention of the Teacher
through the varied expressions of his word and
work. It is as though one were permitted to pass
through the antechambers of an artist's home,
where his finished products are set, and to enter
an inner room, where he may watch the master
busy with his creative task. With a peculiar sense
of reverent intimacy one passes by many other
aspects of the life of Jesus which have detained the
attention of the world, and enters that closet of the
spirit where the Master may be seen in the very
act of moulding men into the character which he
desires.

What then, we ask once more, are the elements
and principles of the Christian character? The
answer to this question may perhaps be best approached if one begins with the opposite inquiry.
What was the kind of character which received
from Jesus special condemnation and rebuke, as
though he felt it to be peculiarly impervious to his

[1] " Psychologisch orientierte Hermeneutik," Jülicher, "Gleich-
nisreden Jesu," I, 73, cited by Weinel (op. cit.), ss. 53, 54: The
succeeding pages are an admirable instance of the method of
" discovering, through the ideas behind the words, the spiritual
experiences behind both."

teaching and almost incapable of being moulded
into his plan? Here at once we meet one of the
most surprising traits of the teaching of Jesus, and
find ourselves called to reconsider our common
classification of virtues and sins. Jesus regards
with extraordinary leniency some of the faults
which the world most unqualifiedly condemns, and
on the other hand judges with surprising severity
much which the world lightly forgives or mistakes
for excellence. He is infinitely patient with the
precipitate Peter; he cannot bring himself to
despair of the treacherous Judas; he is a friend
of those whom the world calls sinners; he accepts
those whom the world calls lost.

What is it, then, in the hierarchy of morals which
seems to him more disheartening and irremediable
than either cowardice or treachery or passionate
sin? Strangely enough, it is the sin of self-sufficiency, the disease of self-importance, the spiritual
satiety of the Pharisaic mind. This is what stirs
Jesus to unmeasured and pitiless rebuke. "Thy sins
are forgiven thee," he says to a sinning woman;
"Woe unto you, hypocrites," he says, on the
other hand, to the bewildered representatives of
orthodox belief. What does this reversal of judgment mean? It means that, to Jesus, character
is not an attainment, but a growth. Under any
test of attainment it was monstrous to condemn
a Pharisee and pardon a Publican. It is not surprising that to many listeners the teaching of
Jesus seemed to reverse all reasonable standards

of respectability and sin. Jesus, however, is contemplating a higher righteousness, a new ideal, a perfected character; and he observes that the obstruction of his purpose which is most insurmountable is not experience of sin, but incapacity for growth. The Pharisees had been attacked by ethical atrophy. They were unteachable, unsusceptible, impenetrable, self-satisfied. The German agitator Lassalle said of the working-men whom he desired to inflame with a sense of wrong, that the chief cause of his exasperation with them was their inability to appreciate how much they lacked, their "*Bedürfnisslosigkeit*," the absence of the sense of need. Something of this same sense of helplessness seems to have fallen upon the mind of Jesus as he saw how much the Pharisees needed and how unconscious of need they were. They did not want to learn; their minds were closed; their self-sufficiency was an absolute barrier to the message of Jesus. "There is no cure," said Frederick Robertson, "for ossification of the heart." "Publicans and harlots," said Jesus, "shall enter into the kingdom before you."

This point of departure in the ethics of Jesus may be further indicated by observing the estimate which his teaching sets on childhood. The Christian world has become so familiar with the scene where Jesus sets a child in the midst and says, "Except ye turn and become as little children, ye shall in no wise enter the Kingdom of heaven," [1]

[1] Matt. xviii. 3, xix. 14; Mark x. 15; Luke xviii. 17; compare Ps. cxxxi. 2.

that it hardly considers how unprecedented a teaching is here given. It is in reality a new note in the history of ethics. Greek philosophy takes no serious account of children except to train them for maturity. Children did not nestle in the arms of Plato or Aristotle as they held their grave discourse. Such a saying as " Whosoever therefore shall humble himself as this little child, the same is greatest," [1] would have seemed in Athens or Rome sheer fanaticism. It might even now be questioned whether it is a reasonable doctrine which makes the child the teacher of the man. Is a child, even though guileless, nearer to the Kingdom of God than a ripened and disciplined character? Would not Jesus have been more of a philosopher and less of a sentimentalist if he had set among his disciples some clear-eyed youth or some wise, calm man, and said: " Except ye become as one of these, ye cannot enter the Kingdom "?

The real nature of the teaching of Jesus, it must be answered, is precisely indicated by the phrase which he employs. He does not say that the childlike spirit is inherently better than the spirit of the man. He does not promise that it shall possess or govern the Kingdom. He affirms only that it is the condition of entering the Kingdom. It is not that the child is better than the man, but that the child stands at the gate of the ideal and takes the first step toward the Christian

[1] Matt. xviii. 4.

G

character.   Docility, receptivity, open-mindedness, the eager, listening spirit of the little child — this is the polar opposite of the unteachable, satiated, closed heart of the Pharisee, and as the latter blocks the way to the kingdom, so the former opens its door.   The teaching of Jesus does not end with the praise of childhood, or confound childlikeness with childishness.   Better things than childhood has to offer are to be gained through the discipline and stress of life, yet entrance to the Kingdom is attained by no other door than the unspoiled, natural, spontaneous spirit of the child, and many a sophisticated and unteachable life will find with a shock of surprise that it has lost the key.[1]

Other aspects of the teaching of Jesus may appear to some minds antiquated or temporary or provincial, but this preliminary demand has peculiar significance for the conditions of the modern world. Pharisaism in its grosser forms of hypocrisy and affectation is certainly not a characteristic sin of the present age.   Candor and contempt of disguise are prevailing virtues.   Yet the underlying state of

[1] The same attitude of mind commends itself to scientific observers. See the noble letter of Huxley to Charles Kingsley, "Life and Letters," 1900, I, p. 219: "Science seems to me to teach in the highest and strongest manner the great truth which is embodied in the Christian conception of entire surrender to the will of God.   Sit down before the fact as a little child, be prepared to give up every preconceived notion, follow humbly wherever and to whatever end nature leads, or you shall learn nothing. . . .   I have only begun to learn content and peace of mind since I have resolved at all risks to do this."

mind in which Jesus found the first obstruction to his purpose is still conspicuous in great numbers of prosperous and respectable lives. It is the condition of spiritual satiety. Circumstances have been so propitious, social traditions so sufficient, and moral inheritances so ample, that many persons are now living on a kind of left-over morality, as they are living on bequeathed estates, and arrive at ethical decisions through transmitted momentum rather than through personal initiative. These persons cannot be classified with sinners. Their instincts make for refinement, self-culture, and physical vigor. They maintain, as a rule, a passive conformity to conventional ethics; but they have lost the capacity for moral enthusiasm, for vigorous decision, for spiritual vision, for social hope.

What is this epidemic disease of modern civilization which fastens so easily on many of the most favored lives? It is what the Germans call " *Verfettung* " — the overnourished and satiated condition created by lack of moral exercise. It is what athletes describe as staleness, the disease of high condition, the loss of moral freshness, the incapacity to respond to strain. Precisely this inertia and unresponsiveness Jesus observed in the respectable Pharisees and contrasted with the teachableness and eagerness of the little child. A large part of what is called modern society has forfeited the taste for simplicity and the appetite for righteousness, which are conditions of moral health. It is often fancied that some great transition in science or philosophy is responsible for this neutrality and lassitude of mind. The fact is, however, that spiritual insensibility is not an intellectual but a moral defect; not a philosophical development but an ethical reversion; the sheer indolence and satiety of a loose and ungirt habit of life.

Such, then, is the first condition of the Christian character. Its primary quality is teachableness. It is unattainable except by the open mind and the receptive heart. Two men go up to the Temple to pray, and of the two the Pharisee is in attainment the better man. He fasts, gives tithes, and scorns the sins of the Publican. He is, however, satisfied and unteachable, and his prayer is unavailing. The other is a self-confessed but penitent sinner, and there is to Jesus more hope in self-reproach than in self-complacency. Two sons go their different ways, — the one to evil, the other to self-regarding virtue, — and Jesus does not teach that the prodigal is better than his brother. The contrast is between satiated virtue and the conscious emptiness of sin. Far as the prodigal has wandered, he has not lost his hunger for love; near to the father as the elder brother has remained, he has remained self-seeking; and to the father's ear there is more hope in the penitent cry: "I am not worthy to be called thy son," than in the unfilial complaint: "These many years have I served thee and thou never gavest me a kid."

Character, in other words, is marked, not by its achievements, but by its desires. It is an unfolding process, a way of education, a moral evolution, thwarted by self-sufficiency, and beginning in docility and love. A child may be immature in morals as he is in form, but Jesus looks upon the child with the love which he felt for all budding and ripening things. He sees the far-off Divine event toward which this moral creation moves. The imperfect is significant as a prophesy of the possible. The ethics of Jesus are not static, but dynamic. He was what the modern world would call an ethical evolutionist. Life to him is not a condition, but a mode of motion. His God is a living God; his discipleship is a living process. " I am come that they may have life, and may have it abundantly." [1]

If this is the starting-point of the ethics of Jesus, then even in the primary demand for teachableness there are involved two other principles which characterize and illuminate all his message. One principle considers the persons to be made into Christians, the other principle considers the way they are to go. One represents the ethical faith of Jesus, the other his ethical method. The first is his teaching concerning moral growth, the second

[1] So, Wellhausen, "Israel. und Jüd. Gesch.," 5te Aufl., 1904, s. 384: " Religion ceases to be the property of experts (eine Domäne der Virtuosen). No art is essential, no refinement of erudition as of Rabbis, but a simple and open mind." (The whole chapter abounds in insight and eloquence.)

is his teaching concerning moral decision.   On the
one hand his acceptance of the tentative beginnings
of   character   indicates   his   confidence   in   moral
growth.   He does not expect the Christian character to bloom in a day.   Having found a receptive
soul, he gives it time to grow.   His loving observation of the ways of nature teaches him the analogy
of the growth of the spirit.   " First the blade," he
says, " then the ear, after that the full corn in the
ear." [1] Let the sower find good ground and he may
wait for a harvest.   Human nature, like the wheat-
fields of Palestine, is a soil where the good naturally
grows.   It has potential capacity.   The forces of
the universe conspire in its germination.   Even
lives which seem sterile or blighted have in them
the latent good.   Precisely as the law of growth
gives significance to each season, however harsh,
and to each storm, however violent, so the law of
growth in the Christian character sanctifies childhood, dignifies experience, and forbids despair.
Where there is growth there is life, and where
there is life there is hope.   What Jesus has in
mind is not primarily the condition of a life, but
its direction.   It was no accident which gave to
the Gospel its original title of "the Way."   Saul's
persecution was directed against those who were
" of this Way "; [2] and Paul, the convert, disputed
with those "who spake evil of that Way," so that
there "arose no small stir concerning the Way." [3]

---

[1] Mark iv. 28.   [2] Acts ix. 2.
[3] Acts xix. 9, 23.   So, "Teaching of the Twelve Apostles," tr.

The Christian religion is a movement, an organism, a faith, a hope, a door, a way.   Let a life be but moving along the way of Jesus, and, like a river, the very motion is a cleansing process, and instead of the malaria of the stagnant pool there is the self-purification of the flowing stream.

Here we meet a characteristic of the moral judgments of Jesus which to many minds has seemed unjustified and extreme.   It is his unconquerable faith in moral capacity, even when such faith seemed mistaken or misplaced.   The third Gospel narrates that when the infant Jesus was brought by his parents into the Temple, a devout old man took the child in his arms and prophesied that through this child the thoughts of many hearts should be revealed.   That is precisely what has happened to multitudes of lives through the teaching of Jesus.   He has revealed to them the thoughts of their own hearts, and taught them that their best self was their true self.   When the prodigal is stirred to repentance, he " comes to himself."   He had been dead and is alive again.   He had lost himself and now it is himself whom he finds.   The faith of Jesus in men produced faith in themselves, and they discovered within themselves thoughts and motives of which they themselves had not dreamed.   It was faith in growth which justified this faith in man.   People who seemed to them-

Hitchcock and Brown, 1884, p. 3: "Two ways there are, one of life and one of death, but there is a great difference between the two ways."

selves fixed in some condition of unworthiness or dulness or sin appeared, to Jesus, as children in the spiritual life, material for education, seed of the Kingdom; and his communication to them of the capacity for growth made them that which they desired to be.

Two dramatic examples illustrate this quality in Jesus. In one his faith was justified, in the other it was disappointed, but in both alike the principle is clear. On the one hand is his apparently unjustified faith in Peter. What could be less descriptive of that unstable character than to say that it should be a rock on which the Church might be built? Was ever a man less like a rock and more like shifting sand than Peter? May not the group of disciples have fancied that the saying was but the playful irony of the Master? Yet Jesus discerns in the man a capacity for leadership, believes in Peter even when Peter does not believe in himself, steadies his impetuous moods of devotion and denial, until at last the sand of his character is hardened by the friction of experience into sandstone, and Peter becomes the rock which his Master prophesied that he should be.

On the other hand is the still more perplexing relation of Jesus with Judas. How was it possible, one asks himself, that the plot of betrayal should ripen without detection or loss of faith? We seem placed between two difficult alternatives. Either Jesus, it may be said, was not discerning enough to discover the purpose of Judas, or else, knowing the

end, he still permitted a traitor to sit among the
disciples and break with them the paschal bread.
In the one case he seems to be an unobservant
leader; in the other case he seems to be playing a
merely dramatic part.   When, however, one recalls
the faith which Jesus had in potential morality,
neither his insight nor his sincerity seems at fault.
The truth appears to be that Jesus could not bring
himself to surrender Judas, and hoped to the last
that faith in him as a disciple might save him from
the fate of a betrayer.   The incidents of the last
days when thus interpreted are unspeakably touching.   Jesus is trying by force of confidence to hold
the disciple from his shame.   This faith is doomed
to disappointment, yet the better nature in which
the Master trusted overtakes the traitor when it is
too late, and Judas hangs himself in self-reproach.
It is startling to think how little was needed to reduce the character of Peter to that of Judas, or to
lift the character of Judas to that of Peter.   Both
were traitors, yet in neither did Jesus find it possible to abandon hope.   Both, he felt sure, still possessed the capacity for moral growth; both he trusted
with a limitless patience and desire.   One friend
he saved, and history has almost forgotten the sin
of Peter in the tradition of his leadership.   The
other friend Jesus seemed to lose, but even the
story of the betrayal is illuminated by the inextin-
guishable faith of Jesus in potential repentance, and
by the fact of that repentance when alas! it was
too late.

Moral education, in other words, begins, according to Jesus, not only with teachableness in the scholar, but with the Teacher's faith in the person taught. Jesus expects much of men. There is little evidence that his chosen friends were men of extraordinary capacities or opinions. They were plain people, with simple fears and hopes, wonders and alarms, yet Jesus, through his faith in them, makes of them heroes and martyrs.[1] "Ye are the light of the world," he says, "ye are the salt of the earth"; "Be ye therefore perfect"; and their natures, easily tempted to doubt or self-seeking or denial, respond at last to his great faith.

A Christian preacher, addressing young men, said not long ago that, just as children were attacked by so many infantile diseases that it was surprising to see them grow up, so youth was attacked by so many sins that it was surprising to see young men grow up good. Precisely the opposite of this teaching is that of Jesus. It is natural, he would say, for young men to be good, just as it is natural for a child to grow up. Hindrances they may have, and crises, and reversals, and some seed will fall on stony and thin soil; but in ethics as in nature

[1] Wernle (op. cit.), s. 65: "He [Jesus] enlarges the sphere of moral possibilities as a scientific discoverer enlarges the sphere of the scientifically possible. . . . The disciples of Jesus were originally no heroes; the whole relation of Jesus with them, up to the denial by Peter, proves this. Yet Jesus made of them a force strong enough to defy the world."

the law of life is not of unproductiveness and decay, but of growth and fruition. The teacher is to expect character, as the sower is to expect a crop.

This is the first lesson of Jesus, the Teacher, to all who profess to teach. Education in any form demands, first, the pupil's teachableness, and, secondly, the teacher's faith. No teacher can penetrate the closed and satiated mind; but the most open mind will shrink from the faithless teacher. To draw out the latent gift, to discover the unexpected capacity, to believe in the pupil even when he does not believe in himself — this is the test of the teacher; and to have this faith justified by the ripening mind and will — this is the teacher's great reward. Nor is this test to be applied to the education of the mind alone. The first condition of all effective leadership is faith in those who are to be led. Many a parent forfeits, by the habit of distrust, his right to guide his child; many a leader finds his followers fail him because they are driven, not led. The good shepherd goes before, and need not turn his head to see if the sheep are following. They know his voice, and follow because he is sure they will. His faith in them kindles their loyalty to him. When Washington at Valley Forge was reviewing his tattered troops, he paused before one feeble regiment and said, " Gentlemen, I have great confidence in the men of Connecticut," and the narrator says, " When I heard that, I clasped my musket to my breast and said, 'Let them come on.'"[1]

Such, then, are the two great assumptions of the teaching of Jesus. The Christian character begins in moral teachableness and is developed by moral faith. It assumes first, humility, and secondly, self-respect. Here is a union of traits which at first sight seems difficult to maintain. If a character is blessed with docility and child-likeness, is it not likely to forfeit initiative and self-confidence? If, on the contrary, it conceives of itself as infinitely precious, is it not likely to be tainted by self-importance and conceit? This antinomy, however, lies on the surface only of morality. Cheap morality may discourage effort; vulgar piety may despise teachableness; but in the deeper experiences of the spirit, receptivity and activity are not conflicting elements, but reciprocal and coöperative. The more one perceives how little he has done, the more the unattained persuades him. The more sincerely one cries, "God be merciful to me a sinner," the more justified in hope he goes down to his house. It is not the sense of ineffectiveness that is impenetrable; it is the sense of sufficiency. The

[1] So, John Watson, "The Mind of the Master," 1897, pp. 238, 239: "He [Jesus] moved among the people with a sanguine expectation; ever demanding achievements of the most unlikely, never knowing when He might be gladdened by a response. An unwavering and unbounded faith in humanity sustained His heart and transformed its subjects. . . . With everything against Him, Jesus treated men as sons of God, and His optimism has had its vindication."

child, sorry that he knows little, is eager to know more. The poor in spirit inherit the earth. Self-effacement is the beginning of self-respect. There is a sorrow, as the Apostle Paul said, which is unto death; but there is also a sorrow which is unto life.

Here is the root of that quality in the teaching of Jesus which has often been described as positiveness. The ethics of the Old Testament are in large degree negative and prohibitory; Jesus translates their "Thou shalt not" into the "Thou shalt" of the Gospels. His judgments concern themselves, not so much with things done which should not have been done, as with things left undone which should have been done. Among the sins which he especially condemns are unproductiveness, unfruitfulness, ineffectiveness, indecision. The servant is rebuked, not because he has lost his talent, but because he has not used it. It seems to him a sufficient defence to say: "Lo, there thou hast that is thine," but because he has not put his money to interest he is cast into darkness. The Priest and the Levite do no positive harm to the man by the wayside, but their sin of omission is their self-condemnation. This quality of positiveness of the ethics of Jesus is the corollary of his doctrine of growth. The prohibitions which leave life where it now is, are supplanted by the summons to action and the demand for progress. "Take up thy cross," says Jesus, not to lean on it, but to follow, with the cross on the shoulder. "Come, ye blessed of my Father, inherit the Kingdom prepared," not for the resigned, the patient, the passive, but for the giver of food to the hungry and the opener of eyes to the blind. The chief contention of Jesus was not with sinners, but with the negatively good. Pharisaic ethics, the code of prohibition, seemed to him the chief obstruction of moral growth. One might obey all these precepts of abstinence and remain an unprofitable servant. His demand is not merely for a good life, but for a life that is good for something; teachable that at last it may itself teach; growing that at last it may be fruitful. First the grain, he teaches, then the ear; but both for the sake of the corn which shall feed the hungry. It is not the virtue one has attained or the things one does not do which makes one a Christian. One may be saved by temperament from many faults which degrade, or saved by prudence from the mistakes of the precipitate; and this illusion of sufficiency may lead him with all sincerity to pray : " I thank thee that I am not as other men are "; but the judgment of Jesus probes this illusory judgment with its positive test. What hast thou done? it asks. What gain has God from his investment in thy soul; what fruit from thy sowing; what added strength or peace or courage, through the loan of life committed to thy care; what fidelity as of the faithful steward ; what watchfulness as of the trusted porter; what integrity as of the righteous judge? When Mazzini heard a man described as good, he asked, "Whom then has he saved?" It is the question of Jesus. The Christian character is not free from blunders or failures; but it grows, through its blunders and failures, toward effectiveness, serviceableness, merciful judgment of others, humble judgment of itself. Its end is not restraint, but generosity. It asks not, "What shall I leave undone?" but "What shall I do?" It mounts on stepping-stones of the dead self to higher things. It finds itself by losing itself; and finally it will be judged, not by its accomplishments, but by its growth; not by its achievements, but by its ideals.

"And this one thought of hope and trust comes with its
        healing balm,
    As here I lay my brow in dust and breathe my lowly psalm;
    That not for heights of victory won, but those I tried to gain,
    Will come my gracious Lord's 'Well done,' and sweet effacing rain."

If, however, the roots of the Christian character begin in teachableness and are persuaded to their growth by faith, what is the form which this growth assumes as it emerges into the air and light? What is the first expression of the Christian character, the point where, as it were, it breaks through the soil of consciousness and rises into the stalk of the conduct of life? What is the specific organ of moral growth, the significant factor of moral experience? At this point we are confronted by the various psychologies of religion, enumerating the possible forms which the spiritual life may assume. Is religious experience primarily expressed through the reason or the emotions or the will? Is character determined chiefly by thought or feeling or volition?

The attention of scholars has been chiefly directed to the place of the first two elements of experience. Either the reason or the emotions has seemed the dominant spiritual force. On the one hand, the distinction of human life is discovered in its rational nature. The truth makes men free. "To place the essence of religion in feeling is self-contradictory, for a religion of mere feeling would not even know itself to *be* religion." "The spiritual life of man . . . rests on the fact that reason or self-consciousness is the form of an infinite content."[1] On the other hand, it has been urged that a spiritual experience which is universal and commanding cannot be reserved for the elect few who may approach it by the way of reason. "The measure of knowledge is not the measure of piety." At one point only does the spirit of the individual have free access to the spirit of the Eternal, as an unobstructed stream empties itself into the sea. It is in the high exaltation of the emotional life. "Your feeling, in so far as it expresses the universal life you share, is your religion."[2] Here is the only way of revelation open to all comers. There is no aristocracy of the spirit. If the life of God is to reach the life of man without discrimination of privilege or condition, it must be in those

[1] John Caird, " Philosophy of Religion," 1880, pp. 170, 291.
[2] Schleiermacher, " Reden über die Religion," 1843, ss. 180 ff.

emotional experiences which all can share. "The spirit searcheth all things, yea, the deep things of God."

In this perennial issue of philosophy between the rationalists and the mystics, there is much on either side which finds itself verified by the teaching of Jesus. It was his knowledge of God which gave him tranquillity and power. "No man," he said, "knoweth the Father save the Son, and he to whomsoever the Son will reveal him."[1] It was, again, his high accessions of spiritual emotion which lifted him above intellectual doubt. "I thank thee, O Father, Lord of heaven and earth, because thou hast hid these things from the wise and prudent, and hast revealed them unto babes."[2] Yet, however rational may be the philosophy of Jesus, and however exalted his moods of mystic insight, it was neither to the reason nor to the emotions that he turned for the initial dynamic of the spiritual life. His appeal is primarily to the third function of spiritual expression, the will. He expects from men a moral initiative. "Follow me," he says. "Sell all that thou hast, and follow me. Take up thy cross and follow me. Whosoever shall do the will of God, the same is my brother and sister and mother. Be it unto thee even as thou wilt." In other words, his teaching is primarily ethical. What he first demands is not verified truth or exalted emotions, but moral decision. He deals with many

[1] Matt. xi. 27; Luke x. 22.　　　　[2] Matt. xi. 25.

persons whose opinions are far from fixed and whose feelings are far from purified; but Jesus takes these lives just as they are, and welcomes the determination of the will as the test of discipleship. The moral decision may be accompanied by a clarifying thought or by an emotional surprise, or by both. It is as if one had lost his path in the dark, but, summoning his will to try the way that seemed most straight, should find it leading quickly to a well-known road and the lights of home. The first step toward safety is in the decision to proceed. The will takes up the march, and the mind and heart follow. Among the obstacles to the spiritual life on which Jesus primarily dwells is the sin of indecision: "He that is not with me, is against me. He that gathereth not with me, scattereth. No man can serve two masters." Neutrality is iniquity. Pilate, though he finds no fault with Jesus, is responsible for his fate. On which side? asks Jesus. What is the direction of desire? "Seek first the Kingdom of God and His righteousness, and all these things shall be added unto you." The Christian character has not, indeed, through this initial decision reached the port toward which it moves; but it is, as it were, launched for its voyage, when the blocks that held it are struck away by one sharp impulse of the will.[1]

[1] So, Wernle (op. cit.), ss. 50, 65: "Jesus, simply because he is a Jew, is far removed from speculation concerning God. . . . But it is equally true that Jesus is no mystic, and demands of no one a

No aspect of the teaching of Jesus is more significant than this appeal to the will.   It is not
a question of origins.   Psychology may still with
justice urge that the beginnings of the religious
life must be sought, either in the primitive speculations of the reason or in the primitive agitations of

mystic self-absorption in God. . . . The teaching of Jesus is a
summons to the will, the faculty of free decision. . . . He doubts
not that one can ; his question is whether one wills."   Modern
psychology has arrived at a similar recognition of the priority of the
will in spiritual growth.   Percy Gardner, " A Historic View of the
New Testament," 1901, p. 37 : " In the nature of man the supreme
element is will, which dominates alike feeling and thought ";
p. 86 : " According to the teaching of the Founder of Christianity,
the will of God is revealed to men in two ways — in the external
and visible world as law, in the moral world as ideal. . . . The
religious view of the will is set forth in the Gospels as it is taught
nowhere else."   Still more striking is the evidence of spiritual autobiography.   " I resolved," wrote John Wesley in 1725, " to devote
all my life to God, all my thoughts, words, and actions, being
thoroughly conscious that there was no medium, but that every
part of my life, not some only, must be a sacrifice either to God or
to myself, that is, in effect, the devil."   " I have been for the last
hour on the seashore," wrote Charles Kingsley on his twenty-
second birthday, " not dreaming, but thinking deeply and strongly,
and forming determinations which are to affect my destiny through
time and eternity.   Before the sleeping earth and the sleeping sea
and stars, I have devoted myself to God, — a vow never (if he
gives me the faith I pray for) to be recalled."   So, Bushnell (cited
by W. Gladden, " Pioneers of Religious Liberty in America," 1903,
p. 231) : " ' Have I ever consented to be, and am I really now, in
the right . . . to live for it, to make any sacrifice it will cost me, —
in a word, to be in wholly right intent, and have no mind but this
forever? '   This was Horace Bushnell's conversion.   He has found
God. . . .   The ethical test will be applied, then, unflinchingly to
theology."

the emotions. The supremacy of the will marks, no doubt, a later stage in social evolution, a late arrival in the history of the soul. Moral decision obviously assumes some knowledge of the objects of choice, and some feeling of attraction or repulsion concerning them. This confession, however, is precisely what gives its exceptional character to the teaching of Jesus. Its primary emphasis is given to a factor of experience of which primitive religion takes scarcely any account. He is not concerned with defining a philosophy of religion, but with communicating a practical religion. He is dealing, not with primitive man, but with developed man, and touching motives of the spiritual life which are not effective in less evolved religions. The origins of faith may be discovered in imagination and wonder, in crude cosmologies, in the sense of dependence, in emotions of hope or fear; but a new step is taken by the teaching of Jesus in his summons to the will. The Christian religion, as Kant taught, is primarily a moral religion. It creates, like other religions, a theology; it feels, like other religions, an emotion; but neither the theologians nor the mystics touch the characteristic note of the teaching of Jesus. What he desires first of all to communicate is not a system of doctrine or a rush of feeling, but an ethical decision. Before his public ministry begins he withdraws from human companionship and faces the special temptations of conscious power, of self-display, and of worldly glory, which threaten him.

Once and for all he fortifies his will against them, and from that time to the day when he gives back his life to God, saying, "Not my will, but thine, be done," [1] the dominating factor, both in his experience and his teaching, is not intellectual achievement or emotional exaltation, but ethical decision. "My meat," says the fourth Gospel, "is to do the will of him that sent me." "I seek not mine own will, but the will of him that sent me."[2] The Sermon on the Mount concludes with the acceptance, not of those who confess "Lord, Lord," but of those who "do the will of my Father."[3] "Whosoever shall do the will of God," says Jesus, again, "the same is my brother, and my sister, and mother."[4] First obedience, then insight; first decision, then precision; first the following of Jesus, and later the understanding of him, — such is the sequence of Christian experience. When modern psychology announces that "The willing department of our nature . . . dominates both the conceiving department and the feeling department,"[5] what is this but a reiteration of the teaching of the fourth Gospel, "He that willeth to do the will shall know of the doctrine"? Among the baffling truths which invite and defy the reason, and the tides of feeling which rise only to fall, the beginnings of

[1] Luke xxii. 42.
[2] John iv. 34, v. 30.
[3] Matt. vii. 21.
[4] Mark iii. 35.
[5] William James, "The Will to Believe," 1897, p. 114. So also, p. 141: "To the end of time our power of moral and volitional response to the nature of things will be the deepest organ of communication therewith we shall ever possess."

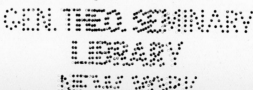

Christian experience are, according to the teaching of Jesus, in the conversion of the will.

> " Our wills are ours, we know not how,
>   Our wills are ours to make them thine."

What is there more disheartening in the history of Christian thought than the meagre recognition of this appeal of Jesus to the will? Systems of theology have been devised in which every virtue is ascribed to God except that of simple goodness, and every hope offered to men except that of moral choice. Creeds have been confidently promulgated by millions as expressing the essence of the Christian faith, which one might utter in entire sincerity without committing himself to personal holiness or ethical decision. It is not surprising that the vulgar estimate of the Christian character should gladly seize on this defect, and fancy that, to the follower of Jesus, dogma is more than obedience and feeling more than righteousness. No single cause, perhaps, has done so much to alienate plain minds from the Christian religion as this divorce of faith from morals. Elsewhere the issues of life are chiefly determined by the will; the best law in other affairs is the law of conscience; the highest occupation to which most men attain is the simple effort to do their duty ; and if the teaching of Jesus gives another principle of conduct, derived either from speculative opinion or from emotional excitement, it becomes an unreal and ineffective teaching among the ordinary problems of unsophisticated men.

The fact is, however, that Christian disciple-ship begins, where all excellence begins, in the dedication of the will to goodness. The first demand of Jesus is not for orthodoxy or ecstasy, but for morality. Seek first God's Kingdom and His righteousness, — this is not the whole of the Christian faith, but it is its first article. The first step to take in the following of Jesus is the resolution to be good. The Israelite without guile is fit to be a disciple. Further disclosures of truth and further accessions of feeling lie along the way of the Christian character; but the direction of its growth is determined by the will. The reason is like the sails of a ship, which give momentum and lift; the feelings are the waves, thrown off tumultuously on either side; but the rudder, which gives direction and control to life, is the will.

At this point, however, where the Christian life hears the summons to the will, there enters a further experience which gives a new quality of poignancy and pathos to the story of the Christian character. It is that experience which the theologians have described as the sense of sin. The will, invited to this definite decision, becomes aware of habits and tendencies whose significance has been unrecognized and whose mastery has been unchecked. It is as though the landscape of life were blurred in outline because seen through an ill-adjusted glass, and as though the action of the will threw the picture of life into focus, so that one saw the perspective of conduct with a new

sense of vividness and precision. As the horizon
of inclination thus takes shape, there comes to the
beholder a shock of surprise and shame. Gross
and startling shapes, at once repelling and irre-
sistible, grow distinct and recognizable. The
action of the will discloses an area of conduct in
which are seen volcanic craters, threatening an
outpouring of evil, from which one recoils with
horror and alarm. Life, which had appeared a
tranquil and orderly growth, seems disordered,
divided, undermined.

Such, for example, was the first effect of Christian discipleship in the experience of so intelligent and controlled a man as the Apostle Paul.
He had learned his lesson in the Law, and had
conformed to its ethical demands. " I had not
known sin," he says, " but by the law. . . . Wherefore the law is holy, and the commandment holy,
and just, and good." [1] Then came the new summons to the Christian character, and that decision
of the will disclosed to Paul a chasm, into which
he had not before looked, and which separated
his Hebrew legalism from his Christian ideal.
" Sin, taking occasion by the commandment,
wrought in me all manner of concupiscence." He
becomes aware of a divided, unreconciled, volcanic
life. Conduct comes into focus before him, and
the foreground of this scene is a battle-ground
where two forces struggle for control. " The good
that I would, I do not, but the evil that I would

[1] Rom. vii. 7-12.

not, that I do. . . .   Oh, wretched man that I am,
who shall deliver me from the body of this death?"
What shall be the end of this spiritual struggle? It
cannot be ignored or pacified or arbitrated. It must
be fought through. The antinomy of character must
be overcome, the strength of sin subdued, until
Paul is able at last to say : " The law of the spirit of
life in Christ Jesus hath made me free from the law
of sin and death. . . . Thanks be to God, which
giveth us the victory through our Lord, Jesus
Christ." [1] It was a victory well won, yet through
all his later life the apostle bore the scars of the
battle, and through all his teaching runs this sense
of internecine conflict between flesh and spirit,
the old man and the new.[2]

When one turns from this tragedy of the conscience which the Epistles of Paul describe, to the
story of moral experience told in the first three
Gospels, the climatic change which has already
been observed is again immediately felt. The
landscape of ethics is not volcanic and appalling,
but sunny and inviting, as of a home country of
the will. " Jesus," a distinguished German Evangelical has remarked, " as the preacher of his
Gospel should take note, has spoken little of sin
in general, and has proposed no doctrine of it, least
of all a doctrine of its origin." [3] If it were true

---

[1] Rom. viii. 2 ; I Cor. xv. 57.

[2] Compare Jacoby, " Neutest. Ethik," 1899, ss. 266 ff., and Stevens,
"Theology of the New Testament," 1899, pp. 338 ff., with notes.

[3] Beyschlag, " Neutest. Theol.," tr. Buchanan, 1895, I, 90.

that the outlook upon life of the "twice-born" is "the wider and completer," or that "the 'heroic' or 'solemn' way in which life comes to them is a 'higher synthesis,'"[1] then the character, not of Jesus, but of Paul, would represent the moral ideal of Christians, as indeed it has dominated much of Christian teaching. The moral experience of Jesus is not a revolution, but an evolution. He meets his own temptations, but he meets them with preparedness and tranquillity, and repels them with authority and contempt. "Get thee hence, Satan: for it is written, Thou shalt worship the Lord thy God, and him only shalt thou serve."[2] The religion of Jesus is not that of the "twice-born," but that of the "healthy-minded." A Christian priest who holds an infant in his arms and says: "Forasmuch as all men are conceived and born in sin, . . . we beseech Thee . . . that this child, being delivered from Thy wrath, may be received into the ark of Christ's Church," has learned his lesson from the Psalmist[3] or from the Apostle Paul[4] rather than from him who said: "Suffer little children to come unto me. . . . Whosoever shall not receive the kingdom of God as a little child, he shall not enter therein."[5] Paul, the man of cities, feels a

[1] William James, "Varieties of Religious Experience," 1902, p. 488.

[2] Matt. iv. 1–11.

[3] Ps. li. 5 : "I was shapen in iniquity; and in sin did my mother conceive me."　　　[4] Rom. v. 9–12.　　　[5] Mark x. 15.

kindred turbulence within himself; Jesus, the interpreter of nature, feels the steady persuasiveness of the sunshine of God, and grows from childhood, in wisdom and stature and favor with God and man.

Beneath these differences, however, there is a deeper sense in which the recognition of sin is as characteristic of Jesus as of Paul. The decision of the will which Jesus asks, while it may not be a dramatic catastrophe, is none the less a deliberate turning or conversion of the nature toward teachableness and childlikeness. "Except ye turn," he says, "and become as little children, ye shall in no wise enter into the kingdom of Heaven." [1] The first call of Jesus is the call to repentance. "From that time forth Jesus began to preach and to say, Repent, for the kingdom of Heaven is at hand"; [2] and his disciples, taught by him, "went out and preached that men should repent." [3]

Jesus is not concerned with Sin, as an abstraction. The word, as used not less than forty times in the Epistle to the Romans, is used but once in the Synoptic Gospels. Of sins, on the contrary, and sinning, and sinful men, Jesus has much to say. He traces acts to their source in the will. " From within, out of the heart of men, proceed evil thoughts, adulteries, fornications, murders, thefts, covetousness, wickedness, deceit, lasciviousness, an

[1] Matt. xviii. 3.
[2] Matt. iv. 17, xi. 21; Mark i. 15, vi. 12; Luke xv. 7, 10; xxiv. 47.   [3] Mark vi. 12.

evil eye, blasphemy, pride, foolishness."[1] Jesus, not less imperatively than Paul, sets at the gates of the Kingdom the plain demand for a will turned toward righteousness, and a conscience sorry for its specific sins. By what road one shall have come to this gate, and through what storms of the spirit he shall enter it, does not seem to Jesus essential to say. The fourth Gospel, in sharp contrast with the reticence of the Synoptics, reports him as prescribing a process of spiritual agony like that of physical child-birth: "Ye must be born again," says Jesus to Nicodemus; and Christian teaching has often found in this travail of the conscience the only sign that the Christian character was born. To Jesus, however, the form is less than the fact. Whenever and however the decision is reached and the will is turned, there the same victory which Paul describes, of the spirit over the flesh, the new man over the old, is won. Compromise is as far from the calm confidence of Jesus as from the brave wrestlings of Paul. "If thy right hand offend thee, cut it off ; if thine eye offend thee, pluck it out." To Jesus as to Paul the sense of a divided will is the essence of the sense of sin.[2]

---

[1] Mark vii. 20–23.

[2] Compare, Jacoby (op. cit.), ss. 56 ff. : "It is noticeable that the judgment of Jesus concerning sin is without severity. It is a sickness (Matt. ix. 12, xv. 14 ; Mark ii. 17 ; Luke v. 31), a folly (Matt. v. 26 ; Luke vi. 49 ; Matt. xxv. 1–13). . . . Three sins are emphasized by Jesus, — hypocrisy (Matt. xxiii. 13–31), hardheartedness (Matt. vi. 15 ; xviii. 23–35), and worldliness (Matt. vi. 24 ; Luke xvi. 13, xii. 15–21, xvi. 19–26). Wernle, "Die Anfänge

At what point in experience, it may be asked, does this consciousness of conflict, this cry of the life rent by two forces, occur? Is it the beginning of religious experience or is it the corollary of an antecedent act of will? Is it a sign of the fall of man or of the rise of man? Is it a witness of death or of birth? It has often been regarded as evidence of the remoteness of human life from holiness, the mark of incapacity for moral growth, the witness of alienation from God. To Jesus, on the contrary, and indeed to Paul, this poignant appreciation of unworthiness is a step, not toward the darkness, but toward the light; a mark, not of alienation from goodness, but of the emergence of character from impenetrability to docility, from the self-satisfaction of the Pharisee to the spirit of the little child. The sense of shame, the confession of sin, the cry for forgiveness, are experiences which meet one, not on his way down, but on his way up. The consciousness of sin is the prophecy of redemption. The publican crying, "God be merciful to me a sinner," is already less a sinner. The prodigal saying, "I am not worthy

unserer Religion," 1901, ss. 65 ff.: "The Hebrew sense of sin . . . had grown to a form of disease. . . . Paul is its great interpreter. . . . Jesus banishes this morbid sense of sin. It disappears before him like the mist before the sun. . . . One would forfeit his right relation to God if he refused to claim God's pardon. . . . Before this faith in the pardon of a fatherly God vanish the beautifully constructed theories of sacrifice and substitution. The one parable of the prodigal son disposes of them. The theology of sin, with sin itself, is left behind by the disciple of Jesus."

to be called thy son," is in fact claiming his sonship. The fear of the Lord is the beginning of wisdom. The confession of sin softens the soil where the seed of the Kingdom grows. Jesus is the friend of sinners, not because he is indifferent to sin or because he confuses evil with good, but because the character he desires to establish grows out of self-humiliation and regret. " I am not come," he says in lofty satire, " to call the righteous, but sinners to repentance." " Come unto me all ye that labor and are heavy laden, and I will give you rest." [1]

Such, then, are the roots of the Christian character. A teachable life is stirred to faith in potential goodness and responds with a decision of the will. Conscious of its faults, confessing its follies, chastened by its new ideals, it yet feels a new sense of power, and turns to the way of Jesus, as roots reach up into the light; and as it thus rises above the ground of consciousness, it is surprised to find its imperfect beginnings and undeveloped traits welcomed by the Master who has bidden it turn that way. It is the surprise which the first blades of spring might feel as they ventured forth into the cold and found the sunshine waiting for them. These, says Jesus, are his disciples, — plain people,

---

[1] So, Stevens, "Theology of the New Testament," 1899, p. 99: " He [Jesus] saw men as they were. . . . In all their unfilial indifference and disobedience they were still, in his view, Sons of God, susceptible to the appeal of a Father's love, and capable both of coming to themselves — their true, normal selves — and of returning to their Father."

with half-formed purposes and half-grown characters, likely to blunder, quick to misinterpret, still
tempted to be ambitious, contentious, hesitating,
even unfaithful; still crying: "Lord, we believe,
help thou our unbelief"; yet welcomed because
turned toward the light, teachable in temper, able
to grow, converted in will, finding the Way. The
roots of the Christian life, fixed in the soil of
moral loyalty and unhindered by the weeds of
hypocrisy, unteachableness, or love of Mammon,
normally grow toward the new moral type; and the
patient Sower, walking his furrow, awaits the harvest, when, from these germinating beginnings,
under the sunshine of God, will some day issue the
ripened fruit of the Christian character.

CHAPTER IV

THE GROWTH OF THE CHRISTIAN CHARACTER

THE beginnings of the Christian character are in the childlike temper, the teachable nature, the responsive will. Repentance enters where self-sufficiency may not tread. Imperfections, mistakes, blunders, are not, to Jesus, insuperable obstacles. What he welcomes is capacity for growth, open-mindedness, the turning of the will; and finding these, he trusts himself and his cause to persons who have little else to offer him except the will to believe. Up through the consciousness of sin grows the Christian experience, until from the initial decision of the will there issues at last a fair and expanding flower of character.

What, then, is the form which this growth of the Christian character assumes; the perfect fruit of this ethical process? The answer to this question may be approached by recalling three great words in the teaching of Jesus which together express the moral ideal of the Christian character. Of these three words the first represents especially the prevailing tone of ethical teaching in the first three Gospels; the second recalls to us the more intimate utterances of Jesus himself; while the third, though appearing throughout the record, is peculiarly characteristic of the fourth Gospel. The words seem to represent distinct moral types. One suggests a character which is upright but severe; another a character which is gentle but soft; the third a character which is large but vague; yet taken together these three words form a logical sequence of ethical definition, and each in turn contributes to the growth and is essential to the completeness of the Christian character.

The first of these three great words is Righteousness. It was no new word to Hebrew tradition, but among the most familiar attributes ascribed to God, and the most essential virtues demanded of man. "If we observe to do all these commandments," says the Book of Deuteronomy, "it shall be our righteousness"; [1] "He shall judge the world with righteousness," says the Book of Psalms.[2] "God that is holy shall be sanctified in righteousness," says Isaiah.[3] When, therefore, those who listened to the teaching of Jesus heard him repeat the ancient word and demand of his followers that

[1] Deut. vi. 25.

[2] Ps. xcvi. 13 ; So, lxxii. 2 ; Is. ix. 7, xi. 2, 4, xxxii. 1.

[3] Is. v. 16. Compare Wendt, "Teaching of Jesus," tr. Wilson, 1897, I, 257: "We must bear in mind that, in the Old Testament phraseology, which governed the religious language of the Jews in the time of Jesus, and which he himself adopted, the word 'righteousness' had a wider signification than that of the Greek word 'δικαιοσύνη'. . . . Righteousness in this sense is the most general designation for the pious God-pleasing disposition or conduct of men which is opposed to sin."

I

they should seek first the Kingdom of God and His righteousness, it may well have seemed to them that his message was a simple reiteration of the Law and the Prophets whose teachings they knew so well.

Jesus is, however, in fact utilizing this large and sacred word of Hebrew tradition to open the way along a path which was familiar to his hearers toward an end which they had failed to see. His preaching was, indeed, the well-known summons to righteousness: "Blessed are they that hunger and thirst after righteousness."[1] "Then shall the righteous shine forth as the sun in the kingdom of their Father."[2] Is this righteousness, however, that same trait of rectitude and conformity of which the Law took account? Yes, Jesus answers, it is essentially that which they of old time have preached. His message reproduces the original intention of the Law. "Go ye and learn what that meaneth," he cites from Hosea; "I desired mercy and not sacrifice."[3] "I am not come to destroy, but to fulfil." Yet Righteousness, as the word is used by Jesus, though it may legitimately claim the ancient title, is immediately distinguished by him from the common usage. "Except your righteousness," he says, "shall exceed the righteousness of the Scribes and Pharisees, ye shall in no case enter into the kingdom of heaven."[4] Righteousness had become the word which gave its authority to the external, legal, ceremonial

[1] Matt. v. 6.
[2] Matt. xiii. 43.
[3] Hosea vi. 6 ; Matt. ix. 13, xii. 17.
[4] Matt. v. 20.

conformity, whose yoke lay with oppressive weight upon the spirit of Israel. "Being ignorant of God's righteousness," wrote Paul, "and seeking to establish their own righteousness, they did not subject themselves to the righteousness of God." [1] To deliver his people from this yoke, to recall them from the righteousness of conformity to the righteousness of the heart, to revive the spirit of righteousness within the forms of rectitude — that, indeed, was to restore the original definition of righteousness, yet it involved such revolutionary demands as to be a practically new command.[2]

Thus, the first task of Jesus is to legitimatize the word which he has spiritualized. He is not come to destroy, yet the righteousness which the Law appeared to teach becomes the first object of his attack. His first controversy is with conformity,

[1] Rom. x. 3. Compare the suggestive view of J. H. Ropes (Journal of Bibl. Lit. 1903, p. 211), "'Righteousness' and 'The Righteousness of God' in the Old Testament and in St. Paul," p. 227: "We have here a significant and instructive illustration of the fact that Paul the Pharisee, like his Master, turned back from the problems and dreams of his contemporaries to the words of the Prophets of Israel, and that he found in them with right the heralds of the Gospel of Christ."

[2] H. Holtzmann, "Neutest. Theologie," 1897, s. 178: "The Sermon on the Mount, in its announcement of the ethical programme of Jesus, discriminates between 'justitia' and 'jus.' Its theme is that 'higher righteousness,' which is the ideal of Jesus. Righteousness is conduct regulated by the standard of the perfection of God. . . . When Jesus commends those who hunger and thirst for such righteousness, the profoundest desire of Israel, its thirst for the Living God (Ps. xlii. 2), gets its highest ethical expression."

conventionalism, externalism, legalism. Righteousness had become, as a distinguished scholar has
said, "not so much a moral quality as a legal sta-
tus."[1] Rectitude by statute had supplanted righteousness of the heart. Was, then, the teaching of
Jesus conservative, in reviving the earlier law, or
radical, in rejecting the popular faith? It was
both. Throughout the Old Testament had been
heard from time to time the same note of spiritual
righteousness. "Man looketh on the outward
appearance, but the Lord looketh on the heart,"[2]
says the Book of Samuel. "Search me, O God,
and know my heart"; "Create in me a clean heart,
O God,"[3] repeat the Psalms. "I, the Lord, search
the heart,"[4] teach the Prophets. To this thread of
spiritual tradition Jesus attaches himself. Not a
jot or tittle of the Law is to be disturbed by him.
In great detail and by a series of instances he
illustrates his interpretation of the ancient word,
the righteousness which was not that of the
Pharisees, but which was the heart of the Law
and Prophets. "Ye have heard that it was said by
them of old time . . . but I say unto you."[5]

The earlier righteousness had concerned itself
with overt acts: "Thou shalt not kill"; the new

[1] Robertson Smith, "The Prophets of Israel," 1882, p. 71:
"The ideas of right and wrong among the Hebrews are forensic
ideas; that is, the Hebrew always thinks of the right and the wrong
as if they were to be settled before a judge."

[2] 1 Sam. xvi. 7.   [4] Jer. xvii. 10.
[3] Ps. cxxxix. 23, li. 10.   [5] Matt. v. 21–28.

righteousness searched the heart: "If thou . . . rememberest that thy brother hath aught against thee." The former righteousness took account of unchaste conduct: "Thou shalt not commit adultery"; the new righteousness judged the desire behind the act: "Whosoever looketh on a woman to lust after her hath committed adultery with her already in his heart." The old righteousness taught consistency between promise and performance: "Thou shalt not forswear thyself"; the new righteousness supplanted protestation by moderation: "Swear not at all." It was the teaching which inspired Newman to say:—

> "Prune thou thy words, thy thoughts control
>   That o'er thee swell and throng;
>   They will condense within thy soul,
>   And turn to purpose strong."

Those of old time had commended justice, reciprocity, an eye for an eye, love for neighbors and hate for enemies; the new righteousness supplanted this equation of rights by generosity, forgiveness, the sacrifice of rights, the recognition of the unrequited beneficence of God: "Love your enemies, . . . do good to them that hate you"; "If ye love them which love you, what reward have ye? Be ye therefore perfect as your Father in heaven is perfect." First restraint, then sacrifice, is the law of the Christian character. Force is reserved that it may be freely spent. "We Florentines," said the old scholar in "Romola," "live scrupulously, that we may spend splendidly."

Here is no new code of social laws. Jesus is not falling in his turn into the legalism against which he had protested, or defining righteousness once more in terms of conformity. He does not legislate concerning non-resistance or judicial oaths or self-mutilation; he substitutes ethical principles for ethical maxims, and displaces the righteousness which is hypocrisy or the acting of a part, by the righteousness which is reality or the expression of a life. Instead of superimposed, external, legal morality, tied to a life as a flower is wired to its stalk, the growth of the Christian character is like the answer of a seed to the sunshine; and this straight normal growth puts forth, as its first shoots, the righteousness of self-judgment, self-control, and self-sacrifice.[1]

Such is the first word of the ethics of Jesus. He sets over against each other the conscience regulated from without and the conscience approved from within, ceremonial conformity and spiritual morality, rectitude and righteousness, an ethical code and an ethical ideal. When one frees this teaching from its Oriental phrases, how modern

[1] So, Herrmann, 14ter Evang.-soz. Kong., s. 20: "How does Jesus discriminate his ethics from the prevailing teaching? Is it enough to say that righteousness to him concerns not outward acts alone, but the inner disposition? . . . This was no new distinction. The word of the Prophets was familiar: 'This people honors me with their lips, but their heart is far from me.' . . . The original element in the ethics of Jesus was the completely practical application of ethical ideas which had already been theoretically developed."

it is! What is there which so much obstructs a teacher of righteousness at the present time as the conventionalism and externalism of modern morality? The permissible without disgrace, the limit of the law, the demands of the social code — are not these the ethical standards which prevail in political, industrial, and even in domestic life? Who shall censure a nation for oppression if the forms of law are maintained; or an industrial movement for injustice if it escape indictment; or a home for divorce if the courts permit; or a church for loss of its soul if it gain the world? Conform, consent, avoid excess, march with the procession, follow the crowd, keep to the middle of the road — such are the moral exhortations which the modern Scribes and Pharisees offer, in many a legislature and home and church, as the secret of social security and worldly wisdom. At such a time it is worth recalling that the first protest of the teaching of Jesus was against the morality of conventionalism. Ethical judgments, he affirms, are not to be determined by majorities, but by principles; not by public opinion, but by universal laws. "The sentiment of virtue," says Emerson, "is a reverence and delight in the presence of certain divine laws." [1] Such was righteousness to Jesus. His teaching is not of ethical prudentialism, but of ethical idealism. Conventional duty-doing is still confronted by that saying which has always perplexed the prudentialist: "When

[1] "Miscellanies," 1875, p. 66.

ye shall have done all those things which are commanded you, say, We are unprofitable servants: we have done that which was our duty to do." That nation follows Jesus which dismisses compromise and pays the price of justice; that industrial order commends itself to him which substitutes coöperation for competition and peace for force; that home is fit for him to enter where domestic unity is not of the lips or courts or church, but of the heart and will; that worship is in his name where form is less than spirit, and orthodoxy is less than truth.

Righteousness, however, is but the first word of Christian morals, an ancient word which seemed to Jesus capable of restoration to its spiritual significance. As his teaching deepens and broadens, a second word begins to displace the first, and enters like a new *motif* into the music of his life. Righteousness as it rises from its roots in the will opens by degrees into a fairer trait, and character blooms into the flower which Jesus calls Love. This also was to his hearers no new word. "Thou shalt love thy neighbor as thyself," said Leviticus.[1] "Love ye therefore the stranger," said Deuteronomy.[2] "What doth the Lord require of thee," said the Prophets, "but to do justly, and to love mercy";[3] "Love the truth and peace."[4] It is the word which Jesus selects from scattered passages of the ancient law, when he is challenged to

[1] Lev. xix. 18, 34.
[2] Deut. x. 19.
[3] Micah vi. 8.
[4] Zech. viii. 19.

name its great commandments.[1] It is his answer
to the question: "What shall I do to inherit
eternal life?"[2] Love then, like righteousness, is
a word which Jesus draws from the tradition of the
past and uses to enrich his ethical vocabulary.

As his teaching proceeds, however, he seems, in
this case, less concerned with establishing the legiti-
macy of his definition, or with the contrast between
the old and new ideals of love. Righteousness, in
his teaching, seems to grow unconsciously toward
a fairer bloom, and one can hardly say where the
stalk ends and the flower begins. Love is the
flower of righteousness. The severer word which
suggests self-scrutiny and self-discipline bears,
like a stiff stem, the fragrant blossom of self-forgetfulness.[3] To this expression of his desire the
mind of Jesus turns with increasing emphasis as
his ministry proceeds. Not righteousness, but
love, becomes the supreme word of Christian
ethics. The note thus struck in the first three

[1] Deut. vi. 5 ; Lev. xix. 18 ; Luke x. 27.   [2] Luke x. 25.

[3] Stevens, "The Teaching of Jesus," 1901, p. 132 : " Love, then, *is*
righteousness" ; and, more precisely, "Theology of the New Testament," 1899, p. 104 : " A very slight attention to the words of Christ
serves to show that love and righteousness are for him practically
synonymous, or at any rate that righteousness is included in love."
So, Wendt, "Teaching of Jesus," tr. Wilson, 1897, I, 350, 358, 363 :
" When we glance over all the various directions given by Jesus
. . . we are filled with wonder at the elevation and consistency of
His conception of love." So, Harnack, " What is Christianity ? "
tr. Saunders, 1901, pp. 76 ff. : " The higher righteousness and the
commandment of love. . . . This is the third head, and the
whole of the Gospel is embraced under it."

Gospels goes sounding on through the New Testament. It reverberates in Paul's great summary of the things which abide: "and the greatest of these is Love." It is heard again like a lingering echo in the reiterated phrases of John: " Beloved, let us love one another: for love is of God; and every one that loveth is born of God." [1]

How strange it seems that this word should have sunk to the soft and sentimental usage so common in Christian teaching; that a love which is the flower of righteousness could be interpreted as a parasitic, clinging, not to say sensual affection, supported by no stalk of duty or root of will! [2] A great part of the literature of Christian love is a tale of sickly sentiment rather than a record of maturing righteousness. " Jesus," it sings,

> " . . . the very thought is sweet,
>   In Thy dear name all heart-joys meet;
>   But sweeter than sweet honey far,
>   The glimpses of Thy presence are."

The love which the Gospels describe is as far as possible from this saccharine sentimentalism. It is virile, authoritative, rational; not neurological, but ethical. Love is the corollary of righteousness. Follow the line of duty and it issues into love. Seek first God's righteousness and you shall find

[1] 1 John iv. 7.

[2] Repelling illustrations in abundance are reported with a devotion worthy of a better theme, by W. James, " Varieties of Religious Experience," 1902, esp. Ch. I, " Religion and Neurology"; Ch. XI–XIII, " Saintliness " ; Ch. XVI, XVII, " Mysticism."

the love of Christ.   The obligations of morality are not detached from the privileges of love.   The ancient commandment held both in one law.   Love is not only a delight, but a duty.   "Thou *shalt* love," say the verses cited by Jesus, "the Lord thy God," and "Thou *shalt* love thy neighbor as thyself." These things, says Jesus in the fourth Gospel, "I *command* you, that ye love one another."   Love to man, like love to God, is not an effervescent, pie-tistic, indiscriminate affection, but the joy of good-ness, the passion of sacrifice, the beauty of holiness. "O how love I thy law," says the Psalmist ; "Thy law is my delight." [1]

This recognition by Jesus of the organic relation of righteousness and love becomes the more impres-sive when his teaching is contrasted with certain modern doctrines of moral growth.   Mr. Spencer, for example, teaches that "the feeling of moral obligation" is to be ascribed "to the effects of punishments inflicted by law and public opinion." By these "is generated the sense of compulsion which the consciousness of duty includes, and which the word 'obligation' indicates, . . . but which has a merely 'illusive independence.' " [2] "This remark," Mr. Spencer proceeds, "implies the tacit conclu-sion, which will be to most very startling, that the sense of duty or moral obligation is transitory and will diminish as fast as moralization increases. Startling though it is, this conclusion may be satis-

[1] Ps. cxix. 97, 77.
[2] "Principles of Ethics," Am. ed., 1893, I, 126 ff.

factorily defended. . . . With complete adaptation to the social state, that element in the moral
consciousness which is expressed by the word 'obligation' will disappear."

It is not to the present purpose to observe the
consequences of this candid hedonism.   In identi-
fying the good with the pleasant, it inevitably
confuses acts which are unmoral with acts which
are morally sublime.   When Mr. Spencer, for
example, concludes[1] that "among the best examples of absolutely right actions " may be named
"the relation of a healthy mother to a healthy
infant," because "between the two there exists a
mutual dependence which is a source of pleasure
to both," it is justly replied that the same absolute
goodness might be affirmed of "free lunches . . .
flattery, bribery, concubinage . . . all of which
likewise combine advantage to one's self with the
pleasure of the other party concerned."[2] Animalism, sensualism, and naturalism become "absolute
morality " when love is detached from obligation ;
and the dictum of Mill that "it is better to be
a dissatisfied man than a satisfied pig " becomes
indefensible.

Precisely the reverse of this doctrine of emancipated and unrestrained morality is the teaching of
Jesus.   Obligation is to him not a limitation, but a
foundation.   External coercion is indeed outgrown,
as the righteousness of externalism is supplanted

[1] p. 261.
[2] J. T. Bixby, "The Crisis in Morals," 1891, p. 74.

by the righteousness of God; but there remains the more imperative coerciveness of ethical idealism, the obligation of sacrifice, the imperative of love. The artist, though he seem free from the laws of art, is in fact free through his mastery, and behind his apparent spontaneity are his discipline and obedience. It is the same with character. Christian love rests on Christian righteousness. Love does not outgrow duty; it grows out of duty, as a flower grows out of its supporting stalk. "Strong Son of God, immortal Love," says Tennyson, with philosophical accuracy as well as poetic insight. Love to be immortal must be strong. Many a home has been built on a love which was emotional, passionate, physical, and has found that, without an underlying sense of obligation, it was built upon the sand. The foundation of a stable love is the recognition of a common duty. Affection cannot endure without respect. Love is not created by law, yet love is not lawless. It is the rational joy which emerges from right relations. "Love is the fulfilling of the Law."[1] As Tennyson finds in Love a strong Son of God, so Wordsworth finds in Righteousness the root of Beauty.

> " Stern daughter of the voice of God,
> O Duty ! . . .
> Stern Lawgiver !   Yet thou dost wear
> The Godhead's most benignant grace
> Nor know we anything so fair
> As is the smile upon thy face.

[1] Rom. xiii. 10.

ugh before thee in their beds,
ance in thy footing treads,
preserve the stars from wrong,
most ancient heavens, through thee, are fresh and
strong." [1]

What, then, is the form assumed by this love
which is thus the flower of righteousness? What
way of expression and what kind of fragrance are
characteristics of Christian love? Love, answer
the Gospels, is to be known, not by its protestation or adoration, but by its utterance in service.
Love is righteousness applied to happiness. It is
not mystical rapture; it is not passive acceptance;
it is duty done with joy. To love God is not an
act of the heart and soul only, but of the mind and
strength; a rational and effective affection. To
love man is to serve one's neighbor. And who is
one's neighbor? It is he, Jesus teaches, to whom
one may show mercy.[2] Love is mercy, considerateness, sympathy, self-forgetfulness, service.

The teaching of Jesus becomes at this point, as
at so many others, inseparable from the person
of Jesus. If the Christian religion were primarily doctrinal, it might have been taught by a
book instead of a person, and have offered a
system instead of a saviour; if it were primarily
emotional, it might have been taught by nature or
experience, in wonder or fear, in joy or pain, by
miracle or sign. A religion which begins in righteousness and is fulfilled in love must, on the other

[1] "Ode to Duty."   [2] Luke x. 29, 37.

hand, be communicated by a person to a person. Will is moved by will. Character answers to character. Love is not felt for a doctrine or a miracle, but for a person. Christian love is not vague ecstasy or limp dependence, but service based on reverence. "The love of Christ," writes his apostle, "constraineth us." It is not a vague, generalized, diffusive affection, but specific, personal, individualized, the direction of desire in the way of Jesus.[1] Christianity, being a way of life, must have its source in a Life; being directed toward conduct, must proceed from a Person. The beginnings of Christian discipleship are not in knowledge about Christ, or in feelings concerning Christ, but in obedience, loyalty, the dedication of the will, the following of Christ.

Many a preacher of the love of Christ has failed to take account of the personal relation which is its essential element. A vast deal of sentiment inculcated as Christian love has dispersed itself in atmospheric forms, such as the comprehensive love of the heathen or the poor or the negro or the human race, instead of being "constrained" or compressed into a relation of a person to a person. The teaching of Jesus deals in no abstract affections. It addresses itself to individuals through individuals. The love it commends is the righteousness of one person applied to the need of another person. One man is going up the Jericho road and helps another

---

[1] 2 Cor. v. 14. Compare the note in Alford's "Greek Testament," 1883, II, 663, with references.

man by the roadside.[1]   One woman pours out her symbolic offering for the sake of One who has pitied her, and he says: " Her sins which are many are forgiven; for she loved much."[2]   The ancient commandment, " Thou shalt love," is applied, not to general principles or to classes of persons, but as a law between thy neighbor and thyself.   Thy neighbor and thyself stand for the moment detached from wholesale programmes of Christian love, and one is called to discern another self in another person, and to love even the unlovely for the sake of the better self one sees.[3]

Many an impulse of Christian love finds its personal application much more difficult than its emotional expression.   Missionary zeal is easily stirred by love of a heathen world, but finds an individual heathen, cast up at one's door, a perplexing and objectionable problem.   Philanthropists bid us love the poor, but a specific poor person is often unpicturesque and sometimes repelling.   Reformers would have us love the human race, but this general principle becomes much obscured when individuals of a race, black, brown, or yellow, are brought into objectionable proximity. Christian love becomes, under such conditions, no

[1] Luke x. 30 ff.   [2] Luke vii. 47.

[3] So H. Holtzmann, "Neutest. Theol.," 1897, I, s. 176: "To love another as oneself is to have the rest of human society with its external and accidental relations retreat into the background, and to be confronted by the moral problem of discovering in the single life of another the life which is thine own.   (' Dass in jedem Du das eigene Ich gefunden und anerkannt werde.')"

easy surrender to general good-nature, but a specific victory of the will. It stands before the complex mystery of another personality, and sees reflected in that neighbor a similar mingling of the desirable and repelling which it discovers in itself, and, by applying reflection to affection, is taught tolerance, justice, patience, and hope. When Paul said, "If any man be overtaken in a fault, ye which are spiritual restore such a one in the spirit of meekness; considering thyself, lest thou also be tempted,"[1] he was but paraphrasing the earlier command: "Thou shalt love thy neighbor as thyself."

No sooner was the Christian religion communicated to the little company of the first disciples than it expressed itself in this individualized love; and with this awakening of personal responsibility a new chapter in the history of philanthropy began. The care of the destitute had played a great part in the Roman world, but it was a wholesale care, a legislative and governmental charity, the virtue of *"Prodigalitas."* The *"Caritas"* of the Christians was personal, continuous, "constrained," definite, the love of the Samaritan for "a certain man," the singling out of the individual from the mass.[2] " Love your enemies," says the teaching of Jesus; but one cannot love his enemies by the wholesale, when gathered in a hostile army, a threatening nation, a corrupt party, a despotic Church. He can, how-

[1] Gal. vi. 1.

[2] Compare, however, the limitations of this contrast, noted in "Jesus Christ and the Social Question," pp. 226 ff., and notes.

K

ever, detach the individual whom he must love from the movement which he must oppose, and be merciful to the wounded soldier or generous to the hostile politician or tolerant to the believer in an irrational creed. The more confident is one's faith in the righteousness of his own cause, the more aware he becomes that the same honorable motives may govern his enemies. Christian liberality is not a blurring of the truth for love, but a "speaking the truth in love."[1] Christian tolerance is the outcome, not of loose sympathies, but of firm convictions. The Christian loves another because he knows himself. Christian charity is not reckless almsgiving or mechanical schemes, but the patient and painstaking gift of a life to a life; not alms, but a friend ; not schemes, but a saviour ; the "constraining" consequence of the love of Christ.

It would seem as if these two words were a sufficient summary of the Christian character; and they are, indeed, the words which the first three Gospels habitually use to express the ethical teaching of Jesus. When, however, he is led to reflect upon character in its wholeness, and, as it were, to watch its growth, from the first stirring of the will through the erect stalk of righteousness to the flower of love, a third word comes to his lips which covers the entire moral process, and holds within itself both righteousness and love. It is the word Life. The ethical growth which we have traced appears to Jesus to be a growth toward life,

[1] Eph. iv. 15.

or an attainment of life, and the end of this process is described by him as the only condition where one can be reasonably called alive.

To speak of life as the end of conduct was, again, no unprecedented use of language. The Old Testament in many noble passages teaches that the issue and reward of righteousness are life. "In the way of righteousness is life," says the Book of Proverbs;[1] "The fear of the Lord is a fountain of life";[2] "He is in the way of life that keepeth instruction."[3] "The just," says Habakkuk, "shall live by his faith."[4] "He is just, he shall surely live," says Ezekiel.[5] Life, however, as thus affirmed by the Old Testament to be the reward of conduct, is, for the most part, life in its ordinary and physical interpretation. "He asked life of thee, and thou gavest it him, even length of days";[6] "With long life will I satisfy him";[7] "In length of days is understanding."[8] Jesus deals with this word as he had already dealt with the word Righteousness. He accepts it as the word which serves his purpose, but gives it a kind of definition which to the prevailing tradition seemed strange and new. Parallel with the physical thought of life and death Jesus discerns, in the earlier teaching, a spiritual interpretation. "The way of life," says the

---

[1] Prov. xii. 28.
[2] Prov. xiv. 27.
[3] Prov. x. 17; see also viii. 35, xv. 24.
[4] Hab. ii. 4.
[5] Ezek. xviii. 9.
[6] Ps. xxi. 4.
[7] Ps. xci. 16.
[8] Job xii. 12.

Book of Proverbs, "is above to the wise";[1] "Whoso findeth Me [Wisdom] findeth life";[2] "He that followeth after mercy, findeth life."[3] "In his favor is life," sang the Psalms;[4] "With thee is the fountain of life."[5] "Wisdom giveth life to them that have it," adds the Book of Ecclesiastes.[6]

To this golden thread of spiritual meaning Jesus boldly attaches his teaching, as though the physical application of the word had been incidental, and its ethical significance were self-evident and essential. With no sense of strain or novelty he quietly carries over the whole conception of life into the world of the spirit, in language which if it were not so familiar would still surprise and bewilder.[7] When the lawyer cites to Jesus the great words of the law concerning love to God and men,[8] Jesus replies: "Thou hast answered right; this do and thou shalt live." Is it of a prolongation of physical existence that the promise speaks? On the contrary, Jesus is recalling the attention of the inquirer to those sayings in the earlier tradition which confirm his spiritual teaching: "Ye shall therefore keep my statutes, and my judgments,

[1] Prov. xv. 24.
[2] Prov. viii. 35.
[3] Prov. xxi. 21.
[4] Ps. xxx. 5.
[5] Ps. xxxvi. 9.
[6] Eccl. vii. 12.

[7] So, Jacoby, "Neutest. Ethik," 1899, s. 12: "While the conception of life in the Old Testament is not yet detached from its physical sense, or, at the most, is but striving to be free, life, to Jesus, is a spiritual possession, which, though already ours in the present world, will be completely developed only in the world of the spirit."

[8] Deut. vi. 5; Lev. xix. 18; Luke x. 25, 28.

which if a man do, he shall live in them." [1]   Fortified by such testimony Jesus does not hesitate to
teach that love to God and love to man are not
merely rewarded by life, but are in fact life itself,
and that until one thus obeys the ancient commandment he does not truly live.

The transfer of meaning is most obvious in the
story of the Prodigal.   When the penitent boy
returns, his father says of him: "This, my son,
was dead, and is alive again." [2]   Is this a merely
rhetorical embellishment of the father's welcome?
On the contrary, it is a statement of fact, of which
physical changes are the imperfect symbol.   This
boy had been actually dead and had risen from the
dead.   Life and death are incidents of the soul.
A man may be physically alive, and yet may experience the whole process of dying and coming to
life again.   At the very beginning of his ministry
Jesus adopts this use of language.   He cites to the
Tempter the ancient saying concerning the manna
in the wilderness; [3] but he translates this special
saying concerning physical food into a general law
of spiritual life: "Man shall not live by bread
alone, but by every word that proceedeth out of the
mouth of God." [4]   Is this a figurative or hyperbolic
use of words?   On the contrary, as Jesus repeatedly insists, this life, which is not nourished
by bread, and into which one enters when he loves
God and men, is the real life of man.   Life and

[1] Lev. xviii. 5 ; Neh. ix. 9 ; Ezek. xx. 11 ; and cited, Rom. x. 5.
[2] Luke xv. 24.   [3] Deut. viii. 2.   [4] Matt. iv. 4.

death are ethical processes. A man may believe himself to be alive when in fact he is dead. He may set himself, as he says, "to see life," when it is but death that he sees. Another man may be dying in the body, yet thoroughly alive. A man's life, Jesus teaches, consisteth not in the abundance of the things which he possesseth;[1] it is more than meat;[2] the way that leads to it is narrow;[3] he that loses it, finds it.[4] "If thou wilt enter into life," he categorically concludes, "keep the commandments."[5]

Such is the word which Jesus borrows from the earlier tradition and appropriates to his own purpose. The Apostle Paul inherits from his Master the same use of language. "To be carnally minded is death," he says; "to be spiritually minded is life."[6] "The law of the Spirit of life in Christ Jesus hath made me free from the law of sin and death";[7] "That we also should walk in newness of life."[8] More specifically, however, and with more sustained reiteration, the new word for the Christian character dominates the fourth Gospel. In this philosophical reflection on the mission of Jesus nothing further is heard of the word Righteousness,[9] and the word Love is expanded

[1] Luke xii. 15. [4] Matt. xvi. 25. [7] Rom. viii. 2.
[2] Luke xii. 23. [5] Matt. xix. 17. [8] Rom. vi. 4.
[3] Matt. vii. 14. [6] Rom. viii. 6.

[9] The word appears only in the reproof of the Comforter, John xvi. 8, 10. Compare Wendt, "Teaching of Jesus," tr. Wilson, 1897, I, 254.

in significance until it comprehends, not only human affection, but the mystical communion of the
Father, the Son, and the brethren.[1]   When, however, the purpose of Jesus is to be completely expressed, no definition seems to the author of the
fourth Gospel capacious enough to hold it but the
great word Life.   " In him," the prologue begins,
" was life; and the life was the light of men."[2]
" I am the bread of life,"[3] goes on the lofty teaching, as though explicitly denying that bread for
the body was the staff of real life.   "The bread
of God is he which cometh down from heaven, and
giveth life unto the world."[4]   "Except ye eat the
flesh of the Son of man, and drink his blood," it
proceeds with still bolder spiritualizing, "ye have no
life in you";[5] "The words that I speak unto you,
they are spirit, and they are life";[6] "That believ-
ing ye might have life."[7]   Thus from its beginning
to its close the fourth Gospel is a psalm of life.   The
life which is created and sustained by communion
with Jesus is the only true life.   The philosophy of
Christian experience is summed up in that great
utterance which has in it the ring of oral tradition :
"I am come that they might have life, and that
they might have it more abundantly."[8]

Nor does this psalm of life cease with its spiritual
interpretation of the present world.   It rises to a
still higher strain in passages, not exclusively the

[1] John xiv. 23 ff., xv. 12 ff.
[2] John i. 4.
[3] John vi. 35.
[4] John vi. 33.
[5] John vi. 53.
[6] John vi. 63.
[7] John xx. 31.
[8] John x. 10.

possession of the fourth Gospel, where Jesus identifies life with eternal life. When the young
man asks: "What good thing shall I do, that I
may have eternal life?"[1] Jesus directs him to the
immediate duties and sacrifices which confront him,
assuring him that this is the gate, not only of
discipleship, but of all which can be called life.
"If thou wilt enter into life, keep the commandments. . . . Come and follow me." Eternal life
is not separable from the life that now is. "This
is life eternal," the fourth Gospel more definitely
announces, "that they might know thee, the only
true God, and Jesus Christ, whom thou hast sent."[2]
"Whoso eateth my flesh and drinketh my blood,
hath eternal life."[3] Life, in its New Testament
usage, has in it what a distinguished preacher has
called a quality of timelessness.[4] It is immediately
accessible and it is eternal. One may enter life
here; and once having entered life, has eternal life.
On through the New Testament echoes the great
word Life, until it dies away in the song of the
New Jerusalem, whose river is a river of life, whose

[1] Matt. xix. 16 ff.; so Mark x. 17; Luke xviii. 18.

[2] John xvii. 3. So, Jacoby, "Neutest. Ethik," 1899, ss. 18, 23:
"We hear [in the fourth Gospel] neither the demand for μετάνοια
nor the command of δικαιοσύνη, nor is there a picture of the
development of righteousness through hunger and thirst. . . . The
Christian life is presented rather as completed unity ('ein in sich
vollendetes Ganzes')."

[3] John vi. 54.

[4] J. B. Mozley, "University Sermons," 1876, pp. 46 ff., "Eternal
Life."

life

food is from the tree of life, whose crown for
him that is faithful unto death is a crown of life,
and whose final blessing is that whosoever will
shall drink of the water of life freely.[1]

Here is the largest name for the Christian character. The root of Christian ethics is in the command: Seek first the Kingdom of God and His
righteousness; the flower of this righteousness is a
rational and serviceable love; but when this growth
from root to flower is surveyed as a whole, the moral
process is found to be nothing else than the process
of life itself. Life to the Christian is the life of
growing character. All else that may be described
as life is but a symbol of life. A man's life consisteth not in the abundance of the things which
he possesseth, whether these things be physical
strength or negotiable securities or titles of respect.
His life consists in the capacity to use his possessions, in the discipline of the body as the instrument of the will, in wealth of righteousness and
love. "Wealth," taught Mr. Ruskin, "is the pos-

---

[1] Rev. xxi. 6, ii. 7, 10, xxii. 17. So, Wendt, "Teaching of
Jesus," tr. Wilson, 1897, I, 243, 248: "Eternal life . . . in the
Johannine discourses, it is spoken of as something already possessed
in the present. . . . Jesus . . . not only exhibits a peculiar use of
language, but also a peculiar thought, not occurring in the sayings
recorded in the Logia and in Mark." Jacoby (op. cit.), s. 11:
"Jesus defines salvation as life, or eternal life. Life, however, in
its limited sense, is an ethical possession, a disposition, a determination of the will. Righteousness is thus a constituent of life. This
relation had already been indicated in the Old Testament, where
life is described as the fruit of righteous men."

session of the valuable by the valiant, . . . To be 'valuable' is, therefore, to 'avail towards life.'"[1] The teaching of Jesus gives a similar definition of life. As a man may seem rich and be in fact poor, so he may seem alive and be in fact dying or dead. When a man considers the problem of his life, his first inquiry should be, not whether he is living well or living ill, but whether he is living at all. As he gives his will to righteousness, and as his righteousness grows toward loving service, he is beginning to live; and as he proceeds in that way of life, he finds it dissociated from the changes of the body and a part of the eternal life. " He that hath the Son," says the Epistle in which love and life seem most at one, "hath life. . . . These things have I written unto you . . . that ye may know that ye have eternal life."[2]

To this height of utterance rises the ethical teaching of Jesus. The Christian character is not a fragmentary collection of detached virtues, or an occasional spasm of excellence, or a passing vision of perfection. It is a normal, healthy, gradual growth, like that growth of nature on which the eye of Jesus was wont to dwell with peculiar joy; a growth not beyond the power of a plain, imperfect, hesitating life, if only its will be firmly rooted in the great decision, which first seeks righteousness and then devotes that righteousness to love. " First the blade," teaches Jesus, " then

[1] "Unto This Last," Am. ed., 1870, pp. 99 ff.
[2] 1 John v. 12, 13.

the ear, after that the full corn in the ear"; [1] and the Apostle Paul, though he turns not to nature but to human life for his figures of speech, describes the Christian character in the same terms of growth. The "perfecting of the saints" is like the development of the body. We are "henceforth no more children," but come unto a "perfect man," unto "the measure of the stature of the fulness of Christ," and "grow up into him in all things, which is the head." [2]

If, however, this series of experiences represents the normal growth of the Christian character, if this dedication of the will to service constituted to Jesus the only life which was rational and secure, what, one finally asks, is to be the fruit of this way of life? What may the Christian character do for one, or rather what may one do with it? What is the practical issue of this kind of life, and what place may it hold among the circumstances and needs of modern men? Such questions are neither trivial nor contrary to the spirit of Jesus. One of the most striking evidences of the sanity of his teaching is the candor with which he points out the rewards of the Christian character. He does not exhort his disciples to act without regard to consequences or to let goodness be its own reward. He says, on the contrary: "Your reward is great"; "Great is your reward"; "Whosoever shall give to drink unto one of these little ones

---

[1] Mark iv. 28.   [2] Eph. iv. 12, 13, 14.

. . . shall in no wise lose his reward." [1]   Conduct
has fruits which it is reasonable to recognize.   As
one sows, so shall he reap.   "By their fruits ye
shall know them"; "For the tree is known by
its fruit." [2]   Even of the hypocrites Jesus says:
"Verily I say unto you, They have their reward." [3]   What, then, is the reward of the Christian character?   Into what condition of conscious
gain does one enter when he has discovered that
righteousness and service make the true life of
man?

The answers which have been given to this
question have been, as a rule, of two opposite
kinds.   On the one hand, the fruit of Christian
discipleship has been found in a condition of joy
and peace, the rapture and exaltation of the saints;
on the other hand, this culmination of Christian
experience has been found in the sense of escape
from the penalty of sin, the salvation of one's soul.
The first view sees in the Christian character a
way of blessedness; the second sees in it a way of
deliverance.   To the first, the purpose of Jesus
is sanctification; to the second, it is redemption.
Two widely different moral types thus come to
represent the Christian character.   On the one
hand are the calm and holy lives of fair, sweet
saints, tranquil in their desires, radiant in their
faith, inheriting the Master's promise: "Be ye
therefore perfect, even as your Father which is

[1] Matt. v. 12, x. 42; Luke vi. 23.
[2] Matt. vii. 20, xii. 33.   [3] Matt. vi. 16.

in heaven is perfect." [1] On the other hand are the heroic experiences of victory over stubborn desires and persistent sins, the bearing of heavy burdens, the discipline of sorrow, the way of the cross. Which of these is the natural fruit of the Christian character ? Is it to be known by its capacity for joy or by its capacity for pain ? Does it grow most luxuriantly in the light or in the dark ? If a life commit itself to the way of the Christian character, will it find that way easy or hard, a way of peace or a way of strife ? Seeking first the Kingdom of God and His righteousness, what are the things which will be added ?

There is much in the Gospels which may serve to fortify each of these views of the fruits of the Christian character. As one listens to the first announcement of the message of Jesus, he hears the Teacher dwelling with fond reiteration on the sense of blessedness, the assurance of reward, the substantial peace, which his disciples will attain. "Blessed," he says in his strain of jubilant confidence, "are the poor in spirit, the merciful, the pure in heart "; "Blessed is that servant, whom his lord when he cometh shall find so doing "; " Come, ye blessed of my Father, inherit the kingdom prepared for you." [2] This note with which the Gospels begin is sustained until their close. The last gift of Jesus to his disciples, according to the fourth Gospel, is this sense of an abiding happiness which the vicissitudes of life cannot destroy.

[1] Matt. v. 48.　　[2] Matt. v. 3–8, xxiv. 46, xxv. 34.

"Peace I leave with you, my peace I give unto you. That my joy might remain in you, and that your joy might be full."[1] Through all these teachings we seem to see the Master trying to communicate to his friends the joyous satisfaction and lofty content which are to issue from the confident acceptance of the Christian character.

No sooner, however, does one listen attentively to this note of tranquil confidence than he hears another and, apparently, a dissonant chord, which seems to be struck in quite another mood. It is the chord of conflict, the warning of pain, the assurance of hardness, the *motif* of the cross. "He that taketh not his cross and followeth after me, is not worthy of me";[2] "Ye shall be hated of all men for my name's sake";[3] "Behold, I send you forth as lambs among wolves";[4] "Think not that I am come to send peace on earth: I came not to send peace, but a sword."[5] The minor note of suffering breaks in with recurring cadence upon the simpler harmonies of blessedness, until at last it seems to dominate the Teacher's mind, and he cries out in his own great agony: "My soul is exceeding sorrowful, even unto death: . . . O my Father, if it be possible, let this cup pass from me."[6]

Must one, then, conclude that the character of Jesus, like the character which he commends, is fundamentally a moral discord? On the contrary, it is precisely at this point that we seem to see, be-

[1] John xiv. 27, xv. 11. [3] Matt. x. 22. [5] Matt. x. 34.
[2] Matt. x. 38. [4] Luke x. 3. [6] Matt. xxvi. 38, 39.

neath the unharmonized and fragmentary record, the expanding experience of Jesus himself, enriching his teaching with more comprehensive elements, as though with new and subtler harmonies. At the beginning of his work, with the gracious promises of his message possessing his mind and pressing to his lips, no cloud overshadows his assurance that what he has to teach is to bring blessedness and joy. " Rejoice," he says, " and be exceeding glad. Ye are the salt of the earth, the light of the world! Blessed are ye, when men shall revile you and persecute you, and shall say all manner of evil against you falsely, for my sake."[1] Throughout the Galilean ministry runs this buoyant strain of tranquil confidence, and the voice of the young Teacher has in it the thrill of delight and the ring of command. Soon, however, — and the point of transition seems clearly indicated, — there is heard a sterner note. " And Jesus went out, and his disciples, into the towns of Cæsarea Philippi, . . . and he began to teach them, that the Son of man must suffer many things, and be rejected of the elders, and of the chief priests, and scribes, and be killed, and after three days rise again."[2] From the time of this

[1] Matt. v. 11, 12, 13, 14.

[2] Mark viii. 27, 31 ; Matt. xvi. 13 ; Luke ix. 22. So, Fairbairn, "Philosophy of the Christian Religion," 1902, p. 395 : " At this point there comes a most extraordinary and unexpected development in the teaching. Coincident with the new emphasis in His person is the new thought of His passion. No one could be less fitly described as the 'Man of Sorrows' than the Jesus of the 'Galilean springtime.' The idea embodied in Holman Hunt's

withdrawal the words of Jesus become touched with a new pathos, and the Beatitudes give way to more poignant utterances. It is as though a calm and sunny dawn were succeeded by a sombre and threatening day. As Jesus "goes up to Jerusalem," the shadow of the cross falls across his road. His way is leading, not through unclouded blessedness, but through conflict and pain. "From that time forth began Jesus to shew unto his disciples, how that he must go unto Jerusalem, and suffer many things." [1] "And Jesus going up to Jerusalem took the twelve disciples apart in the way, and said unto them, Behold, we go up to Jerusalem, and the Son of man shall be betrayed unto the chief priests and unto the scribes, and they shall condemn him to death, and shall deliver him unto the Gentiles to mock, and to scourge, and to crucify him." [2]

His teaching becomes colored by this assurance of his destiny. Instead of promises of reward, there are warnings of conflict and calls to vigilance.

'*The Shadow of the Cross*' is false to nature and to history. . . . The morning of His ministry was a golden dawn. . . . The new development in His teaching occurs, then, at the moment when the disciples had come to conceive Him as the Christ." So, Wernle, "Anfänge unserer Religion," 1901, s. 53 : "It is a sublime fact that Jesus first calls for this confession at Cæsarea Philippi, where he and the disciples are threatened by danger. A faith without danger and suffering had never been commended by him ; . . . but now the confession is necessary because the suffering is near. . . . Jesus does not hesitate to make the readiness to suffer a part of discipleship." Compare also O. Holtzmann, "Leben Jesu," 1901, Kap. XI, "Auf heidnischem Boden."

[1] Matt. xvi. 21.   [2] Matt. xx. 17-19.

"Whosoever will save his life shall lose it; he that shall endure unto the end, the same shall be saved. Many are called, but few are chosen. If any man would come after me, let him deny himself, and take up his cross, and follow me." [1] As the great word of the Sermon on the Mount is blessedness, so the word which now springs to the lips of Jesus is watchfulness. Characters are tested by their readiness or unreadiness. The wise servant is ready for the reckoning; the foolish virgins stand before the fast-shut door; the faithful porter watches for his Lord's coming. "What I say unto you I say unto all, Watch." [2] Thus, the teaching of Jesus deepens and broadens like a river which receives new tributaries along its course as it proceeds. His mind had at first turned with delight to the rewards of discipleship, and he had perceived that the only rational and permanent happiness was to be found in the life he had to teach. This doctrine of the end is now amplified by a doctrine of the way. The path to blessedness, though it will reach that end, runs through a region of misinterpretation, solitude, and discipline. Jesus does not retract the Beatitudes. The supreme satisfaction in life is to be gained by none other than the poor in spirit and the pure in heart. Blessedness is, however, not separable from suffering; and among the things which are added

[1] Matt. xvi. 25, xxiv. 13, xxii. 14, xvi. 24; Mark viii. 34; Luke ix. 23, xiv. 27.

[2] Matt. xxv. 1, 13, 19, xxiv. 42; Mark xiii. 34, 37; Luke xxi. 36.

L

to one who seeks God's Kingdom is the bearing of one's own cross.

Such is the paradox of the Christian character. It is to be blessed, but it is not to be sheltered. It hears the word: "My peace I give unto you," but it hears also that other word: "Not as the world giveth"; it is the saving of the soul, but the saving is through losing; it is the house built upon a rock, yet the porter of that house must watch.[1] The teaching of Jesus evades neither the problem of pleasure nor that of pain. The Christian character takes account of both. It leads to blessedness, but it anticipates hardness. Its end is reached, not by escape from trouble, but by victory over trouble. The peacemakers are to be blessed; but the peacemakers are not so much those who avoid war, as those who contend for equity. They are not seekers of peace; they are makers of peace. What they are seeking is the Kingdom of God and His righteousness; and the blessedness of peacemaking is thus added to them. The outcome of righteousness is blessedness; but the process of righteousness is sacrifice.

Frankly, however, as Jesus recognizes this paradox of ethics, which has divided the hedonists from

---

[1] Mark xiii. 34. The contrast of types and the Christian solution of the antinomy are admirably stated by Hugh Black, "Culture and Restraint," 1901, pp. 329 ff. : "In all Christ's teaching on self-denial it must never be forgotten that it always meant to Him some larger good. . . . The surrender of self to the will of God makes all necessary self-denial not worthy to be mentioned."

the ascetics, there remains in his teaching a further quality which separates him from both these moral types. Clearly as he notes these incidents of pleasure and of pain, he is strangely indifferent to them. The experiences, both of blessedness and of cross-bearing, are to happen along the way that he is going, but they are plainly not the end which he is most concerned to reach. Jesus is neither hedonist nor ascetic. Pleasure and pain are not the motives of his conduct, but the corollaries of his conduct — the environment, as it were, through which conduct has to go. It is as though one, while walking his chosen path to his predetermined end, had time to note the scenery along his road and to take account both of the sunny heights and sunless valleys through which his pathway led. The Christian character goes its way with a purpose which lies quite beyond the changeful light and shadow of its path ; and while it marches along looks about it on either hand.[1]

And what is this end toward which the Christian character proceeds, and in which its growth is ful-

---

[1] Tolstoi, among many excesses of interpretation, notes this moral detachment in Jesus (Vol. XXII, "The Christian Teaching," tr. Wiener, 1905, p. 458) : "A man who lives a Christian life does not ascribe any great meaning to his joys . . . but looks on them as accidental phenomena which meet him on the path of life ; . . . and does not look upon his sufferings as something that ought not to be, but looks on them as an indispensable phenomenon of life, like friction at work." So, Jacoby, "Neutest. Ethik," 1899, s. 103 : "Jesus applies the motive of reward, but at the same time is free from it. . . . The essence of reward is eternal life."

filled? The answer to this question becomes obvious when one recalls the total impression which was made by the character of Jesus himself. The first effect of his personality upon his hearers was, as has been said, an effect of power. His word was with power; he taught with authority. Behind his tenderness, his sympathy, his patience, uttering itself in his insight, leadership, and tranquillity, was this quality of force and mastery, the effect of a commanding personality, the power of character. Such power may manifest itself both in action and in repose. There is a power to lead and a power to calm; a strength of expression and a strength of reserve. Both these forms of power were illustrated by Jesus. His word had power both to stir and to calm. He was strong to defy and strong to suffer. He was equally powerful when he drove the traders from the Temple, and when again he was accused of Herod and "answered him nothing." [1] Nor is the secret of this power obscure. It lay in singleness of desire. Jesus had committed himself without reservation to the work which had been given him to do. His horizon was clear from obstructing aims. His business was to preach the Kingdom of God, and this singleness of desire clarified his mind and gave simplicity and consistency to his duty. He was sure of himself because he was not concerned about himself. His detachment from the world gave him power over the world. Being lifted up from the world, he

[1] Matt. xxvii. 12 ; Mark xiv. 61 ; Luke xxiii. 9.

drew men unto him. The secret of his poise of character was the completeness of his idealism. He made himself the instrument of his Father's will, and the blessedness or pain of his experience was, as it were, the shifting landscape through which he walked his way.

This quality of power is the perfect fruit of the Christian character. In many a vivid phrase Jesus describes the power which his disciples receive. "Behold," he says, "I give unto you power to tread on serpents and scorpions."[1] "And he called unto him the twelve and gave them power against unclean spirits." "And to them," adds the fourth Gospel, "gave he power to become the sons of God."[2] The Apostle Paul reiterates the same thought: "According to the power which the Lord hath given me,"[3] he says, "that the power of Christ may rest upon me."[4] The Christian character, that is to say, as it grows through righteousness to love, is discovered to be not only life itself, but life at its full power. Character means effectiveness, force, capacity, serviceableness, an instrument with which things may be done, a power by which things may be moved, or resisted, or overcome. "Character," said Emerson, "is centrality, the impossibility of being displaced or overset. . . . The natural measure of this power is the resistance of circumstances."[5] The purpose of

---

[1] Luke x. 19.

[2] Matt. x. 1 ; Luke x. 19 ; John i. 12.

[3] 2 Cor. xiii. 10.

[4] 2 Cor. xii. 9.

[5] "Essays," 2d series, 1869, pp. 96 ff.

Jesus is not accomplished when character has become meek, enduring, long-suffering, calm. Beneath these evidences of self-control there is a certain volcanic quality in the Christian character, capable of sudden expression in indignation, passion, or rebuke. The same Jesus who recalled the prophecy of a Man of sorrows acquainted with grief, turned upon the traders in the Temple with righteous wrath and lashed the Pharisees with passionate irony. The same Paul who was an instrument of persecution became through the very passion of his nature the most serviceable instrument of the new faith. Leadership, mastery of oneself and of the world, mark the character derived from the influence of Jesus Christ. The teaching of Jesus ends as it began, by rejecting the self-satisfied, the self-important, the consequential, and accepting the poor in spirit, the childlike, the burden-bearing; but his teaching does not end without imparting to those whom it accepts a new gift — the gift of power. It promises to the self-distrustful a new sense of capacity; to the crushed a new strength of resistance; to the insignificant a place in the world; to plain people a spiritual democracy; to the mourners the comfort of self-forgetting service; to the solitary the sense of companionship; to the poor in spirit the Kingdom of Heaven within. What all these, and many more ineffective, effaced, and hesitating lives, most need is an assurance of significance, a sense of power; and their response to the ethics of Jesus is that of Paul: "When I am weak, then am I strong."[1]

Whence does such moral power proceed? It issues, as in Jesus himself, from single-mindedness of desire, and from subordination both of pleasure and of pain. So long as a character hovers between competing ends, computing the consequences of pleasure and of pain, balancing the expediency of self-interest and of self-sacrifice, its spiritual momentum slackens. It is like a vessel that hangs in the wind until her steerageway is lost. Movement involves decision, as a vessel obeys its wheel. To seek righteousness first is to have other things added; to seek other things first is to find that the more they are gained, the more of life they subtract. The divided life is without moral power. Control of circumstances is gained by detachment from circumstances. The only mastery of the world is for those to whom its apparent issues are indifferent, and to whom its service is essential. Only those who are lifted up from the earth draw men unto them. The world is possessed by those who are not possessed by it. The momentum of love is the source of power.

Has such a character a place among the special conditions of the modern world? What is it, indeed, for which such a world is waiting but an accession of spiritual power? What are the traits demanded by the perplexing circumstances of social and industrial life? They are efficiency, service-

[1] 2 Cor. xii. 10.

ableness, moral force, strength of character. Institutions, governments, industrial machinery, political schemes, are elaborately prepared to accomplish their ends if they can but be supplied with the motive power of idealism. How to take command of circumstances instead of being their slave; how to own one's wealth and not be owned by it; how to rule one's spirit as well as to take a city; how to be among the leaders and not among the led; how to labor together with God instead of becoming a cog in some great machine; how to maintain peace of mind amid the disasters, illusions, and tragedies of experience, — this is the cry for power which goes up from many a life, ensnared — as whose is not? — in the mechanism and materialism of the world.

To this cry for moral power among unprecedented conditions there comes with new force the answer of Jesus Christ. One cannot be, he says, both the servant of circumstances and their master, the slave of the world and its freeman. What hinders characters from efficiency is their divided aim. They want blessedness, but they want things inconsistent with blessedness. They seek the Kingdom of God and His righteousness, but they seek other things at the same time. They want pure politics, but they want also political success; honesty in business, but profit in business; simplicity for their children, but luxury for themselves; happiness, but not suffering; humility, but not humiliation; leadership, but not the leadership of love. The teaching of Jesus tolerates no such ethical bimetallism. The source of power is discovered by him in the undivided dedication of the will to righteousness and service. The incorruptible statesman, the just employer, the self-effacing mother, the wise giver, not of alms alone, but of the mind and the strength,—these are not only characters to be commended, but they are instruments of power through which the world's redemption is to come. The only effective utilitarians are the idealists. The heart of the world turns with its final loyalty to lives untainted by self-seeking and greed. He that would be the greatest must be the servant of all. The modern world is a vast mechanism which waits for power to do its work, and the form of power most applicable to the mechanism of the modern world is the Christian character.

CHAPTER V

THE PERSONAL CONSEQUENCES OF THE CHRISTIAN
CHARACTER

WE have set before ourselves the Teacher and
the teaching. The Teacher is not impracticable
and visionary, but convincing and sane. The
teaching is not emotional and extravagant, but
natural and consistent, a doctrine of moral growth,
a call to the Christian character. We turn from
the past to the present; from the character presented to us in the Gospels to the character demanded by the conditions of modern life. What
relation does the one bear to the other? Is the
teaching of Jesus applicable to the circumstances
of the modern world? Has the Christian character a place in an environment so remote from that
in which the teaching of Jesus was delivered?
Are we still Christians? Is it possible to adjust
the Christian character to the needs of the present
age?

It is frequently urged, both by critics of the
present age and by critics of the Gospels, that the
perpetuation of the Christian character under
the conditions of modern life is possible only
through a pious self-deception, which is soon

proved to be untimely and impracticable. "If Christianity," it is categorically laid down, "is to mean the taking of the Gospels as our rule of life, then we none of us are Christians, and, no matter what we say, we all know we ought not to be."[1] The circumstances under which the teaching of Jesus was delivered, were, we are reminded, even in that distant age, exceptional. "It was," said Strauss, "as though a preacher, during a Russian occupation of Poland, should address the native population on their immediate duties."[2] Under such conditions many problems which might concern the rest of the world would be overlooked, and many sayings, applicable to the special needs of an oppressed and despairing people, would be colored by the peculiar and pathetic traits of the time and place. "The life of the family," said Strauss again, "falls into the background of the teaching of this man without a family; he is at least neutral toward the State; property is not only rejected by him because of his vocation, but obviously opposed; and practically everything which concerns art or the æsthetic interests of life lie beyond the horizon of his mind."[3] "Jesus," said Schopenhauer, "transformed the optimism of Israel

---

[1] F. H. Bradley, *International Journal of Ethics*, October, 1894, p. 25.

[2] "Der Alte und der neue Glaube," 6te Aufl., 1873, s. 25, cited by H. Holtzmann, "Neutest. Theologie," 1897, I, 177, note.

[3] "Leben Jesu für das deutsche Volk bearbeitet," 1864, s. 626, cited by Luthardt, "Gesch. d. christl. Ethik," 1888, s. 73.

into the pessimism of India. . . . The New Testament must be in some way of Indian descent. Its ethics are thoroughly Oriental, and issue into the morals of asceticism, its pessimism and its Avatar." [1] To the same effect is the comparison of Strauss: "Sakya Muni was a nihilist; Jesus, a dualist. . . . Nothing which contemplates human activity as an end or object has for him any worth." [2] All these historical judgments lead to the same conclusion. We are not Christians. The Christian type of character was local, Hebraic, Palestinian, and has been inevitably outgrown. A new world must construct a new moral code and create a character fit for its new needs.

This conclusion of critics concerning the unfitness of Christianity for modern life has been greatly fortified by two literary influences which have had a profound effect on many minds. Tolstoi, the John the Baptist of the nineteenth century, preaching in his Russian wilderness a message of repentance, simplicity, and universal love, identifies this teaching with the Gospel of Jesus. The future of society depends, he affirms, on a revival of religion, an emancipation from "personal life," a discovery of essential Christianity, a return to the Gospel. The Gospel, however, demands the complete abandonment of the complexity of the modern world, and a reversion to simplicity, non-resist-

---

[1] Werke VI, Kap. XV, "Ueber Religion," ss. 407 ff.
[2] "Der Alte und der neue Glaube," 6te Aufl., 1873, ss. 61 ff.

ance, perfect flexibility of social relationship and
superiority to the claims of family, friendship,
or State.[1]

What is the effect on the modern mind of this
interpretation of Christianity? The sins of civilization, it may be confessed, deserve grave indictment,
but is the conversion of civilization to this social
creed either conceivable or desirable? Is it possible
to detach the personal conscience from the world of
other people and to determine conduct as though the
social order were unreal and social duties were in-

---

[1] "My Religion," tr. Smith, 1887, pp. 3, 16, 94, 153: "My
faith was chiefly shattered by the indifference of the Church to
what seemed to me essential in the teaching of Jesus. . . . The
command 'Resist not evil' is the central point of Jesus' doctrine.
. . . It is verily the key to the whole mystery. . . . The entire
doctrine of Jesus inculcates renunciation of the personal, imaginary
life." "Never resist evil by force; never return violence for violence; if any one beats you, bear it; if any one would deprive you
of anything, yield to his wishes; if any one would force you to
labor, labor; if any one would take away your property, abandon
it at his demand." With more appearance of system and with great
nobility of utterance the ethics of Tolstoi is summed up in "The
Christian Teaching," 1897, tr. Wiener, 1905, Vol. XXII of Works,
where the "personal life" and the "true life" are contrasted (p.
375), and the five offences enumerated which ruin men: the personal offence, the family offence, the offence of work, the offence
of companionship, and the offence of the common good (pp. 397 ff.).
The first offence justifies one's conduct by its being "useful to
men"; the second by its being good for one's children; the third
by the desire to finish one's work; the fourth by its usefulness to
friends; the fifth by its being for the "good of the State, of the
nation, of humanity." "To live according to Christ's teaching a
man must destroy the obstacles which interfere with the true life"
(p. 413).

significant?   Ought one to divorce his own business from God's business, and "be at all times prepared to throw up any business as soon as the execution of God's work calls him"?   Ought one to "do the same for any stranger that he wishes to do for his family"?   Ought one, "under no condition, to prefer the people of his own nation or country to the people of another nation or country"?[1]   If this is the Christian religion, if the teaching of Jesus is inconsistent with devotion to one's business, one's home, and one's country, then these teachings are plainly not adapted to the modern world. Here and there some noble protestant against the lusts and strife of civilization may retreat to primitive solitude, but the great multitude must stay where the work of the world is done, and meet their moral problems within the circle of their commercial, domestic, and political life.   What the monastic system was to the mediæval world, — a retreat for the elect whom the unsanctified must maintain, — that is the Christian anarchism of Tolstoi amid the prosaic trade and toil which turn the wheels of the world.   If on no other terms we can be Christians, then Christians we are not and cannot be, and must be content with what has

[1] Compare Hugh Black, "Culture and Restraint," 1901, pp. 334 ff.: "'Entangle not thy heart with any creature,' says à Kempis, but it is part of the divine education of life that we should be so entangled.   The sweetest and noblest qualities of human nature . . . are alone developed through the ties that bind us to our fellows, in the family, the Church, the state."

been called an *interim* ethics, adapted to life as it must be lived.[1]

On the other hand, there is heard at the same point the more defiant prophecy of Nietzsche. The Christian ideal, gentle, compassionate, ascetic, is to be frankly regarded, not only as antiquated, but as repulsive to the modern mind. Social stability rests on a more virile doctrine of the survival of the fit and the victory of the strong. Christianity is "a religion of decadence." "Every instinct which is beneficent or contributory to life or establishing the future is mistrusted." "To live so that one shall not care to live, becomes the problem

---

[1] Paulsen (*Deutsche Monatsschrift für das gesamte Leben der Gegenwart*, October, 1903, ss. 119 ff., "Die Ethik Jesu in ihrem Verhältniss zur Gegenwart") confirms the interpretation of Tolstoi, and concludes that "the ethics of heaven cannot be at the same time the ethics of earth. We need an interim ethics for this life." Compare Herrmann, "Die sittlichen Weisungen Jesu," 1904, s. 30 ff.: "Tolstoi bears the stamp of . . . Russian culture and the Russian Church. The best in the Russian Church is devoted to tradition. In this Tolstoi is its true son. He submits to the sayings of Jesus even when he cannot convert them to reality. He finds it essential to follow as universal the principle of Jesus that one resist not evil ; but he cares nothing for the responsibility for discord which would ensue. Such responsibility does not concern the Russian Church ; it is buried in the happy sense of reverence for tradition. . . . The energy of a man is applied to reduce human life to the condition of a child." So A. Harnack, "What is Christianity ?" tr. Saunders, 1901, p. 86 : "To him [Tolstoi], too, the shunning of the world is the leading characteristic of Christianity. There are thousands of our 'educated' readers . . . who at the bottom of their hearts are pleased and relieved to know that Christianity means the denial of the world; for then they know very well that it does not concern them."

of life." "Christianity is the one great curse, the one great spiritual corruption, the one great instinct of revenge, for which no means are too poisonous, secret, subterranean, or mean."[1] Virtue must be freed from "moralic acid." Ethics has been hitherto tedious and soporific, and morality a weariness (*eine Langweiligkeit*).[2] "When one has learned the symptoms of decadence, he understands morality and what is concealed under its sacred names and formulas, — the impoverished life, the desire to end it, the weariness of it. Morality is the negation of life."[3] "How a conscientious theologian can remain a Christian is more than I can understand. . . . It is a matter of honor . . . to hold one's faith pure from belief in God. . . . We are not Christians. We have outgrown Christianity, not because our lives have been too far from it, but because they have been too near. . . . It is our more strenuous and instinctive piety which forbids us to continue Christians."[4] "Would that he [Jesus] had remained in the desert, far from the good and righteous. Then perhaps he would have learned to live and to love the earth — even to smile. . . . He died too soon. Had he lived to my age [38] he would have renounced his teaching."[5]

[1] F. Nietzsche, Sämmtl. Werke, Leipzig, 1895 ff., VIII, 270, 272, 313, "Der Antichrist."

[2] VII, 78, 183, "Jenseits von Gut und Böse."

[3] VIII, 88 ff., "Götzen-Dämmerung."

[4] XIII, 313, 317, 318, "Die Befreiung vom Christentum."

[5] VI, 107, "Also sprach Zarathustra." Citations might be multiplied, as in XIII, 120, 130, "Zur Kritik der Moral" : "As Optics is

To such a philosophy of life the Christian character with its sympathy, compassion, social responsibility, and love of the unlovely appears an
anæmic survival.[1] The "Superman," as one of
the most audacious of Nietzsche's disciples calls
him, "will snap his superfingers at all Man's present trumpery ideals of right, duty, honor, justice,
religion, even decency."[2] Christian sentimentalism
must be supplanted by virile aggressiveness. The
Christian character has no place among the problems and programmes of the present age.

Here are two teachings which seem as remote
from each other as light from darkness, or peace
from war. One is a gospel of non-resistance, the
other of force; one is a programme of reversion,
the other a war-cry of revolution; one is a doctrine
of the spirit, the other a doctrine of the flesh. Both
teachings, however, are expressions of social pessimism. Behind both is the shadow of the philosophy
of Schopenhauer.[3] Both coincide in the conclusion

forgotten in seeing, so is Ethics in morality." "One no longer eats
his food for duty's sake, he will soon do nothing for duty's sake."
"Der Fall Wagner," VIII, 85: "The *praxis* of the Church is hostile
to vitality." The language of abuse finally becomes untranslatable,
VIII, 272 : " Alles Missratene, aufständisch Gesinnte, schlecht Weg-
gekommene, der ganze Auswurf und Abhub der Menschheit."

[1] Compare C. F. G. Heinrici, "Dürfen wir noch Christen blei-
ben ?" 1903; "Ist die Lebenslehre Jesu zeitgemäss ?" 1904.

[2] G. Bernard Shaw, "Man and Superman," 1904, "The Revolutionist's Hand-book," p. 194.

[3] The relation is traced in the case of Nietzsche by Rittelmeyer,
"Friedrich Nietzsche und die Religion," 1904, s. 12: "Nietzsche
became an atheist on the day when, as a student in Leipzig, he

that the Christian type is inapplicable to the world as it is. Tolstoi proposes a new world, Nietzsche proposes a new man; but the inference concerning the adaptation of the Christian type to the present world is in both cases the same. Either the world is not fit for the Christian character, or the Christian character is unfit for the world. We are not Christians. Either a new man is needed to cope with things as they are, or a new world must be created to fit the Christian character.

These strictures and prophecies appear, however, to involve two misconceptions. They misapprehend, on the one hand, the nature of the teaching of Jesus, and on the other hand, the nature of the present age. The teaching of Jesus is, it is true, not to be violently detached from the circumstances and problems of his own time. He was a Galilean, teaching other Galileans. He was a Hebrew, applying and fulfilling the Hebrew law. In form and manner his teaching was applied to conditions remote from our own, and the adjustment of its precepts to modern life is quite impracticable. This admission, however, instead of reducing the teaching to insignificance, indicates precisely where its significance is to be found. The method of Jesus was, it is true, occasional, incidental, contemporary. He was not posing before the future; he was dealing with people as they met him, with

discovered at a bookseller's the works of Schopenhauer"; and in both cases by M. Adams, *International Journal of Ethics*, October, 1900, "The Ethics of Tolstoi and Nietzsche."

the temptations, prejudices, and possibilities of their Palestinian lives. He speaks to them, not to us. Yet, occasional though the teaching be, its fundamental intention was to lift those lives of his own time into the sense of the timeless and eternal, and to disclose to them, through the interpretation of their own experience, the permanent principles of the Kingdom of God.

Is not this problem, which thus lay before the mind of Jesus, precisely the problem which presents itself to each succeeding generation as it interprets the message of Jesus? The form of Christian teaching is occasional, but the intention of Christian teaching is universal. The modern student of the Gospels is called, as Jesus was called, to see the timeless through the medium of the temporal, and to interpret, through the occasionalism of the present age, that which was expressed by Jesus through the occasionalism of his own age. To revert, with Tolstoi, to the literal reproduction of the circumstances of the Gospels, is thus not only impracticable, but contrary to the intention of the Gospel. To dismiss from consideration, with Nietzsche, the teaching of Jesus, because it was addressed to another civilization and another age, is to mistake the temporary for the permanent, and instead of solving the problem of Christian ethics to leave that problem unapproached. The relation of Jesus to his own age is the subject of Christian archæology; the discovery of the principles which underlie the relation of Jesus to his own age is the subject of Christian ethics. The circumstances of Palestine in the time of Jesus were, it is true, like the condition of the Poles under Russia ; yet it is possible to infer from the conduct of the Czar of Russia, in his dealing with the specific problem of the Poles, what general principles of governmental control would be applied by him in a widely different case. The occasionalism of the Gospels is the frame in which the principles of the Gospels are set. Through the incidental looks out the picture of the permanent. Christian ethics is not a reiteration of the maxims of the Gospels ; it is the rational inference concerning conduct to be derived from the facts of the Gospels.

On the other hand, these critics of the Christian character misapprehend the nature of the present age. On the face of things it may seem to be a time of brutal competition and material success, a commercial, militant age, a time when it is as impracticable to follow Tolstoi in his heroic reproduction of the circumstances of the Gospels, as it is to urge against Nietzsche that the principles of the Gospels are still applicable to society. When, however, one listens more attentively to the tumult of the time, does he not hear beneath these harsh noises of the present age an undertone of serious desire, quite distinct from its obtrusive discords ? Is there not, at the heart of the time, a deep sense of dissatisfaction with material gains, with luxury and ostentation, with political aggrandizement and commercial power ? Riches increase, but are not great numbers of the rich seriously considering the peril and the use of riches? Commerce expands, but does not commercial success leave many a life with a confession of emptiness and failure? Wars still scourge the nations, but is not the hope of international peace being converted from a Utopian dream into a practical programme? "Ill fares the land," said Goldsmith,

> "To hastening ills a prey,
>   Where wealth accumulates and men decay,"

and many a modern prophet is repeating the warning of the "Deserted Village." Do not these deeper aspects of the time suggest that it is a preparatory, preliminary age, to which the Christian character may be for the moment ill adjusted, but which is prophetic of a new world in which the Christian character may be an effective force? Nothing could be more contrary to the facts of social evolution than to assume, with Nietzsche, that the movement of civilization is proceeding from morality to naturalism, from good and evil to passion and force. On the contrary, the process of social evolution moves, though with many halts and reversions, toward a more humanized world, and registers not only the descent, but also the ascent of man. Beneath the scum and eddies which are conspicuous on the surface of the time, a deeper current of thought and feeling sets toward a revival of idealism, and the stream of tendency is purified of its uncleanness by the very swiftness with which it flows.

If, then, it may be not unreasonably believed that the Christian character is applicable to the modern world, we are led to consider in some detail the special qualities of this ethical type. What kind of person is naturally created by the influence of Jesus Christ? How does such a person lead his own life, and how does he conduct himself among his fellow-men? What are the personal consequences, and what are the social consequences of the Christian character? It is, of course, impossible to fence off from each other these two fields of ethics, as though one might have, first, a character of his own and then might carry over that character into the world of social good. All morality is social morality. Ethics is a sociological science. The moral life is a life in common. The sense of obligation is a sense of being tied to other people. Personal character does not grow in a vacuum, but in the soil of the common life and the atmosphere of the social world. For convenience, however, it is possible to consider character, first in its own inherent traits, and later in its uses as an instrument of social good — to think of a person first as a moral being, and then as a moral force. What sort of person, then, is the natural product of the Christian character? How does the teaching which we have traced affect and mould the various functions of personality? How does the Christian determine his duty, first, in the concerns of his body, secondly, in the interests of his mind, and finally, in the affections and desires of his emotional life?

The ethics of the body has seemed to many sincere followers of Jesus Christ to present one of the most perplexing of moral problems. They have heard in the teaching of Jesus an unmistakable note of asceticism, summoning them to physical repression and sacrifice. What, they ask, are the concerns and conveniences of the body compared with the welfare of the soul? What shall it profit us ·to gain all else and lose our souls? Does not Jesus command us to cut off the offending hand, to pluck out the sensual eye? Is it not better to enter the Kingdom halt and lame than with a sound body to be cast into hell? Each new wave of religious exaltation which has been set in motion by Christian faith has borne on its crest the foam of this ascetic discipline. The call to self-denial came to a world dominated by a Greek philosophy of self-culture and a Roman tradition of worldliness; and classic morals seem pallid and unsatisfying to those who were touched by the passion of the Cross. The tide of monasticism swept over Europe and bore away from the temptations of the flesh the choicest of those who heard the call of the spirit.

> "She heard it, the victorious West,
>   In crown and sword arrayed!
>   She felt the void which mined her breast,
>   She shivered and obeyed.
>
> *   *   *   *   *   *   *   *
>
>   She broke her flutes, she stopp'd her sports,
>   Her artists could not please;

> She tore her books, she shut her courts,
> She fled her palaces;
> Lust of the eye and pride of life
> They left it all behind,
> And hurried, torn with inward strife,
> The wilderness to find.
> Tears wash'd the trouble from her face!
> She changed into a child!
> 'Mid weeds and wrecks she stood — a place
> Of ruin — but she smiled!"[1]

No one can review this history of the soul in its struggle against the body without a sense of admiration. The supremacy of the religious sentiment was never more manifest than in its power to dictate bodily sacrifices and rejoice in bodily sufferings. Yet the final judgment of history can but conclude that Christian asceticism, with all its heroism, was one of religion's glorious mistakes. At the very time when the world most needed the Christian character, thousands of those whose mission was to relieve the world fled from the world, and in the caves of the desert and the cells of the monasteries forgot what was written of their Master: "He saveth others; himself he cannot save." Asceticism was not a solution, but an evasion, of the ethics of the body. It did not fight the battle of life; it fled from that battle. The battle had to go on, and the great working, productive, tempted multitude had to fight it through; while those best equipped to win the battle were heroic runaways.

[1] Matthew Arnold, "Poems," 1889. "Obermann, once more," p. 237.

Nor was even the soul delivered from the body by this flight. The more rigidly the body was repressed, the more violently it turned upon its oppressor, and tortured him with imaginary sins. They pursued the hermit to the desert, and hid beneath the cowl of the monk. "When me they fly," they said, with Emerson, "I am the wings." Self-denial was no escape from self-consciousness; and behind the forms of sacrifice lurked the spirit of self-consideration and pride. The ethics of the body, in a word, offered a problem which must be answered, not by change of place, but by change of heart, and which must be finally answered nowhere else than in that place where the body found its natural duties and desires.

This is precisely the view of the body which meets us when we pass from the spirit of monasticism to the teaching of Jesus. It is like passing from an anchorite's cell, solitary in a sterile desert, to some happy scene of fields and homes, and the natural vocations of the common life. Jesus does not counsel deliverance from the body by retreat from the world. He finds no antinomy between the life of the body and the life of the soul. He does not, like John the Baptist, call his followers to the coarse food and raiment of life in the wilderness. On the contrary, he meets human lives just where they are, among their natural incidents of pleasure and pain, temptation and joy, social resources and private needs. Among all these varied lives, rich and poor, saints and sinners, he goes his way, not demanding of them change of condition, but discerning in each condition its significance and service.

One of the most striking facts of the ministry of Jesus is the fact that, for the most part, he left people in the same vocation where he found them. He bids them forsake all and follow him; but this loyalty involves no abandonment of their habitual tasks. His first disciples were fishermen washing their nets, at the beginning of the Gospel of Matthew; and they were fishermen, still washing their nets, at the end of the Gospel of John. Obedience to their Master did not drive them to the wilderness, but held them to their work. They forsook all and followed him, yet the circumstances of their lives remained just what they were before. Thus it happens that the discipline of the body, which has played so great a part in Christian history, holds no important place in the ethics of Jesus. The temptations which he regards as most alarming are of a more subtle kind. He has more to say of worldliness, hypocrisy and care, than of the sins of the flesh. When the tempter approached his own life, he was, it is written, " an hungered "; yet the temptation to make stones into bread was a temptation, not of hunger, but of power and self-display. When physical asceticism is demanded by him, it is always for a purpose behind itself. When the body has become an impediment to the soul, then the hand is to be cut off and the eye plucked out. It is not an act of merit, but a penal discipline applied to a member which offends. When the young man is withheld from entering life by his " great possessions," Jesus does not hesitate to say : " Sell whatsoever thou hast . . . come, and follow me."[1] The teaching of Jesus is not that of bodily mortification, but of bodily sanctification. The body is an instrument of the soul.

At this point meets us once more the word which made its mark on the record as expressing the moral aim of Jesus. The Christian character is a form of power. As righteousness rises into love, and love discovers itself to be life, there issues a new quality of effectiveness, vitality, capacity for service, spiritual force. The Christian comes to regard himself, not as a detached problem to be solved, or an isolated creation with its own laws of conduct, but as a means, a member, an agent; or, to use the more human language of the Gospels, as a servant trusted by his master, a porter bidden to watch, a steward to whom much is committed, a son to whom the father confides his affairs. From this point of view the ethics of the body gets a wholly new significance. It deals, not with an enemy of character to be subdued, but with an instrument of character to be used. Asceticism, as the New Testament commends it, is not a negative term of denial or abandonment or renunciation ; but a form of exercise, a way of discipline, a kind of spiritual athletics, which

[1] Matt. xix. 21; Mark x. 21; Luke xii. 33.

trains the soul for effective living. "Herein," says
Paul, "do I exercise myself"; "Exercise thyself
rather unto godliness";[1] and Ignatius Loyola accurately describes his self-discipline under the title
of "Spiritual Exercises."[2] As the Christian
character is itself a form of power, so the various
organs of life are agents of this power. Whatever
condition or action of the body sustains, steadies,
and amplifies moral power, is right. Whatever
reduces moral effectiveness, self-control, poise of
judgment, and ethical confidence, is wrong. If a
conflict of interests arises between the body and the
character, if the flesh instead of serving the spirit
dominates and degrades it, then there must be immediate moral surgery. Cut off the offending member; pluck it out. Surgery, however, is not for
normal, but for pathological, conditions. The body
is not made to be amputated, but to be educated.
There is a mortifying of the flesh, but there is also
a dignifying of the flesh. "I am not come to
destroy, but to fulfil," might have been said by
Jesus of the body. The body which is conformed
to his ethics is not a despised and distrusted member, but full of serviceable life. Character, to be
power, must have its machinery in full command;
and the alertness, responsiveness, and endurance
of the body are the mechanism which conveys

[1] Acts xxiv. 16 ; 1 Tim. iv. 7.
[2] So, Dorner, "Christian Ethics," tr. Mead, 1887, p. 405:
"Ascetics is the doctrine of the purification, preservation, and
strengthening of the spiritual life."

moral power. It is possible to be good and to do good with a weak and shattered body; but it is much easier to be good if one's body be sound, and much easier to do good if one's body be the ready instrument of one's will.

This teaching of Jesus may be more specifically illustrated in the case of two virtues which concern themselves directly with the ethics of the body. The passion of sex has been controlled by chastity; the passion of drink has been subdued by temperance; and both these forms of bodily discipline have profoundly affected the history of Christianity. Chastity seemed the most obvious evidence that the spirit had gained its victory over the flesh. Saintliness, therefore, knew no sex; and celibacy was the first mark of the higher life. Temperance, in its special application to intoxicating drink, is the modern expression of the same asceticism. As chastity came to be identified with celibacy, so temperance has come to signify abstinence. Both celibacy and abstinence assume that the physical life is essentially hostile to the spirit, and must be rigidly repressed and subdued.

There are, no doubt, many circumstances where this ethical antinomy is real. The sensuality of Rome under Tiberius and Caligula forced the chastity of Christians to take the form of celibacy; the circumstances of many a modern life and of many a modern country permit no temperance which is not abstinence. A celibate clergy may have been the best protest which the Christian ministry could make against the corruptions of the mediæval Church ; as a pledge of abstinence is beyond doubt, for many persons to-day, the best safeguard of self-control. There are those, says Jesus, with unflinching sternness, "which have made themselves eunuchs for the kingdom of heaven's sake." [1]   " If meat make my brother to offend," says Paul, " I will eat no flesh while the world standeth, lest I make my brother to offend." [2]   Yet to identify chastity with celibacy, or temperance with abstinence, is to forget that in the teaching of Jesus the body is not an end in itself, but a means to character. Chastity is not a virtue pertaining to one condition of life.   There may be unchastity within the marriage bond, and even in the condition of celibacy. There is, on the other hand, no purer chastity than in the union of chaste lives.   Chastity is such maintenance of the body that it shall be the willing and effective servant of the Christian character ; and unchastity is the domination by lust and appetite of a life which should be an instrument of the Kingdom of God.   Celibacy takes account of the immediate virtue of the single life. Chastity contemplates the future and presents to another life, for whom it would gladly sacrifice itself, an unstained body, fit to be an offering of love.   It takes account of one who is as yet unloved, and of others who are as yet unborn.   The same enlargement of definition must be given to

[1] Matt. xix. 12.   [2] 1 Cor. viii. 13.

temperance.   Under many conditions of life temperance can be best assured through abstinence; yet temperance is more than abstinence.   To be temperate is not to escape temptation, but to hold the physical life to its maximum of service.   Temperance tempers the body as the artisan tempers a sword, so that it resists and reacts without breaking.   Abstinence may contribute to temperance; but temperance is, as the word is rightly rendered in the Revised Version of the New Testament, the capacity for self-control.[1]

Who, then, is the Christian in the concerns of his body?   He is not to be found in any single condition of life.   The celibate may be unchaste in desire; the abstinent may be intemperate in speech.   The Christian use of the body is its maintenance as the mechanism of the spirit.   Chastity and temperance are not forms of contempt of the body, but forms of control of the body.   The body is not to be ministered unto, but to minister.   Its health, composure, restraint, self-mastery, are conditions of power.   Even its ills may contribute to patience, humility, and peace.   Bodily passions which obstruct ease of moral movement are to be unhesitatingly repressed.   The Christian does not shrink from moral surgery.   The healthy body is, however, an agent of the healthy soul, and is normally utilized, not when it is amputated, but when it is dedicated to the Christian character.

---

[1] ἐγκράτεια, 2 Peter i. 6 : "Add to your knowledge . . . self-control."   So Acts xxiv. 25 ; Gal. v. 23.

When we turn from the ethics of the body to the ethics of the mind, we meet in Christian history a different situation. While the body has been for the most part regarded as a hostile force threatening the Christian character, the mind, on the contrary, has often been accepted as the special organ of Christian discipleship. From this point of view the acceptance of Christian dogma is the first of Christian duties, and intellectual doubt the most deadly of sins. At times the ethics of the mind has appeared to prescribe as Christian duty a restriction of thought; at other times an adjustment of thought to the standards of the Church; at still other times an attack on one form of thought called science, by another form of thought called religion. All these limitations and controversies have proceeded from the assumption that religion is a way of thinking, a conclusion of the reason, a state of opinion, a consent to proof.

The first important heresy in Christian history was a consequence of this intellectual interpretation of Christianity. Gnosticism regarded Christian faith as a form of knowledge, a chapter in the history of philosophy, an esoteric doctrine to be interpreted by adepts alone. What was at first heresy has often become orthodoxy; and many a definition and persecution, when not directed against Gnostics, has itself expressed the spirit of Gnosticism. To regard knowledge as the essence of faith, to affirm with Hegel, the prince of Gnostics, that "religion is a knowledge reached by finite spirit of its real nature as infinite spirit," is to close the door of the inner kingdom on all who do not hold its key of speculative truth.   "For much of the Agnosticism of the age," a great teacher has remarked, "the Gnosticism of theologians is undeniably responsible."[1]

These heresies and orthodoxies of Christian history are, it must be recognized, encouraged by one aspect of the Gospels which is often overlooked. Whatever else may be found in the teaching of Jesus, it certainly exhibits an extraordinary quality of intellectual elevation and insight, which easily tempt the speculative mind to believe that they are the supreme elements of the Gospel ; and it is not surprising that the philosophers have found material for elaboration in the deep sayings of Jesus concerning both God and man.   His intellectual mastery would have given him a place among the great idealists, even if he had failed to establish his authority in the ways of duty and faith.

When, however, one examines the teaching of Jesus in its application to the mind, it becomes obvious that nothing could be more remote from the spirit of his ethics than the spirit of Gnosticism. Jesus is neither a philosopher unfolding his system nor a theologian enforcing his creed.   Religion is to him, not a form of thought, but a way of life.   He approaches the ethics of the mind at a much earlier and a much more critical point than

[1] Martineau, "Study of Religion," 1888, I, xi.

N

that of intellectual conformity.   He considers not so much the morality of opinions as the morality which creates opinions, the motives of reasoning, the moral perspective in which the mind is set, the attitude of the thinker toward truth.   The intellectual sins which appear to Jesus most alarming are not those of imperfect faith or hesitating doubt.   He does not reject Thomas because of his scepticism, or rebuke the disciples who confess their unbelief.   Intellectual immorality, to him, begins, not in incorrect opinions, but in irreverence, unteachableness, satiety of mind; and intellectual morality gets entrance to a mind when it is open to the truth, childlike and unperverted, unafflicted by formal philosophy or Gnostic self-sufficiency. There are, in short, antecedent ethical conditions which direct the mind toward truth.   Behind Christian truth lies the Christian character.   The blessing of the pure in heart is not in their purity alone, but in the fact that their purity permits them to see God.   They are blessed, not only with moral simplicity, but with intellectual discernment.

Here is an order of procedure precisely the reverse of that which the Gnostic proposes.   He that knoweth the doctrine, says an intellectual Christianity, will do the will.   The fourth Gospel, on the other hand, finds in obedience the path to knowledge: "If any man will do his will, he shall know of the doctrine."   Sound knowledge and straight thinking issue from moral loyalty; the flippant or reckless mind lacks the ethical conditions of intellectual achievement. "Let knowledge grow from more to more," says Tennyson, "but more of reverence in us dwell." Jesus goes farther, and affirms that the higher knowledge will not grow from more to more, unless an antecedent reverence in us dwell. It is not an accident that in the great summary of the fourth Gospel Jesus sets the truth between the way and the life. The way of Jesus leads to his truth, and the truth becomes thus, not a doctrine merely, but a life.

Who, then, is the Christian thinker? He is not to be recognized by his opinions alone. There may be immorality in conformity as well as in heresy, and more faith in honest doubt than in half the creeds. Nor is the Christian thinker endowed with a special kind of knowledge, which may be contrasted with the scientific habit of mind. All paths to truth are sacred to the Christian thinker. Good science is good theology. The only issue between science and faith is between faithless science and unscientific faith. What distinguishes the Christian thinker is the ethical background of his reasoning. He is reverent, teachable, self-controlled, pure in heart. "God desireth," says the Psalmist, "truth in the inward parts;" and it is in the inward parts that a Christian thinker equips himself with the desire for truth. "Thou shalt love the Lord thy God," quotes Jesus from the earlier law, not with thy heart alone, but "with thy mind." The Christian thinker makes his mind an organ of sympathy, appreciativeness, love. His will to do the will enriches his knowledge.   His purity of heart makes him see.   His Christian character has its consequence in his Christian creed.

To the ethics of the body and the mind there is added in the Christian character the ethics of the emotional life; and here the contrasts of opinion are much more confusing.   To many minds the emotions appear to give to life all its richness, color, and charm; to many other minds feeling seems an intrusive and perilous element of experience, which is likely to mislead the reason and to enervate the will.   The æsthetic temperament finds in emotional expression an ultimate satisfaction.   Art for art's sake is its maxim.   Beauty is its own excuse for being.   Morality is an interloper when it invades the sphere of the beautiful. To the ethical temperament, on the other hand, this delight in the sensuous, the harmonious, the artistic, appears to weaken moral fibre, and to threaten the world with a new wave of heathenism.

The same conflict of opinion is met in Christian teaching.   To great numbers of devout believers, the only adequate expression of the religious sentiment seems offered by the feelings.   "The measure of knowledge," they repeat, with Schleiermacher, "is not the measure of piety. . . .   Your feeling, in so far as it expresses the being and life common to you and to the universe, is your religion. . . . There is no feeling which is not devout, unless it indicates some diseased and impaired condition." [1]

---

[1] Sämmtl. Werke, "Zur Theologie," I, 1843, ss. 184 ff.

This faith of the mystic lifts him above reasoning, even above action, into the higher region of passive or ecstatic communication with the Divine. It is the religion of the revivalist, with its emotional expressions and ejaculatory faith; it is the religion of music, of color, of processions, of art. In all such forms of piety feeling becomes the main channel of revelation. " To seek life and to find it in immediate feeling — that is religion."

Nothing, on the other hand, is more repelling to many thoughtful minds than this religion of feeling. It appears unbalanced, vague, delusive, extravagant. The mystic mistakes sensual raptures for Divine communion. The revivalist excites to a remorse or joy which satisfy themselves in utterance and make no mark on character. The worshipper is stirred to vague emotions by beauty of sound or sight, but this æsthetic delight is often an unmoral and sometimes a demoralizing joy. There is, as a distinguished theologian has said, "an enormous monotony" in mysticism. Its experiences " have no history," but are immediate and return upon themselves; and their differences are only those of intensity of feeling.[1]

What is it which gives this impression of instability to the emotional life? Why is it that the feelings may become either the organ of the highest good, or the source of the most insidious evil? How may one trust himself to his emotions without

[1] W. Herrmann, "Der Verkehr des Christen mit Gott," 1886, ss. 12 ff.

falling a victim to their treachery or deceit? The answer to these questions is plain when one considers the genesis of emotions. Feeling is not a self-originated or isolated function. It refers itself to some antecedent suggestion, either of the body or the mind. An e-motion is a motion from. It is a pleasure or a pain emerging from an act or thought. In itself it is spontaneous, unreflecting, immediate; but it assumes an intention to be achieved, a desire to be satisfied, an adjustment of body to environment or of mind to fact. Feeling, therefore, has in itself no moral value. Strictly speaking, there is no ethics of the emotions. The emotions are corollaries to be drawn, rather than problems to be solved. They are the wave which leaps up in light and color on the crest of the heaving ocean. If the sea is deeply stirred, its crest will inevitably carry the foam of feeling; if the sea is sluggish and flat, the white-caps of emotion cannot be induced to break. The ethics of emotion, then, is to be sought, not in the emotion itself, but in the source from which it proceeds. Feelings which are apparently akin may be, ethically, strangers to each other. The sense of the beautiful may be either a spiritualizing and refining grace, or a degrading and sensual self-indulgence. Religious mysticism may express itself either in exalted vision or in fleshly ecstasies. Even the supreme emotion of love, whether to God or to man, may represent loyalty, sacrifice, and service, or may exhaust itself in ineffective sentimentalism and pious rapture.[1] The ethics of the emotions is concerned, therefore, not so much with their form or intensity, as with their origin and background. Is the feeling of the beautiful detached from this moral background, or does it stand out against this background as the beauty of holiness? Does the mystic's vision of God lift him so high above the plains of duty that he loses sight of its prosaic details, or does this vision give him a clearer and broader view of duty, and verify the promise that the pure in heart shall see God? Is Christian love an isolated passion, which may utter itself without committing conduct to a moral pledge; or does love presuppose righteousness, as a flower involves its stalk?

No aspect of the teaching of Jesus is more instructive for the present age than his declaration

[1] One of the most instructive transitions in the history of philosophy is that of Schleiermacher, from his original confidence in feeling as altogether sacred, to the more restrained teaching of his maturer years, where the religious feeling becomes specific, contemplative, and humbling. "Reden über die Religion," 1843, s. 264 : "The true nature of religion is not one or another form of thought, but immediate consciousness of Deity. . . . In the midst of time to be one with the Infinite and in every instant to be eternal, that is the immortality of religion." "Christliche Glaube," 1861, I, 15, 167 : "In all expressions of religion the common element, which distinguishes religion from other feelings and make the essence of piety is this — that we are conscious of an absolute dependence, or in other words, of relation with God. . . . This consciousness of absolute dependence [is] the only way in which the finite being and the infinite God can be consciously one." (Compare *Unitarian Review*, August and September, 1880, F. G. Peabody, "The History of the Psychology of Religion.")

that Christian emotion has worth only as a consequence of the Christian character. The detachment of feeling from obligation, the satisfaction of the religious sentiment with æsthetic expression, even the scorn of rigid ethics among the circumstances of the modern world — all these perversions of Christian faith still afflict the Christian church. When a negro convert in a Southern prayer-meeting shouts, " I'se done broke all de commandments, but praise de Lord, I'se got my religion," it seems a grotesque separation of faith from morals ; but it is, in fact, not more ludicrous, and it is much less shameless, than the practices which, to many cultivated people, appear consistent with Christian discipleship and Christian worship. How does it happen that ostentatious prodigality, habitual gambling, and looseness in marriage occur, not only among those who have abandoned religious obligations, but among those to whom religious conformity is a part of good manners and good taste ? It is because religion is regarded, not as a moral law, but as a comforting emotion. The commandments may be broken, while the solace of religion is retained. Such is the travesty of religion, when it becomes æsthetic instead of ethical. It is well to be stirred by religious feeling, but, as Phillips Brooks once remarked, " you must ask of its parentage and its offspring." [1]

The same lesson concerning the ethics of emotion

[1] "The Influence of Jesus," 1879, Lect. III, " The Influence of Jesus on the Emotional Life of Man."

is taught on a larger scale, and in a more positive
form, by a great historical transition, of which this
looseness of contemporary morals is one expression.
Among the creative forces of religion in America,
the most important was the spirit of Puritanism.
It subdued a wilderness, established popular government, bred a learned ministry, and set religion
at the centre of the State. Its morals, however,
were severe; its judgments harsh; its recoil from
the laxity of English customs made it hostile to
mirth and play. It is not surprising, therefore,
that a reaction has come, and that one hears much
ridicule of the spirit of Puritanism. Instead of
the earlier rigidity we have the new tolerance;
instead of unlovely morals, a new appreciation of
the beautiful; instead of self-discipline, self-culture
and delight in life. Is this transition a moral gain
or a moral loss? That must depend on the relation between the new æstheticism and the earlier
Puritanism. If what we are witnessing means
simply a reaction from sternness to license, from
hardness to softness, as Puritanism was itself a
reaction from the laxity of its own age, then it is
simply one more swing of the pendulum of opinion
which merely registers the course of time. To be
a moral gain, these generous instincts of a kindlier
world must be, not an outgrowing of Puritanism,
but a growth out of Puritanism; not a revolution,
but an evolution; not the swing of a pendulum, but
the blooming of a flower; not the withering of the
Puritan conscience, but the unfolding of it under

a more genial sun. First the sternness of duty-doing, then, and then only, the fairer traits of attractiveness and charm; first the Puritan self-discipline, and then an age of sweetness and light, — this is the only order of a sound moral growth. Puritanism was like a bulb, brought — as Puritanism was brought — from Holland, of rough exterior and without apparent beauty or grace, but which, set in a Southern window, unfolds into a flower which a Puritan might have thought too fair. "Seek first the kingdom of God and His righteousness," said Jesus, "and all these things shall be added unto you." To seek righteousness first is to find in other things the natural flower of the expansion of righteousness; to seek other things first is to attempt the impossible task of developing a moral creed from the seeds of sensualism, self-indulgence, and scorn.

Who, then, is the Christian in his emotional life? He is not to be recognized by his ecstatic utterances or turbulent repentances or demonstrations of passionate affection for a visualized Christ. These states of feeling may be the best expression of the Christian character, or may, on the other hand, have no moral significance. Christian emotion is an instrument of Christian consecration. The Christian has his exalted moments of emotional communion with God, like those in which Jesus said, "All things have been delivered unto me by my Father"; but these mounts of vision rise out of valleys of common duty-doing, as when Jesus, in the same passage, said to the weary and heavy-laden, " I will give you rest." The Christian, like his Master, has his mount of transfigured feeling; but at its foot waits the life of service, as Jesus went down to heal the demoniac boy. The Christian feels the passion of indignation, as when Jesus drove the traders from the Temple; but his indignation is impersonal, unselfish, " a zeal for the Father's house." The Christian is touched by the feeling of compassion; but it is a conscientious and continuous compassion, as when the Samaritan set the sufferer on his own beast and took care of him. Behind Christian feeling stands Christian thoughtfulness; behind Christian passion, power in reserve. The emotions are not superficial agitations of nervous excitement, like little waves tossed up by a passing steamer with its churning wheels; they are the crests that lift themselves when the depths of nature are stirred, and the whole character is lifted, like a heaving roller, to the surface of life.

If, then, the Christian character has these personal consequences in the affairs of the body, the mind, and the emotions, what is the total effect which is thus produced? What is the moral type which naturally issues as the product of the Christian character? What kind of person normally represents the influence of Jesus Christ? What are the distinctive marks by which we recognize the Christian, in his moral bearing, attitude, and influence?

The first of these distinguishing traits of character may be described as Poise. The body, the mind, and the emotions, being the instruments of moral intention, are held in balance, and perform their functions without excess. It is this trait which makes it so difficult to define or classify the character of Jesus himself. He is in his physical life neither ascetic nor self-indulgent; in his intellectual life neither scholar nor peasant; in his emotional life neither prosaic nor visionary. The inclinations which distinguish temperaments are held in poise by him. He meets the scholars with the learning of their law, but he welcomes the spontaneity of the little child; he is stirred by deep emotions, yet he is calm when others are most moved. It is the same with the Christian character. Many a devoted enthusiast has committed himself to the imitation of Christ, and has seemed to find ample support in the teaching of Jesus for some moral protest or exhortation, but has precisely missed that poise of character which made it possible for Jesus to be a revolutionary innovator without eccentricity, extravagance, or bitterness. The Christian character is neither excited nor temporizing; it is balanced and sound. The duties of body, mind, and feeling, being determined by their contribution to moral power, get steadiness and poise.

From this trait follows the second mark of the Christian character, which is known in the New Testament as Simplicity. "In simplicity," says

Paul, " we have had our conversation." [1]   " I fear lest . . . your minds should be corrupted from the simplicity that is in Christ." [2]   Simplicity, however, is not so simple a quality as the word may seem to imply.   It is not attained by elimination of desire. Life is not simplified by becoming barren.   Simplicity means, not meagreness, but singleness; the simplifying, not of the content of life, but of the direction of life.   It is better known as single-mindedness, the uncomplicated directness of a life which moves toward a thoroughly determined end. In the Revised Version the saying of Paul reads, not " The simplicity that is in Christ," but " The simplicity that is toward Christ."   The movement of a life toward Christ simplifies character by giv-ing it a way to go.   The Christian character has poise, yet it is not the poise of rest, but the poise of motion ; as a bird, which seems to lie inactive on the air, is borne straight to its aim by the perfect balance of its wings.   " If therefore thine eye be single," says Jesus, " thy whole body shall be full of light." [3]   Single-mindedness throws its light on the path of life, and the crooked problems of experience become illuminated and simplified.   What compli-cates life is its divided aim, its double standard, its uncertainty of direction.   When it turns with un-deviating directness toward Christ, then simplicity meets it on the way.

To the poise and single-mindedness which mark the Christian character, there is added a third trait,

[1] 2 Cor. i. 12.   [2] 2 Cor. xi. 3.   [3] Matt. vi. 22.

which, as exhibited by Jesus himself, deeply impressed his disciples. It is what the Gospels, with constant reiteration, describe as Peace. "To guide our feet into the way of peace,"[1] prophesied Zacharias of John the Baptist; the angels sang at Bethlehem : "Glory to God . . . and on earth peace;"[2] and Jesus himself at the beginning of his ministry promises to the weary and heavy-laden the gift of rest. It was a strange prophecy, strangely fulfilled ; for the life of Jesus was as unrestful as a career could be, and those who came to him for peace were confronted by his other words, "Suppose ye that I am come to give peace on earth? I tell you, Nay; but rather division";[3] "I came not to send peace, but a sword."[4] Yet it remained true that the final impression left by the influence of Jesus upon his friends was that of peacefulness; and his last promise, as enshrined in the fourth Gospel, was that this gift should be their permanent possession. "Peace I leave with you, my peace I give unto you"; "These things have I spoken unto you, that in me ye might have peace."[5] When the Apostle Paul recounted the blessings of his new faith, none was more constantly in his mind than the gift of peace, "from God our Father, and the Lord Jesus Christ."[6]   "The fruit of the spirit,"

---

[1] Luke i. 79.
[2] Luke ii. 14.
[3] Luke xii. 51.
[4] Matt. x. 34.
[5] John xiv. 27, xvi. 33.
[6] Rom. i. 7; 1 Cor. i. 3; 2 Cor. i. 2; Gal. i. 3; Eph. i. 2; Phil. i. 2.

he says, "is love, joy, peace";[1] "Christ came and preached peace to you which were afar off, and to them that were nigh";[2] "Now the Lord of peace himself give you peace always by all means."[3]

What was this peace of Jesus, this restfulness of spirit, which so impressed those who had been with him that Peter, in commending the new faith, describes it as "preaching peace by Jesus Christ"?[4] Certainly it was not a peace to be attained through escape from conflict or retreat from trouble or freedom from misapprehension. Never was a life more continuously involved than that of Jesus in incidents which would seem destructive of peace. The peace of Jesus Christ is, however, not created by external events. It is a freedom from inward conflict, the peace of single-mindedness and poise, the tranquillity of a character at one with itself. Jesus knew what it was that was given him to do; and his meat and drink were to accomplish it. "I do not mine own will," he says, "but the will of the Father that sent me." Here was the secret of peace. He was not primarily concerned with the praise or blame that met him on the way. These were the scenery of light and shadow which he passed. His task was to finish the work which was given him to do, and this distinctness of desire gave peace of mind. Misunderstanding might environ him, friends might doubt him, enemies

<hr>

[1] Gal. v. 22.   [2] Eph. ii. 17.   [3] 2 Thess. iii. 16.
[4] Acts x. 36; so Eph. ii. 14, 17; Col. i. 20.

might threaten him; but in the midst of these storms he is at peace. When he was gone, his friends remembered what he said: " In the world ye must have tribulation;" but they also remembered that he said: "Peace I leave with you." " I have overcome the world." [1]

It is the same with those rare characters which represent most perfectly the influence of Jesus Christ. They are not the most sheltered of lives, retreating from the world into the peace of inactivity or stagnation. Peacefulness is not inconsistent with activity. The opposite of rest is not work, but restlessness; and the source of peace is not inaction, but single-mindedness. This is the life of undistracted service, which Matthew Arnold has described as one of " toil, unsevered from tranquillity." Poise of character gives simplicity, and simplicity gives peace. Such persons trudge along the highway of life, not looking here and there for a peaceful spot by the wayside, but travelling toward home, and going, though wearily, yet peacefully, with a song upon their lips. They steer their course across the ocean of life, not as those who are lost in the vastness of the Universe, and know not whither they are bound, but as those whose compass points true, and who can steady their course with peaceful hearts because they are sure of their course and their port.

Poise, simplicity, peace — all these mark the character which issues from the teaching of Jesus;

[1] John xiv. 27, xvi. 33.

but when his followers wished to sum up in a single phrase the most dominant aspect of this moral creation, and the special blessing which it received from him, they turned to one further word, which soon became the accepted form of benediction in his name. It was the word Grace. "Full of grace and truth," said the fourth Gospel of him. "They wondered at the gracious words," wrote Luke of his first teaching. "The grace of our Lord Jesus Christ be with you all,"[1] conclude most of the Epistles. What is this grace of Jesus Christ, which thus lingered like an aroma where he had been, and for which Christians in their worship still unite to pray? It is the issue of poise, simplicity, and peace, the total impression of a harmonious, unruffled, and disciplined character. Grace is not so much a virtue as an acquired instinct, not so much a duty done as a way of doing duty. External manners may be cultivated to become what is known as gracefulness; but graciousness is the unconstrained expression of the kindly, self-forgetting, and tranquil mind. Sometimes one sees a child blessed with this sweet reasonableness, this natural winsomeness. Such is —

> "The gracious boy, who did adorn
> The world whereinto he was born,
> And by his countenance repay
> The favor of the loving Day."

[1] John i. 14, 17; Luke iv. 22; Rom. xvi. 20; 1 Cor. xvi. 23; Phil. iv. 23; 1 Thess. v. 28; etc.

o

Sometimes a man or woman is endowed with this same gift, — a beautiful way of doing things, an instinctive generosity, considerateness, and tranquillity. This is the gracious man, the gracious woman; and when the disciples recalled their Master it was this elevation of nature and compelling grace which dwelt in their memories so vividly that their letters and their worship could not end without this final prayer, that the grace of the Lord Jesus Christ might be with them all.

Here is the final consequence of the Christian character. Much goodness, though it compels respect, repels affection. It is severe, restless, strained, uncomfortable. We admire, but we do not love. We wish there were more persons so excellent, but we do not wish them near to ourselves. Much which has been mistaken for the Christian character has had this repelling and exasperating quality. The saints have not been the pleasantest of neighbors. Precisely the reverse of such saintliness is the type which reproduces the character of Jesus. Beyond the poise, simplicity, and peace of these rare lives, there is the abiding sense of their charm. They are not incapable of severity, of indignation, of rebuke; but their characteristic quality is graciousness, considerateness, patience with defects, insight for the excellent in uninteresting lives. They do not strive or cry for leadership; they go their way and speak their word, and men are drawn to them by the natural law of attraction, which draws small bodies to greater. The sheep hear their voice and follow. They do not drive, they draw. When one thinks of them, he recalls not so much their greatness as their grace. They have received the final benediction of the Christian character, the grace of the Lord Jesus Christ.

CHAPTER VI

THE SOCIAL CONSEQUENCES OF THE CHRISTIAN CHARACTER

THE social consequences of the Christian character are not to be approached as though they were independent of its personal consequences. Life is not like a ship with water-tight compartments, one of which may be submerged while another floats. Among the most familiar of moral failures is the attempt to do good without the antecedent resolution to be good. Social morality is a corollary of personal morality. If simplicity and tranquillity in social conditions are to be attained, it must be by increasing the number of lives whose characteristics are poise, simplicity, peace, and grace. The Christian character is the key of the Christian world.

Here we meet a distinguishing characteristic of the Bible. Its ethics are, as a rule, personal; yet the consequences of its ethics are, as a rule, social. The Old Testament habitually addresses the individual as though he were alone with his duty and his God. "Thou shalt not sin; Thou shalt love." "The word is very nigh unto thee, in thy mouth and in thy heart." Yet the individual is at the same time the member of a chosen people whose holiness and redemption are the peculiar task of Jehovah. The secret of national welfare is in personal morality. The nation may be saved by a remnant of the righteous. Economic prosperity is the social consequence of personal righteousness; political prosperity is the corollary of individual holiness.

Even more explicit is the teaching of Jesus. He concerns himself scarcely at all with the organization of society or the adjustment of social conditions. The New Testament is not a text-book of political economy or of social science. Jesus gives himself to the inspiration of individuals, leaving the form and order of the Kingdom in the hands of individuals. "Ye are the light of the world," he says to his handful of followers: "Ye are the salt of the earth." The Christian character is to illuminate the darkness of the world with its light, and savor the flatness of the world with its salt. The field of the purpose of Jesus was the world; but the good seed which was to fructify the field was the children of the Kingdom. To plant in the soil of the world the strong seed of the Christian character was to be certain of an abundant harvest of social consequences.

It is interesting to remember that precisely this sequence of events immediately succeeded the teaching of Jesus. Though he had so little to say of the social perils and problems which confronted his own age, his followers were at once thrown among these perils and problems; and the new faith, planted in a few responsive lives, gave an early harvest of social change. Jesus was not an organizer of charity; yet the immediate effect of his teaching was a bloom of charity more luxuriant than the world had ever seen. He was not a labor agitator; yet his teaching undermined the Roman system of society, gave new hope to the slave, and new self-respect to woman. So dramatic were these social consequences of the teaching of Jesus that it has been frequently described as essentially a doctrine of social transformation, as though industrial and political rather than moral and spiritual changes were his primary aim.[1] Far from the truth as this conclusion may be, it indicates the ethical scope of the Gospels. They may be searched almost in vain for social regulations, yet they have become an unparalleled source of social inspiration. Their social principles have transformed the moral code of the world; yet these principles are not prescriptions of the Christian teaching, but social consequences of the Christian character.

---

[1] So, Nitti, " Catholic Socialism," 1895, pp. 64 ff. : " We are bound to admit that Christianity was a vast economic revolution more than anything else. . . . Most of the great schisms and conflicts by which the Catholic Church has been torn, were simply economic conflicts." So, Herron, "The New Redemption," 1893, pp. 30 ff.: " The Sermon on the Mount . . . is a treatise on political economy. . . . An industrial democracy would be the social actualization of Christianity." Compare " Jesus Christ and the Social Question," pp. 26 ff.

What, then, are these social principles, which are thus involved in the teaching of Jesus, and which, even in their incomplete application, have created a new order of social duties, ideals, and hopes? There are three such principles explicitly stated in the Gospels, interdependent in their effects, but distinguishable in their form. Each of the three has appeared to many minds not only impracticable and visionary, but even destructive of social stability, and has been opposed by important tendencies of philosophy and theology. Each principle presents itself in the form of a paradox, whose very statement repels many minds; yet by these paradoxes the Christian character, as a social force, must stand or fall, and through these paradoxes Jesus most distinctly announces the social consequences of the Christian character.

The first of these principles is the paradox of sacrifice, the principle of self-realization through self-surrender, or — in the less academic language of Jesus — the finding of life through the losing of it.[1] This principle makes a line of cleavage not only between ethical systems, but between personal types of character. Self-development, self-culture, self-realization, — the Greek ideal of a harmonious and symmetrical nature, — is an end of conduct which cannot be lightly dismissed as discreditable. Self-realization is the primary law of life. It is not selfish to cultivate one's faculties or to utilize

[1] Matt. x. 39, xvi. 25 ; Mark viii. 35 ; Luke ix. 24.

one's opportunities. Faculties and opportunities are possessed only as they are developed and used, and without cultivation shrivel and disappear. Jesus himself teaches this truth, with unusual elaboration, in his parable of the talents. The gifts of life, according to this impressive picture, increase in the using and shrink through disuse. To cultivate one's powers is to multiply them, and from him who fails to increase his stock is taken away that which seemed his own. This note of sanity and reasonableness is heard throughout the literature of self-culture. We seem to stand on safe moral ground. We are not beguiled into the misleading paths of self-sacrifice, but find before us a plain way of conduct. Realize thyself! Invest thy talents! Know thyself! To thine own self be true! — what can be more rational and convincing than these familiar maxims of prudential philosophy?

The difficulty of conforming to these maxims, however, begins when one discovers that this self which is to be thus realized is itself not a fixed self, with a definite signification, but a variable and developing self, so that one self is reached only to be passed in the search for a better self. There is, as Professor James has remarked, a physical Me, a social Me, and a spiritual Me.[1] Self-realization, in other words, may mean anything, from the realization of animal instincts or the most undisguised ethical egoism, all the way to the highest visions of ethical idealism. Self-

[1] Compare " Principles of Psychology," 1890, I, 292.

culture may mean either the surrender to the lower self or the emergence of the higher self. The moral process is thus not so much the outgrowing of self, as the detachment of one self from another self, and the discovery of the true self in the "spiritual Me." How to develop the existing self into the better self; how to —

> "Move upward, working out the beast
> And let the ape and tiger die;"

how to give to the potential self control over the actual self — that is the problem of self-realization which has given to the philosophy of self-culture its spiritual power.

Yet even with these qualifications, self-realization has always appeared to many minds an unsatisfying ideal. What is this little life of the individual, they ask, that it should be taken so seriously? Is it not rather an instrument than an end of duty? So long as it remains in the region of self-interest, where it computes its own advantage and balances its own insignificant pleasures and pains, can it be fairly said to have entered the region of moral obligation at all, or to have reached the knowledge of duty as a universal law? It is not until one transcends the personal and surrenders himself to the universal that he passes from expediency to morality, from the calculations of prudence to the categorical imperative of ethics.

These reflections, more or less consciously expressed, displace, in many lives, the ethics of self-realization by the ethics of self-sacrifice. Instead of sagacious maxims of self-interest there is heard the call to the heroic, the self-forgetting, the larger good. "He that taketh not his cross, and follow-eth after me," said Jesus, "is not worthy of me."[1] "What is the reason," said Thomas à Kempis, "why some of the saints were so perfect and con-templative? Because they labored to mortify themselves wholly to all earthly desires; and therefore they could with their whole heart fix themselves on God."[2] Self-abnegation, self-efface-ment, even the scorn of self, becomes the mark of positive morality; and the self-considering, computing, prudential spirit is a sign that posi-tive morality has not yet begun. This conflict of moral creeds may occur even within the bounds of a single human life. It cultivates itself, by education and opportunity, only to find in some high moment of moral purpose that all these gains of self-realization must be abandoned for some ad-venture of self-sacrifice. What, then, is my duty, cries out, in grave perplexity, this life which finds itself rent by opposing motives — to develop myself, or to deny myself; to hear the command of Jesus bidding me invest my talents prudently, or to hear his other command bidding me sell all I have, take up my cross, and follow?

What is the answer of Jesus to this antinomy of ethics, which makes the daily, and often the tragic, problem of many a self-scrutinizing life? Jesus

[1] Matt. x. 38 ; so xvi. 24 ; Mark viii. 34 ; Luke ix. 23, xiv. 27.
[2] "Imitation of Christ," Bk. I, Ch. XI.

meets the issue with his paradox of sacrifice. There is, he teaches, no such schism in life between gain and loss, self-cultivation and self-abnegation, the finding of life and the losing of it. The field of duty-doing is not a battle-field, where duties to oneself contend against duties to others; it is a field, where human life, like other living things, is growing; and growth, by its very nature, means transmission, expansion, the giving of the root to the stalk, and of the stalk to the flower, — a loss which is gain, and a death which is life. In short, when Jesus announces the paradox that to save life is to lose it, and that to lose it is to save it, he is transferring to conduct the general law which the processes of Nature had disclosed to his observant eye. The life, alike of the corn and of the conscience, was, as Jesus saw it, a process of development through service, of self-realization through self-sacrifice. The life that withheld itself was checked and dwarfed; the life that yielded itself was enriched and confirmed. Assimilation and elimination, receiving to give, dying to live — such was the rhythm of nature which Jesus discerned, alike in the fields of Galilee and in the life of man.

The modern world has verified this law of rhythm. The same paradox is observed in biological organisms, in physiological tissues, in intellectual achievements, even in economic progress. Physical health, which seems to depend on that which the body receives, depends in fact quite

as much on what is exhaled and excreted.   Intellectual growth seems a matter of accumulated
learning; but an undigested mass of erudition leaves
one a bookworm rather than a scholar, and productive expression alone clarifies and sifts the scholar's
mind.   The movement of trade is on its surface a
mere scramble of self-seeking; but in its total action
economic life is a vast tidal process of production
and distribution, of multiplying by investing, of
increase through use.   To hoard one's possessions
is to lose their increment.   " Thou oughtest therefore to have put my money to the exchangers," says
the capitalist of the parable, "and then at my coming I should have received mine own with usury." [1]

Nothing could be more remote from the spirit
of the Gospels than to conceive of Jesus as consciously arguing from such analogies, or deducing
from them, by a process of logic, his philosophy
of life.   His mind was that of a poet rather than
that of a logician; he saw rather than reasoned;
he overleaped logic rather than trudged through
it; yet there are many indications that the paradox
in which he states his ethics was confirmed by his
observation of a general law.   " Except a corn of
wheat fall into the ground and die," he says of the
world of nature, " it abideth alone : but if it die, it
bringeth forth much fruit." [2]   " Not that which
goeth into the mouth," he says of the body, " defileth a man; but that which cometh out of the
mouth, this defileth a man." [3]   " Take therefore

[1] Matt. xxv. 27.   [2] John xii. 24.   [3] Matt. xv. 11.

the talent from him," he says of the unused gifts of God, "and cast ye the unprofitable servant into outer darkness."[1] The same principle is formulated in his paradox of sacrifice. He does not ask that life be thrown away; on the contrary, he points out how life is to be saved. He does not compare personal duty and social duty, self-development and self-surrender, as alternatives from which conscience must choose. On the contrary, the only complete self-realization is, according to his teaching, to be reached through self-sacrifice. A hoarded life, like hoarded money, fails of increase. Throughout the Gospels runs this assurance, that the law of rhythm binds together both development and sacrifice. " Blessed are the merciful,"[2] says Jesus, not only in the mercy they show, but also in the mercy they receive. Judge not, for in the judgments made on others thou thyself art judged. The re-actions of mercy and the recoils of judgment bind together duty to another and duty to oneself. The other is, in fact, another self; and the self which forgets itself in another rediscovers itself in the other whom it serves. This is the truth summed up in the Golden Rule, — golden, not only because it is a rule of self-effacement, but because it is also a law of self-realization. In the other self thou seest thine own self. What, therefore, ye would that the other should do to you, that do ye also unto him.[3]

---

[1] Matt. xxv. 28, 30.   [2] Matt. v. 7.

[3] So, Paulsen, " System der Ethik," 1889, ss. 298 ff., " Egoism and Altruism": " All conduct which promotes or disturbs the healthy

Such is the first social consequence of the Christian character. Many followers of Jesus and many critics of his teaching have conceived that the character derived from him is a stunted and truncated type, which flings itself away in self-abandoning and self-scorning altruism. The fact is, on the contrary, that the paradox of sacrifice indicates the only way of deliverance from the stunted and truncated life. Nothing shuts in a life and shuts out satisfaction and joy like the self-considering temper and the self-centred aim. Such a life, though it may seem to itself self-developing, is in fact self-deceived. Instead of growing richer in its resources, it finds itself growing poorer. The more it cultivates itself, the more sterile it grows; the more it accumulates, the less it has; the more it saves, the more it is lost. The paradox of Jesus is the picture of a character which is enriched by spending, developed by serving, happier itself because it makes a happier world, finding itself in losing itself, discovering the unity of the moral world, where sacrifice is growth and service is freedom.

It would be ungracious to illustrate this contrast of types by any personal reference had not a striking instance been of late forced upon public

development of the individual has at the same time the tendency to promote or disturb the common life. But the converse is also true: The fulfilling of duties to others, and the possession of social virtues, have the tendency to promote personal welfare, and the lack of these virtues . . . works injury to one's own life."

attention by the self-confession of a remarkable man. Mr. Herbert Spencer had hardly crowned his colossal system with the theory of ethics which he regarded as its crucial test, when failing health forbade further ventures in philosophy, and he gave himself to the study of his own character and mind. His autobiography is singularly lacking in incident, but almost without parallel as the scientific analysis of a human type, and as an unconscious illustration of the writer's ethical creed. He had already expounded, in theoretical terms, the distinction between absolute morality and relative morality, the hopelessness of attaining ideal right, and the duty of adjusting oneself to expediency with the least friction of desire; and he has now reported the experience of a life consistently directed by a creed of relative ethics. What was the moral product of such a creed? What type of character, according to the philosopher's own confession, issued from the habitual balancing of competing ends? Was this balance of desires possible to maintain, or did it involve an experience of meagre satisfactions, scanty resources, and trivial decisions? In substituting for the paradox of sacrifice the pursuit of a judicious self-interest, did the happiness and scope of life increase, or did that which seemed the gain of life become its loss?

These interesting questions are answered with fulness in the curious story of high thinking and meagre living which Mr. Spencer himself has told. It is sufficient to recall a single chapter, which

bears the startling title, "A Grievous Mistake."
It recounts what Mr. Spencer describes as "the
most unfortunate incident" of his career. What
was this great disaster? It was the mishap of
yielding to an instinct of indignant sympathy.
The tendency of English politics toward aggression over weaker races stirred his sense of justice,
and he permitted himself to attend a meeting and
to make a speech. This interruption of his regu-
lar routine, however, brought temporary harm to
his health and a consequent delay in the comple-
tion of his philosophical system. He was smitten
with a sense of self-reproach, and proceeds at considerable length to speculate whether the effort to
do good does not generally bring more harm than
benefit. His one attempt at public service remained in his memory as "a grievous mistake."
For the rest of his life every circumstance is tested
by its bearing on his own productive power and
his own peace of mind. Even the love of children
is a cultivated resource; and he sends for them to
play in his room because he finds that they quiet
his nerves and restore his power of work.[1] Never,

[1] "An Autobiography," by Herbert Spencer, 1904, II, 443 ff. :
"The actions I have narrated above were prompted exclusively by
the desire to further human welfare. . . . But right though I
thought it, my course brought severe penalty and no compensations
whatever." II, 523 : " During early years, and throughout mature
years, there was no sign of marked liking for children. . . . When
at Brighton in 1887, suffering the *ennui* of an invalid life, I one
day, while thinking over modes of killing time, bethought me that
the society of children might be a desirable distraction. . . . Mrs.

perhaps, was there so candid a disclosure of a wholly self-considering career, or a more explicit contrast with the Christian paradox of sacrifice. From this point of view the career of Jesus, ending at the age of thirty, with its task, as it seemed, half done, its disciples despairing, and its teaching not even preserved in literary form, would have certainly seemed "a grievous mistake." Would not the world have been richer if Jesus, like the English philosopher, had lived to a ripe old age, and left behind him, not a few beatitudes and parables, but a complete system of religion and ethics such as his later years might have produced?

The answer to this criticism is sufficiently given by the unconscious evidence of Mr. Spencer himself. He had set himself to write a universal philosophy; but, with a candor which no critic would have dared to use, he points out how meagre was the material for such a philosophy which could be drawn from his own emotions and desires. He did not permit himself to enter the region of life where Jesus found not only the joy of living, but all that he understood under the name of Life. Mr. Spencer's narrow range of experience disqualified him from interpreting experience. The severest indictment of his ethics is his autobiography. Love and pity, service and sacrifice, are

W. Cripps let me have two of her little ones for a fortnight. The result was . . . to awaken in a quite unanticipated way the philoprogenitive instinct . . . and the two afforded me a great deal of positive gratification."

P

subordinated by him to the task of explaining human life; but the subject which was his theme was precisely the subject he had left unexplored, and when his Ethics was set, as a capstone, on the great structure he had built, the writer regarded it with a sigh of disappointment, as though aware that his system was soon to be a historical monument, marking a point where the procession of thought had for a few years paused.[1]   The fragmentary ethics of Jesus remains the interpreter of the modern conscience, while Mr. Spencer's System, in comparison with which a generous impulse seemed a grievous mistake, has, like many another system, had its day and ceased to be.   The whole story is told in a conversation with Professor Huxley.   As they walked together one day Mr. Spencer said: "I suppose that all one can do with his life is to make his mark and die."   "It is not necessary to make one's mark," replied Huxley; "all one need do is to give a push."

To the paradox of sacrifice in the teaching of Jesus is added, as a second principle, the paradox of service.   It is the answer of the Gospels to the inevitable desire of healthy-minded human beings for success, achievement, power, mastery.   Jesus

[1] See Preface to "Principles of Ethics," Vol. II, 1893: "Now that . . . I have succeeded in completing the second volume of THE PRINCIPLES OF ETHICS, . . . my satisfaction is somewhat dashed by the thought that these new parts fall short of expectation.   The Doctrine of Evolution has not furnished guidance to the extent I had hoped."

takes life as it is, with its ambitions, its hope of reward, its desire to control. He does not counsel the abandonment of these normal desires, but on the contrary says to many an inquirer: "Your reward shall be great." He does not depreciate success or greatness; he teaches what it is to be successful and what is the mark of greatness. When, however, he announces his paradox, how irrational and impracticable it seems! "Whosoever," he says, "will be great among you, let him be your minister; and whosoever will be chief among you, let him be your servant."[1]

When such a teaching is confronted by the facts of the world, does it not sound like sheer rhetorical extravagance? Is not greatness more concerned with ruling than with ministering? Is there to be no distinction between master and servant? Is not success, under the conditions of the real world, reserved for self-assertion, aggression, leadership, rather than for the desire to minister and the passion for service? Is not the law of natural selection verified in social life as in the physical world? Do not the few that are fit to survive succeed in the social struggle, and the many that are unfit to be great become ministers and servants? Is it not better to accept this inevitable law and to adjust life to its compulsion than to substitute a sentimental for a scientific world? Though the ways of nature are merciless, do they not in the end prove more merciful than the ways of sentiment?

[1] Matt. xx. 26, 27.

Let the fit survive, let the strong rule, let the weak slip down by the easiest path, unobstructed by mistaken philanthropy, toward degeneration, sterility, and extinction; until at last, through much pain perhaps, yet by an unhindered process of social evolution, the better world arrives, when those who are great shall rule through their greatness, and those who are fit to be first are the masters of all! Such is the new animalism, so cleverly disguised as scientific wisdom and worldly common sense, which finds in superior force and unbridled license the most effective instruments of social peace.

It would not be difficult to oppose these doctrines by a saner view, even of the physical processes on which this new naturalism rests. Is it true, one might ask, that social evolution invariably advances through the same internecine conflict which in the physical world has eliminated inferior types, or is it rather true that as progress becomes human it proceeds under a new law of ministry and service? The inventor of a new industry, the explorer of a new continent, the discoverer of a new law of nature, the advocate of a new cause — have these, whose names make epochs in human history, become great at the cost of others or rather through service to others? Behind the competitions of the industrial world is there not disclosed a system of social service, where, in spite of many evasions of its laws, he that would be greatest ministers to some general need and becomes the ser-

vant of all? Do not the poet and the artist become
great by ministering to an ideal which others recognize but cannot utter? Is there not a temporariness
in success through mastery, and a permanence in
success through service? Does not the world
finally withhold its honor from those who compel
admiration and give it to those who deserve
gratitude?

Such considerations, even though they may not
cover the whole area of social life, at least limit
the range of the brutality and mercilessness which
it at times exhibits. It would be, however, a most
inadequate statement of the teaching of Jesus to
find in it merely this observation of the kindlier
aspects of civilization and progress. His paradox
of service goes quite beyond the statement of laws
which govern the world as it is, and proposes a
new law for the world as it might be. He is raising an issue with the ordinary principles of social
life, rather than stating an analogy which they
confirm. It is not the correspondence of his
thought with accepted truth, but the originality and
improbability of his paradox which give it a place
in history. Jesus is himself the discoverer of a
new moral process, the explorer of a new moral
continent; and the paradox which he announces
must always appear incredible to those who use
the ordinary moral processes or live in the familiar
continents of conduct. His teaching, as he explicitly says, is not one which can commend itself
to worldly wisdom, but one which must be verified

by personal experience. He prefaces his paradox by saying: "Ye know that the princes of the Gentiles exercise dominion over them, and they that are great exercise authority upon them. But it shall not be so among you."[1]

What, then, is this moral process which he discovers, this moral continent which he explores? It is a process which reverses the ordinary classifications of goodness, a continent in which recognition and primacy are given to a kind of conduct which is elsewhere lightly regarded or doubtfully praised. In the history of ethics character has been generally described as a personal possession, to be cultivated and maintained as an endowment of the individual. Its ideal expression is in what is called integrity, — the clean, straight, honorable way of life. It is an ethical attitude like that physical attitude which the body assumes when at its best, a condition of uprightness, a moral posture of steadiness, erectness, and poise. Nothing in the teaching of Jesus discredits this self-respecting integrity. The literature of his nation abounded in the praise of uprightness. Noah, it is written, was an upright man; Job was an upright man; David walked in integrity. "Mark the perfect man," says the Psalmist, "and behold the upright"; "The just man walketh in his integrity."[2] This is the unbending and unflinching habit of life to which Jesus applies the word righteousness. Uprightness is the external expression of righteous-

[1] Matt. xx. 25, 26.   [2] Ps. xxxvii. 37; Prov. xx. 7.

ness; righteousness is the spiritual principle of uprightness. It is at this point that the ethics of Jesus begin. "Seek first the Kingdom of God and His righteousness"; "Blessed are they that hunger and thirst after righteousness." The Christian character is, first of all, upright, erect, integral, righteous.

When, however, Jesus passes from the elementary beginnings of morality to its finer expressions, and considers the marks which distinguish moral greatness, he enters into a new region of conduct, as though he were ascending the heights of life and had come to a new zone of vegetation and a new horizon of outlook. "Whosoever would be great among you," he says, "shall be your minister, and whosoever would be first shall be your servant." This is not only uprightness, but uprightness which bows itself; not only erectness, but the capacity of erectness to stoop and serve. Integrity, to Jesus, is not merely a possession, but an instrument; not an attitude which is unbending, but a strength which can bow itself to minister. His whole teaching gives an extraordinary dignity to the humblest forms of service. "Come, ye blessed of my Father," he says, in language of the loftiest commendation, "inherit the kingdom prepared for you from the foundation of the world."[1] What makes these blessed ones the heirs of the Kingdom? It is that they have fed the hungry, received the stranger, clothed the naked, befriended those in

[1] Matt. xxv. 34.

prison.   The servants of those which are least are the heirs of that which is most.   They are chief because they are ministers.

The most touching illustration of this teaching is that in which the fourth Gospel adds to the sayings at the Last Supper an act of the most impressive and suggestive symbolism.   Jesus, after the Supper, says the passage, knows that the Father has given all things into his hands, and that he is come from God and goes to God.[1]   It is his last opportunity to confirm his leadership and to demonstrate to his friends his great commission.   How does he teach this lesson of spiritual primacy?   He rises from the table and, laying aside his garments, washes the disciples' feet, saying unto them : " For I have given you an example, that ye should do as I have done to you."[2]   The evidence that he had come from God and was going to God was in his taking on himself the form of a servant.   His right to lead was in his desire to minister.   His mastery of men was in his service of men.   The disciple of Jesus was to prove his discipleship by the capacity to stoop and serve.

When the Apostle Paul desires to reiterate his Master's principle of service, he also is led to express it in the same language of paradox.   " Bear ye one another's burdens," he says, " and so fulfil the law of Christ."[3]   The law of Christ is the law of service.   To say: " Bear ye one another's burdens," is but to repeat the saying of Jesus,

[1] John xiii. 3.   [2] John xiii. 15.   [3] Gal. vi. 2.

"As I have washed your feet, ye ought also to wash one another's feet." Yet in almost the same breath Paul goes on to announce an opposite and apparently contradictory law. "Every man," he says, "shall bear his own burden;" as though now repeating that other word of Jesus: "If any man would come after me, let him take up his own cross and follow me." Is this transition sheer inconsistency in the apostle's thought, or does the essence of his teaching lie in its paradox? Who are they, he seems to ask himself, who can fulfil the law of Christ and bear the burdens of others? It is not every one who wishes to be a burden-bearer who is able to carry the load. Not every tender heart can be effectively sympathetic. They only can bear others' burdens who quietly and firmly bear their own. The principle of service involves the possession of strength. To stoop in pity one must first stand erect. Each one who bears his own burden has added to him the further blessing that he may bear others' burdens too. The paradox of service states not only the duty, but the condition of usefulness. He that is strong to bear his own burdens is able to be the servant of all.

This aspect of the teaching of Jesus immediately impressed his followers and gave a peculiar quality to primitive Christian life. Among the earliest traditions concerning the death of Jesus was that "being put to death in the flesh . . . he went and preached" to the spirits in prison before he as-

cended "to the right hand of God."[1] "He descended into hell," says the so-called Apostles'
Creed,[2] " he ascended into heaven."   The first act
of his ascension was a descent.   His freedom from
the flesh made him the servant of those in bonds.
His first step toward heaven was not up, but down.
This new ethics at once characterized the new faith.
A new responsibility for the weak, the sick, the
outcast, the prisoner, the slave, for women and
children, became the primary evidence of discipleship.   The earliest records of Christian worship
report as an essential part of ritual the deposit of
alms for the relief of the needy.   The earliest
expressions of Christian prayer gather up into the
petition of the congregation, the help of the helpless
and the cry of the poor.[3]   The Christian religion

[1] I Peter iii. 19, 22.

[2] So, XXXIX Articles, No. VIII: "That which is commonly
called the Apostles' Creed."

[3] Justin, "Apology," Ch. LXVII: "At the close of the prayer, as
we have before described, bread and wine with water are brought.
The President offers prayer and thanks for them, according to the
power given him, and the congregation responds the Amen.   Then
the consecrated elements are distributed to each one, and partaken,
and are carried by the deacons to the houses of the absent.   The
wealthy and the willing then give contributions according to their free
will, and this collection is deposited with the President, who therewith
supplies orphans and widows, poor and needy, prisoners and strangers, and takes care of all who are in want."   So, "Teaching of the
Twelve Apostles," tr. Hitchcock and Brown, 1884, Ch. XII, XIII :
"Let every one that cometh in the Lord's name be received, but
afterward ye shall test and know him ; for ye shall have understanding, right and left.   If he who comes is a traveller, help him
as much as ye can ; but he shall not remain with you, unless for

became a vast movement of philanthropy. Compassion, sympathy, charity, brotherhood — these words were superimposed in the structure of the Christian character on rectitude, uprightness, righteousness. Christian discipleship was not complete until the disciple, like his Master, rose from the table of abundance and bent as a servant to minister to human needs.

Here was a new classification of virtues. The primacy of compassion, the dignity of sympathy, the lordship of service, made a teaching strange to Roman ears and still presents a perplexing paradox to many a modern mind. However noble the teaching appears to be, is it — one may still ask — a teaching which should be unhesitatingly obeyed? Has it been to the advantage of the world that these softer sentiments should have such precedence? Has not Christian compassion prolonged many superfluous lives; has not Christian charity supported in idleness those who should

two or three days, if there be necessity. But if he will take up his abode among you, being an artisan, let him work and so eat; but if he have no trade, provide, according to your understanding, that no idler live with you as a Christian." . . . "Every firstfruit, then, of the products of wine-press and threshing-floor, of oxen and of sheep, thou shalt take and give to the prophets; for they are your high-priests. But if ye have no prophet, give it to the poor." So, "Epistle of Clement to the Corinthians," tr. Lightfoot, 1877, Appendix, p. 376 : "We beseech Thee, Lord and Master, to be our help and succour. Save those among us who are in tribulation; have mercy on the lowly; lift up the fallen; show Thyself unto the needy; heal the ungodly; convert the wanderers of Thy people; . . . raise up the weak; comfort the faint-hearted."

have learned the hard lessons of thrift? Is one's life best employed in ministering to the weak; or will one in the end accomplish more for the world, as well as for himself, by finding for himself a place among the strong? Might not Jesus have occupied the last hours of his life with some task more useful than the washing of his disciples' feet?

The answer to such questions must finally depend on the antecedent conclusion which one may reach concerning the nature of human society. Is the social order essentially a fratricidal or a fraternal world? Is it a chaos or a cosmos? Is it a scramble or a family? Must those who rise climb over the bodies of those who fall; or is there, on the contrary, no permanent security for those at the top unless there be a corresponding lift of those at the bottom? Can there be a survival of the fit unless there be also a corresponding revival of the unfit? Is civilization most secure where a ruling class represses an illiterate peasantry, or where a democracy insures civil rights to all? Is a community rich which spends nothing on its paupers, its blind, its insane; or is it true, as a historian of the English Poor Law has remarked, that "the moral life of the community is incompatible with the spectacle of unrelieved indigence"?[1]

The teaching of Jesus presupposes what the answer to such questions must be. If it were true

[1] Fowle, "The Poor Law," 1881, p. 10: "This law or fact we may express in the following terms: That every society upon arriving at a certain stage of civilization finds it positively necessary

that society is merely the organization of selfishness, that the elevation of the few involves the degradation of the many, that progress and poverty must increase together, that mastery must rest on servitude; — then the teacher who should propose that the great should be servants and the first should be ministers, is too ignorant or too defiant of social laws to be a trustworthy moral guide. If, on the other hand, human society is an organism, where the strength of the whole is dependent on the health of each part, and where the neglect or atrophy of any part threatens the vitality of the whole; if the chief peril of the social order is created by the isolation and hostility of social classes; if the first conditions of social security are mutual understanding, fraternalism, coöperation, the spirit of industrial and political democracy; if there is a law of the equilibration of characters, as of the equilibration of forces, by which power is transferred from the strong to the weak, and the balance of life restored; — then no teaching could be more sane and rational than that which exalts the work of ministering and affirms the dignity of service.

It is interesting to observe how many modern tendencies of thought tend to confirm this view of social progress. Sociology and economics, politics

for its own sake, — that is to say, for the satisfaction of its own humanity, and for the due performance of the purposes for which societies exist, — to provide that no person, no matter what has been his life, or what may be the consequences, shall perish for want of the bare necessaries of existence."

and philanthropy, have been led to appreciate, in an unprecedented degree, the unity and interdependence of human society. It has become plain that a condition of prosperity for the few and a condition of degradation for the many creates, not a stable society, but a social volcano, which is threatened every day by eruption from beneath. We have learned through the tragedies of war in the East that political autocracy is the seed of political weakness and revolution. We have become aware, through tragedies near at hand, that the life of the garment-wearer in a luxurious home is at the mercy of the health or disease of the garment-worker in the tenement. We have become convinced that the defective classes must be protected if the State is to be secure; that the social order, though it be built by self-interest, must be cemented by compassion. In spite of all the greed and self-seeking of the modern world, it is already recognized that those are first in honor who heal social divisions, establish democracy, free the slave, help the helpless, deliver the oppressed. The heart of the time responds to the *dictum* of Emerson : " Every step so downward, is a step upward. The man who renounces himself, comes to himself." [1] Human society, in short, is not a fixed condition, where a single law is adequate for its interpretation ; it is a living, moving organism, a process of growth, from the animalism and brutality which still threaten its advance, to the humanity and altruism which

[1] " Divinity School Address," p. 67.

are already real possessions. The teaching of Jesus addresses itself to the ideal society, the coming social order, the superman. To the lower instincts of human beings his law is an absurdity, but to their higher moments it is demonstrable truth. Here is the issue between Christian civilization and social reversion. The whole structure of modern philanthropy and social responsibility — our hospitals, our charities, our science of relief, our industrial schemes of mutual welfare — rest on the paradox of Jesus. The passion for service, which is so conspicuous a mark of modern life, is nothing else than a social consequence of the Christian character.

There remains a third paradox in the teaching of Jesus, less explicitly announced and less directly related to the conduct of life, but involved in all his teaching, and of the utmost social consequence. It is the paradox of idealism. As one reviews the intellectual, literary, and social tendencies of the present time, he observes, among much that is reckless and superficial, an extraordinary revival of the sense of reality. Instead of conventionalism in literature, formalism in art, and artificiality in manners, there is a new respect for facts, a new confidence in candor, a renaissance of realism. It is a phase of civilization which is full of promise. Honesty is better than affectation; facts are more romantic than fiction; sincerity is more convincing than conventionalism, and realism than unreality.

What is it, however, which to modern realism seems most real? What are these facts which are thus substituted for unreality? To what end is this new passion for sincerity and unaffectedness devoted? Is it not true that realism, instead of offering a satisfying creed, often presents a pathetically meagre and colorless picture of life? In its reaction from the fictitious and the metaphysical, is it not inclined to content itself with facts which are insignificant, and in its respect for truth to take for its material truths which are not even respectable? Realism at its worst has become merely another name for the art of the flesh and the literature of the sty; and, even at its best, realism, in the effort to be real, runs grave risk of missing the very touch which gives to art or literature permanent reality. It is steadying to have one's feet on the ground, but it is not unreasonable to look up to the stars. It is honest to recognize the scum on the surface of the stream of life, but it is not dishonest to remember the clear current below. It is a dramatic surprise to discover — as realism has discovered — that poetry may be wrought out of steam-engines and barrack-rooms and light-houses; but Mr. Kipling's writings would be no more than a passing literary fashion unless at times he touched the note of the heroic, the spiritual, the sublime. In short, the revival of realism renews the question of the nature of reality. Is human life real when it is at its worst or when it is at its best? To be sincere must one be brutal, fleshly, cynical? Is the scum of life real and not its deeper waters? Is the mud real and not the star? Is there, in a word, any fundamental issue between the real and the ideal, or is the ideal the most real of human possessions, and are the best interpreters of reality the idealists?

To such questions the greatest of the world's sages, prophets, philosophers, artists, and seers give but one reply. Human life does not come to its own until it comes to its ideals. The thirst for reality is unslaked by the temporary, the accidental, the fleshly; and is satisfied by nothing less than the permanent, the spiritual, the ideal. " The things which are seen are temporal; but the things which are not seen are eternal," says St. Paul.[1] "Our heart can find no rest until it rests in Thee,"[2] says St. Augustine. " We seek the better because we conceive a Best," says modern philosophy.[3] " Man is an ideal-forming animal," says modern ethics.[4]

" 'Tis not what man does which exalts him, but what man
     would do,"

says modern poetry.[5]

[1] 2 Cor. iv. 18.   [2] " Confessions," I, 1.

[3] T. H. Green, " Prolegomena to Ethics," 1883, p. 325: "No one doubts that a man who improves the current morality of his time must be something of an Idealist. . . . That idea cannot represent any experienced reality. If it did, the reformer's labour would be superfluous."

[4] John Grote, " A Treatise on the Moral Ideals," 1876, p. 392: " Whatever else we consider about man, we must add to this — what constitutes indeed the practical significance of our calling him a rational animal — that he is an ideal-forming animal."

[5] Browning's " Saul."

Q

"What I aspired to be,
And was not, comforts me."[1]

"Was ich besitze, seh' ich wie im weiten,
Und was verschwand, wird mir zu Wirklichkeiten."[2]

In this serene company of witnesses of the spirit the teaching of Jesus finds its place. He is the greatest of idealists, not as a philosopher expounding a system, but as a character consciously sustained by an ideal aim which to him is the supreme reality. At the beginning of his ministry he repeats to the tempter the words of Deuteronomy: "Man doth not live by bread only, but by every word that proceedeth out of the mouth of the Lord;"[3] and this conviction that the real life is fed by the sense of the ideal colors his teaching and conduct to the end. "The life," he says, "is more than meat."[4] "A man's life consisteth not in the abundance of the things which he possesseth." "Thou fool," says the parable, of him that "layeth up treasure for himself, and is not rich toward God."[5] "My meat," says the fourth Gospel, "is to do the will of him that sent me."[6] Thus by word and deed Jesus testifies that the real life is life directed toward its ideal. His teaching is not a theory of reality, but a discovery of reality. He does not evade material facts; he translates

[1] Browning's "Rabbi Ben Ezra."
[2] Goethe, Faust, 1te Theil, "Zueignung."
[3] Deut. viii. 3.
[4] Luke xii. 23.
[5] Luke xii. 15, 20, 21.
[6] John iv. 34.

material facts into his idealism. Nature, business, the play of children, the work of life, all speak to him the truth of the spirit in the language of the real. The subjects of his parables are the commonplace and trivial incidents of life, but the purpose of his parables is the idealization of the commonplace and trivial. The way of his discipleship is through prosaic deeds, like feeding the hungry, clothing the naked, or caring for the stranger; but the prose becomes poetry and the real becomes ideal when Jesus says, "Inasmuch as ye have done it unto one of these least ye have done it unto me."

Thus, behind the paradox of sacrifice and the paradox of service in the teaching of Jesus stands always this paradox of idealism. The reason one is sure that to lose life is to find it, and that to serve is to command, is because he is antecedently sure that the world is not what it seems to be, — a world of material gains and glory; but that the real is the ideal, and that the unseen things are eternal. Here is the explanation of the curious mingling of conservatism and radicalism in the teaching of Jesus which has perplexed many an observer. He comes, not to destroy the Law, but to fulfil it; yet his teaching proves a radical departure from the Law and an offence to the legalists. How can he be at once a destroyer and a fulfiller, a radical and a conservative? It is because he finds the reality of the Law in the ideals of the Law; and in destroying the formal law he is fulfilling the ideal law, as the ripening of a seed involves the bursting of its shell.

Such, for instance, is the attitude of Jesus toward the law of the Sabbath. He is conservative in conformity, yet radical in interpretation. He shares the common worship, and takes his part in its ritual; yet his conduct on the Sabbath day appears to many blasphemous. "The sabbath," he says, "was made for man, and not man for the sabbath."[1] The reality of the Sabbath was to be sought in the ideal of the Sabbath. Its authority is not formal, conventional, repressive; it is human, enriching, spiritualizing. What makes a man more a man is a Christian use of the Sabbath; but a man is not more a man when he is undevout, ungirt, or torpid. Jesus does not lower the level of the day of rest; he lifts it, and it becomes a real day of the Lord through its revival of the ideal life of man.

These details, however, are but illustrations of one comprehensive conception in which the idealism of Jesus is fully expressed. "He came into Galilee, preaching the gospel of the kingdom of God."[2] It was a social ideal which still seems to many minds the Utopian dream of a visionary enthusiast; yet to Jesus this unattained ideal was the supreme reality which gave direction to his entire work. The Kingdom of God, as described by Jesus, has many aspects. It is, at one time, remote, external, millennial; again it is near, accessible, spiritual. In its fulfilment it was to be a divine harvest of the

[1] Mark ii. 27.   [2] Mark i. 14.

world; but the seed of that harvest already lay in
the faith, love, and prayers of the little company
of believers. "Fear not," he says, "little flock;
for it is your Father's good pleasure to give you
the kingdom." "I will give unto thee the keys
of the kingdom of heaven."[1]

Was ever idealism so audacious as this? What
seemed the real world, with its Roman power, its
Hebrew prejudices, its human neutrality and timid-
ity, shrank into insignificance before the mind of
Jesus, as the ideal of his faith, the better world,
the brotherhood of man, the Fatherhood of God,
became to him the great reality for which he might
live and die. The paradox of idealism made his
teaching extravagant and unintelligible to many
hearers, as it still remains an offence to the wisdom of the world. Why should we be guided, one
asks, by illusory dreams, when the realities of life
bluntly contradict this vision? Why should Christian congregations still pray that God's kingdom
may come on earth, when after nineteen centuries
it is as far away as ever? Is it not better to take
the world as it is than to imagine it as it cannot be;
to content oneself with the real rather than to
dream of the ideal? The Christian character, on
the other hand, inherits from Jesus his inexpug-
nable idealism. The world as it is, prosaic, hard,
commercial, is the raw material of the world as it

[1] Luke xii. 32; Matt. xvi. 19. Compare the various views of the
nature of the Kingdom as contrasted in "Jesus Christ and the
Social Question," pp. 91 ff., with notes.

is to be. The Christian is an optimist, not with the reckless assurance which calls evil good, but with the rational faith that good is to overcome evil, and that : —

> "Step by step, since time began,
>   We see the steady gain of man."

When one surveys the history of moral progress, what does it teach but the justification of this idealism? What is it that has created a better world but the antecedent faith of the idealists? Each reform in industrial conditions, in the protection of the unprotected, in the abolition of slavery, — whether it be chattel slavery or commercial slavery, — in the treatment of the criminal and the prisoner, has been first dreamed and then accomplished. The idealist endures " as seeing him who is invisible."[1] God chooses "the things which are not, to bring to nought things that are."[2] First comes the idealist with his impracticable hope, and then follow the legislatures and the nations with their practicable measures. First comes the prayer for God's kingdom, and then the realization of that kingdom in some corner of the world. The idealist does not argue with the world as it is; he simply creates the world which has been proved to be impossible. The sagacious Pilate smiles at the zeal of Jesus for a kingdom of truth and withdraws from this hopeless idealism to the realities of the kingdom of the Cæsars; but the realist is soon

---

[1] Heb. xi. 27.   [2] 1 Cor. i. 28.

remembered only because he once ridiculed the idealist, and the kingdom of the Cæsars surrenders to the kingdom of the truth.

Such are the paradoxes of the teaching of Jesus and their social consequences. The Christian character, with its sacrifice, its service, its idealism, must always appear perplexing to the selfish, the grasping or the worldly. Why is it, then, one is led finally to ask, that, in spite of these paradoxes of character, the heart of the world has turned toward such a teaching, and that worldly sagacity has been unable to arrest the progress of this idealism, even when it seems so easily disproved? It is because life itself is so complex, many-sided, and contradictory that nothing short of the paradoxical is its adequate interpretation. One of the most instructive of intellectual experiences is to watch a system-maker as he follows his passion for the simplification of truth. He sets at the head of his task some clew or formula, and the facts which present themselves fall in like a procession behind. It may be the origin of religion which he is examining, or the nature of society or the history of ethics, and in each the complexity of truth is reduced to the limits of one astonishingly simple law. We are on the brink of consenting to the theory proposed, — a worship of ancestors, it may be, or a law of imitation or a doctrine of utility. Truth, which had hitherto baffled us with its complexity, is opened by a single key. Then, of a sudden, another truth looks, as it were, over the shoulder of the principle thus presented and mocks our simple faith.   Instead of presenting to us one calm face, truth is like a throng of faces, varying in expression and confusing in their complexity.   The simple formula was ingenious, but it was not ample enough to hold the many-sidedness of truth.

There is the same story to tell of the simplifying of conduct.   Do what the philosophers may to reduce life to a formula, it remains a paradox.   Shall we define life as pleasure or pain, as gain or loss, as rich or poor, as long or short?   It is all of these, a series of mingled and bewildering experiences, a quick shifting of light and shadow, of sunshine and storm, of achievement and regret, of living and dying.   To find life simple is not to have lived; to miss the complexity of experience is to miss the meaning of life.   Each life holds many lives.   There are truths which are false on one level of experience and which become true only as one ascends.   There are experiences which are fictitious to one age or condition, but which are the supreme sources of joy or peace as one grows fit to use them.   The same truth, Jesus taught, may be convincing to some minds and quite inaccessible to others.   He that has ears to hear, alone can hear.   "Unto you," he said to his friends, "it is given to know the mysteries of the kingdom of God; but to them it is not given."[1]

[1] Luke viii. 10; Matt. xiii. 11.

There were things which he desired to teach which did not come into view until one went up with him to the height of his teaching; where that which seemed to those below a paradox became the most obvious of realities.

How is it, then, that the paradoxes of Jesus may be applied to the paradox of life? They cannot be accepted as theories; they can be verified by experience alone. The appeal of Jesus is always to experience. "Follow me," he says. "Sell all that thou hast and follow me." "Come unto me." "I am the way." The paradox of sacrifice must seem to those who do not go the way of sacrifice, a foolish teaching which leads to loss of life; but those who follow this way to its end, discover that it is life which they have found. The paradox of service is for the poor in spirit alone to verify, yet through their self-effacing service the poor in spirit reach the kingdom of heaven. The paradox of idealism is to the realist the most illusory of dreams, yet the idealist creates the reality in which he alone has believed. Not one of these paradoxes is a truth open to demonstration. They are apparent contradictions, precisely as life itself appears to be a contradiction; but the apparent contradictions of truth are among the most impressive evidences of the many-sidedness of life. The social paradoxes of Jesus are not propositions of the Christian reason; they are consequences of the Christian character.

CHAPTER VII

THE ASCENT OF ETHICS

In all that has been thus far said there is a manifest sense of incompleteness. The ethical teaching of Jesus, though it may interpret many of his words and works, brings us repeatedly to a point where the Teacher seems to pass beyond the province of ethics and to use a language which ethics does not comprehend. His summons to righteousness, his command of love, his conception of life, all move in the sphere of ethics; but when at any point he indicates the sources of his moral authority, the motives which direct his will, the grounds of his ethical confidence, he crosses the boundary of ethics, and, while still discoursing of character, enters a region where character is consciously controlled by communion with God. Jesus, in short, is fundamentally not a teacher of morals, but a witness of religion. The supreme motive of his conduct is his relation to the Father. "Wist ye not," he says in youth, "that I must be about my Father's business?"[1] "All things are delivered unto me," he says of his commission, "of my Father."[2] The interpretation of the teaching of

[1] Luke ii. 49.   [2] Matt. xi. 27; Luke x. 22.

Jesus in terms of ethics leads, as it were, to a threshold, which the Teacher crosses to enter a room of which ethics has no key, and of which he says : " I am the door."

This impression which one receives from the teaching of Jesus, that, though ethical in its content and aim, its motives and sources are super-ethical, meets one again as he examines the modern literature of systematic ethics. These analyses of conduct proceed with their classifications of virtues, appetites, and desires, where the student feels at each step that there is solid ground under his feet; yet he cannot escape the suspicion that these ethical distinctions, though substantial so far as they go, do not touch the bottom of the material with which they deal. It is as though one's way led over a series of stepping-stones, each of which was firm, but beneath which ran an unexplored and mysterious stream. Beneath the questions of ethics, even when these are answered, run deeper questions of religion, issuing from sources which lie back of ethics, and flowing to an end which is beyond ethics. The footpath of ethics follows the course of this current of religion, and one looks down from the stepping-stones of morals and wonders whither this unexplored river would bear him if he gave himself to its control.

In the preface of Dr. Martineau's " Study of Religion" he quotes "an eminent English positivist" as commenting on John Fiske's treatise on the "Destiny of Man." "It only proves," said this advocate of naturalistic ethics, "what I have always maintained, that you cannot make the slightest concession to metaphysics, without ending in a theology!" The criticism was to be anticipated; but, as Dr. Martineau proceeds to remark, it was a naïve confession that "If once you allow yourself to think about the origin and end of things, you will have to believe in a God and immortality."[1] That was precisely what had happened to John Fiske. He had permitted himself to think about the evolution of morality, and the implications of ethics had led him across the threshold of religion.[2] Ethics, in short, while it has a certain stability and coherence of its own, has the marks of a preliminary, suggestive, propædeutic science. A theory of morals is like a house by the wayside, where one may rest securely for a night, but which is not the journey's end. Ethics is a sign-post on the way to religion.

This lack of finality has a striking illustration in an Association which has made important contributions to contemporary morals in the name of "Ethical Culture." Here is a movement which, superficially regarded, is neutral or hostile to the

[1] "Study of Religion," 1888, pp. vii ff.

[2] "The Destiny of Man, viewed in the Light of his Origin," 1884, pp. 104 ff.: "Now what is this message of the modern prophet but pure Christianity? . . . When have we ever before held such a clew to the meaning of Christ in the Sermon on the Mount? . . . Our new knowledge enlarges tenfold the significance of human life, and makes it seem more than ever the chief object of Divine care."

formal teaching of religion, and deliberately restricts its programme to moral education. The metaphysics of Christianity are dismissed from consideration as superfluous and obstructive, and attention is recalled to the obvious and immediate truths of ethical responsibility and human service. It is an indictment which the churches should take to heart, an appeal from feeling to conduct, from theology to life. When, however, one observes more closely the literature of Ethical Culture, he is surprised to observe that, though its title seems repressive, its intention is comprehensive. Its "culture" represents not merely the practice of morality, but the philosophy of idealism. Its hope is not to reduce religion to morals, but to expand morals into religion. Its language is that of ethics, but its motives are those of faith. Ethical idealism may shun the phrases of religion; but its emotions, its impulses, its spiritual attitude, are identical with those of rational piety. Faith in the moral order of the Universe, in the categorical imperative of duty, in the fitness of man for ethical culture, may not express the whole of religion, but it is certainly the point at which the teaching of Jesus began. Lives which are trained to recognize the universal authority of the moral law may not name the name of God, but they are doing the will of the Father. Ethical culture is suppressed Theism.[1]

[1] Compare *e.g.* "Ethics and Religion," edited by the Society of Ethical Propagandists, 1900, Lect. I, J. R. Seeley, "Ethics and Religion," p. 26: "My advice is that instead of waging war, open

If, then, it be true that ethics, whether in its modern forms or in the teaching of Jesus, bears this mark of preparatoriness, as though preliminary to an end beyond itself, what is the principle which distinguishes these two ways of conduct? Can religion exist without morality? Can morality exist without religion? Is religion merely morality touched with emotion? Is morality merely religion freed from superstition? Theologians have spoken slightingly of mere morality or mere works; moralists have regarded with equal indifference mere theology or faith without works. Religion often appears unmoral or even immoral, whether in cruel rites of barbaric tribes or in limp emotions of modern sentimentalists. Morality often acts without consciousness of religious sanctions, whether in Stoic philosophers or in modern Agnostics. How, then, shall one discriminate ethics from religion? What is it in these two sentiments, which have

or covert, you enter once for all into the heartiest and most reserved alliance with Christianity"; Lect. II, Felix Adler, "The Freedom of Ethical Fellowship," pp. 50 ff.: "The teachings of Jesus . . . are that it is necessary to live the spiritual life in order to understand the spiritual truths. . . . The symbols of religion are ciphers of which the key is to be found in moral experience. . . . The new religious synthesis which many longed for, will not be a fabrication, but a growth. It will . . . come in time as a result of the gradual moral evolution of modern society." Lect. IV, W. M. Salter, "Ethical Religion," pp. 88 ff.: "Ethics realized in its meaning is religion. . . . Aspiration, reverence, awe, . . . are but uncompleted morality; and when the moral act is done, ecstasy is its sign, — ecstasy, which is the grace heaven sets upon the moment in which the soul weds itself to the perfect good."

directed so great a part of human history, — the sense of duty, and the sense of God, — which at the same time demonstrates their affinity and denies their identity ?   How is it that ethics comes to have this preliminary and unconclusive aspect, as though it were a threshold across which one passed to faith ?

The answer to these questions is suggested when one observes the different circles of relationship in which the two sentiments habitually move.   Ethics is sociological, human, contemporary.   It considers the adjustment of each individual within the circle of his social relations.   The elementary truth which makes the starting-point of ethics is the truth that the individual is not alone, but is a part of the social order.   Through the performance of its function by each part, the social organism, like physical organisms, survives and thrives ; the discovery by the individual of his part in the social whole is his problem of ethics ; and the performance of that part is the doing of his duty.   Individuals are not wandering atoms which at times collide and then rebound into isolation ; they are inevitably associated in the organic life of the social body.   Thy neighbor and thyself are interdependent atoms ; and the moral law, " Thou shalt love thy neighbor as thyself," is imperative, because it describes the fact that thy neighbor and thyself are members one of another.[1]

[1] Compare Royce, "The World and the Individual," 1901, Lect. VIII, "The Moral Order," p. 349 : " The essence of this consciousness

If this is the field of ethics, what is that of religion? Here also the individual finds himself part of an organic life, in which he is to find and fulfil his function; but the circle of relationship in which he is now set is no longer limited by the human, social, contemporary world. Association with the Eternal, loyalty to the Ideal, communion with God, — the characteristic attitudes of the religious life, — assume that the individual is set within a universal order, whose total movement, whether of man or nature, of pain or pleasure, of personal or national experience, is the movement of a spiritual intention, the evolution of a Divine plan. To conform to that plan and coöperate with it becomes the supreme desire. Discernment of that plan is the end of theology; coöperation with it is the end of religion. To fulfil one's function in the universal organism; to recognize in one's own experience not an unmeaning accident, but an essential incident in the vast design; to do not one's own will, but the will of Him who sends us, — that is the habit of mind which expresses the peace, courage, and consecration of a religious faith.[1]

[of Ought] is that the Self is to accomplish the object of its search through obedience to an order which is not of its own momentary creation "; Seth, " Ethical Principles," 1902, Ch. XI, " The Social Life "; Wundt, " Ethik," 1886, ss. 386 ff., " Das Verhältniss des Einzelnen zur Gesammtheit "; Mackenzie, " Introduction to Social Philosophy," 1890, Ch. III, " The Social Organism."

[1] So, Sabatier, " Religions of Authority and the Religion of the Spirit," tr. Houghton, 1904, pp. 350 ff.: " If the law of duty is the immanent law of the life of the spirit; . . . if humanity makes no

Here, then, are two circles of conduct which in one aspect are identical, but in another are distinct. The problem of conduct is in each case the same. Morality and religion are alike concerned with the adjustment of the part to the whole, the atom to the organism, the person to the world; but the areas of conduct within which adjustment is to be found are of different dimensions. What ethics proposes within the circle of social life religion accomplishes in the larger circle of the universal order. The two circles are concentric. At the centre of each stands the personal life, with its own problems and needs; but while the radius of one circle runs out to the circumference of human companionship, the radius of the environing circle is protracted as far as thought and feeling have the strength to go. It is not surprising, then, that ethics, though having a certain completeness of its own, betrays the sense of a greater environment. The outer edge of ethical inquiry is the inner margin of larger problems. Prolong the radius of duty-doing, and one enters the territory of faith. Ethics goes its own way toward its own end; but the end of ethics is no sooner approached than there appears beyond it a further ideal, as one

progress . . . except by obedience ; . . . if this law commands universal evolution . . . does it not become evident that . . . the law of duty shares in the objectivity of cosmic laws themselves?" So, G. H. Palmer, "The Field of Ethics," 1901, p. 201 : "Ethics is . . . occupied with earthly conditions. The finite is its field; but . . . the moral man is ever seeking to manifest the connection of the finite with the infinite."

R

reaches what seems the summit of a mountain only to discover a higher peak beyond.

May ethics, then, exist without religion? Such independence, it must be answered, may unquestionably be maintained; but it is maintained by restricting the radius and scope of duty. Small ethics, conventional conduct, decent conformity, may be comfortably fortified within a very limited circle of principles and sanctions; but no sooner does conduct reach out toward heroism, initiative, leadership, idealism, than the circle of ethics expands into that of faith, and instead of conformity to conventional maxims feels the compulsion of categorical commands. May religion, on the other hand, exist without morality? This detachment, also, it must be admitted, appears practicable. Religion has an outer circle of emotion and expression in which one may dwell without retiring to the inner circle of practical morality. The contemplation of God may become so absorbing that it may induce sheer inactivity, meditation or ecstasy.[1] The manifestation of religion may be mistaken for religion itself, and religion may be defined as though it occupied an outer circle of ritual, ceremonial or theology. Yet this rupture of the outer circle of experience from the inner is like the breaking of a living growth, where the part cut off withers and the part abandoned shows the scar. Religion, as a way of life, is a flower of the whole of life. It does not outgrow morality, it grows out

[1] So, Palmer, "Field of Ethics," 1901, pp. 180 ff.

of morality. It is no more to be defined by the form it assumes than a person can be defined by the clothes he wears. Ritual, ceremony, theology, are the clothes of religion, and religion itself is the life within. Normal religion is an extension of the radius of morality. It is conduct persuaded by the call of God, life set in the circumference of the Eternal, participation in the universal order, enlargement of experience by contact with the permanent. "Wouldst thou find thy way to the Infinite?" said Goethe, "Push on into the finite as far as thou canst go." [1] Even the immoralities which have often characterized the history of religion confirm the principle that religion is an extension of morality; for it is the sense of obligation, perverted but compelling, which has given to these immoralities their authority. The imperfect ethics has penetrated the developing faith, as a wavering radius vitiates a circle. Pure religion, whatever else it may contain, is a circle of experience at whose centre are those who are unspotted from the world.

What, then, is the relation of morality to religion? It is the relation of the part to the whole, of the smaller to the larger world, of the antechamber to the presence-chamber, of companionship with humanity to companionship with God. The second commandment, "Thou shalt love thy

[1] " Gott, Gemüth, und Welt " : —
  " Willst du in's Unendliche schreiten,
    Geh' nur in's Endliche nach allen Seiten."

neighbor," is not only like the first, "Thou shalt love the Lord, thy God"; it is in reality the same commandment in a preliminary form. Love of one's neighbor, the problem of ethics, is the same task of self-adjustment within the social organism which makes the problem of religion in the universal order. Ethics is thus, in its form, identical with religion, but in its content distinct from religion. The interior circle of conduct is in itself complete, but it is environed by the larger circle.

In one of the noblest passages of ethical literature, Dr. Martineau, applying the analogy suggested by Kant, describes the relation of duty to faith as that of an island to an environing ocean.[1] The islander has firm ground under his feet, he may live and work in the thickets of the interior and may "remain quite unaware of any relations beyond this circle, and work within it as a complete and rounded whole." If, however, he goes up some day to the heights of his conduct, there, on every side, he finds the unexplored and mysterious circle of the sea. "Ethics, therefore, on their outer margin, bring us face to face with the momentous question, whether their supreme intimations are verifiable, and their relations eternal. . . . Conscience may act as human, before it is discovered to be divine. . . . Ethics must either perfect themselves in religion, or disintegrate themselves into Hedonism."[2] "Sometimes," said Lowell, translating into one of

[1] "A Study of Religion," 1888, I, 20 ff.
[2] *Ibid.* pp. 16 ff., "Why Ethics before Religion?"

the highest utterances of modern poetry this philosophy of life,

> "Sometimes at waking, on the street sometimes,
> Or on the hillside, always unforewarned,
> A grace of being, finer than himself,
> That beckons and is gone, — a larger life
> Upon his own impinging, . . .
> To which the ethereal substance of his own
> Seems but gross cloud to make that visible,
> Touched to a sudden glory round the edge."[1]

One of the most impressive of modern preachers has developed the same thought in still more spacious language under the title of "The circular and the onward movement."[2] In the solar system where we dwell, he points out, there are two forms of motion, first the rotation of the planets round the sun, and secondly a vast onward movement, sweeping both sun and planets in infinitely greater orbits round some infinitely distant centre. How is it, he asks, that this second motion, whose scope is beyond all observation, can be proved? The onward movement, he answers, is discovered through the patient observation of the orbits which can be seen. Perturbations in the solar system are interpretable only by conceiving this mighty sweep of all which can be observed in a movement which is invisible. So, says this inspiring teacher, the system of duty lies within the system of faith, and the in-

---

[1] "The Cathedral," 1870, p. 34.
[2] Mark Hopkins, "Strength and Beauty," 1874, Sermon XVI, p. 311.

visible truths of the universal order are disclosed by the patient observation of the smaller system where one's duty, in its orbit of daily tasks, revolves.[1]

When one turns from these discussions of modern scholars to the teaching of Jesus, he finds himself, it must be admitted, in quite another climate of experience and expression. Jesus does not speculate concerning the relation of ethics to religion in philosophical language or by astronomical analogies. Without apparent consciousness of logical processes, his discourse moves freely among the problems of duty and faith; yet the ascent of ethics to religion, which these modern masters describe, is the way which he summons men to go. Jesus is, first of all, a teacher of morals. The Sermon on the Mount is an ethical discourse. The Beatitudes are ethical promises. Conduct is the test of discipleship. "Whosoever heareth these sayings of mine, and doeth them, I will liken him unto a wise man, which built his house upon a rock." [2] The commendations of Jesus are for moral fidelity, conscientiousness, watchfulness, unselfishness. The faithful servant, the diligent woman, the watchman at the gate, the maidens with their lamps burning, represent the moral type which he desires to create. When, however, these ethical judgments and instructions are traced by

[1] See also, G. H. Palmer, "The Field of Ethics," 1901, p. 187: " Morality precedes religion, but morality fulfils itself in religion."
[2] Matt. vii. 24.

Jesus to their causes or their consequences, or are explained by him in their full significance, they are taken up into his religious consciousness, and are illuminated by his sense of God. Thus at many points it is not easy to say whether Jesus is a teacher of ethics or of religion. He speaks of conduct, but he looks past conduct. Phrases which begin in one key end in another. The radius of his thought prolongs itself from the circle of duty to the comprehensiveness of God.

One can hardly open the Gospels without coming on an illustration of this transition in his thought. The Beatitudes, for example, are for the duty-doers, the meek, the peacemakers, the pure in heart; but the consequences of this duty-doing are super-ethical, the inheritance of the Kingdom of Heaven, the title of the children of God, the capacity to see God. Character is the object of the teaching, but character is discovered to be a part of the Divine plan. The parables of Jesus follow the same path of ascent, and though their way runs through the valley of duty, it mounts to the heights of faith. It is as though the Teacher lifted his eyes while he spoke, and saw, as those who listened did not see, the distant view beyond. He speaks of servants and their talents; but he sees, beyond the problem of their duty, the Lord of those servants who will come and make a reckoning with them. He speaks of the sower and his seed; but beyond the sower's task he sees the harvest which is the end of the world and the reapers who are the angels.

He commends the porter watching at the gate, but translates his fidelity into a universal law : " What I say unto you, I say unto all, Watch ! " He speaks, with infinite pathos, of the prodigal's repentance, and it seems a purely ethical transition. The boy " comes to himself," as though it were the recovery by himself of his real character ; but as Jesus traces farther this moral regeneration, he sees in it another factor of reform, and beyond the self-discovery of the prodigal hears the call of the waiting Father.   Thus, the near and the far, the contemporary and the universal, the immediate duty and the consummate revelation, are so intimately blended in the teaching of Jesus, that as it ascends from the less to the greater, from the plains of duty to the summits of faith, it is one path which he follows, unbroken in its continuity and familiar to his feet.   The point of departure is from the obvious facts of duty ; but the path of duty leads to a view beyond duty ; the corollaries of conduct give significance to the problem of conduct ; to him that is faithful in that which is least there is added the capacity for faithfulness in that which is much, and for him who learns the lesson of the Mammon of unrighteousness there are reserved the true riches.   To the follower of Jesus the ascent of ethics is like the ascent of a mountain with a trustworthy guide.   Through the level facts of duty one may trudge a well-trodden way ; but as the slope grows more precipitous, and the plains of commonplace recede, and what seems the summit is reached only to disclose a higher peak beyond, the climber is sustained by the assurance that the guide knows the path, and has the right to say, as one having authority : " Follow me."

One may begin this ascent at any point where one strikes the path of duty. Even a single virtue or repentance or resolution gives a point of departure. The Canaanite woman says in self-abasement : " Lord, help me " ; " The dogs eat of the crumbs which fall from their master's table," and Jesus welcomes this humble teachableness and says : " O woman, great is thy faith." [1] The father of the sick child cries : " Help thou mine unbelief " ; and Jesus accepts the half-belief as the hesitating beginnings of a faith to which "all things are possible." [2] The woman " which was a sinner " has little to offer to Jesus but the lavishness of her love ; but Jesus accepts this also and says : " Her sins, which are many, are forgiven ; for she loved much." [3] It is the story of the growth of character told once more, but ascending from character to faith. Not conscious attainment, not the theological satiety of the Pharisee, but each genuine impulse of humility or loyalty or regret has in it the potential development of Christian faith. " A Christian," said a great German theologian, Julius Müller, " is never made, but always making. He therefore that is already a Christian is as yet not a Christian." The ethical method of Jesus is prophetic, preliminary, a doctrine

---

[1] Matt. xv. 27, 28.   [2] Mark ix. 23, 24.   [3] Luke vii. 47.

of the way, with an assurance of the end, the
method which, as Wordsworth says,

> "hath among least things
> An under-sense of greatest, sees the parts
> As parts, but with a feeling of the whole." [1]

Even in the ministry of Jesus himself it is, perhaps, possible to trace a deepening of his message,
as though the channel of his teaching were broad-
ened by the increasing abundance of his thought.
In the Sermon on the Mount the Kingdom of
Heaven is described in the language of ethical
prophecy. "Whosoever therefore shall break
one of these least commandments . . . shall be
called the least in the kingdom of heaven." [2] In
the later teaching, however, this Kingdom takes
the form of a day of the Lord or of a coming of
the Son of Man in his glory. The calm, grave
Teacher of righteousness becomes more distinctly
the spiritual Messiah, whose mission is the fulfilment of the Father's will; and instead of summa-
rizing his teaching in a law of ethics, "Therefore
all things whatsoever ye would that men should
do to you, do ye even so to them," [3] he expresses
the heart of it in a prayer of faith: "Not as I
will, but as thou wilt." [4]

Nor does this influence of the teaching of Jesus
cease at the Master's death. Jesus seems aware
that a teacher may so dominate the minds of his

---

[1] "The Prelude," Book VII. [3] Matt. vii. 12.
[2] Matt. v. 19. [4] Matt. xxvi. 39.

followers that, as the fourth Gospel says, it is expedient for him to go away if the Spirit of truth is to come to them. That is what the later experience of the disciples seems to prove. "Follow me," he teaches, and they follow, though with hesitating steps; but the Master's death, which seemed the end of their hope, becomes in fact the beginning of their ascent from obedience to faith. Their eyes were opened, and they knew him, says the third Gospel, as he vanished from their sight. Not till they tarried in the city after he was gone were they "endued with power from on high."[1] This is the tradition which is amplified in the fourth Gospel, where Jesus repeatedly points beyond his own teaching for its interpretation. "These things have I spoken unto you, being yet present with you. But the Comforter, which is the Holy Ghost, whom the Father will send in my name, he shall teach you all things, and bring all things to your remembrance, whatsoever I have said unto you."[2] The ascent of discipleship was to be continuous and life-long, a progressive revelation, from loyalty to insight, from the plains of duty-doing to the heights of communion, from things to God, from obedience to vision, from the teaching of Jesus to the teaching of the Comforter, from the righteousness of the Kingdom of God to the truth of all that had been said unto them.[3]

[1] Luke xxiv. 49.   [2] John xiv. 25, 26.
[3] Compare the striking treatment of E. M. Chapman, "The

When one turns from contemplating these characteristics of the teaching of Jesus and recalls the teachings which have been offered in his name, is he not met at many points by a most disheartening contrast? Have the expositors of Christian duty and Christian faith consistently recognized that in the mind of Jesus these two elements of experience were parts of a continuous process which has its natural growth and fruit? Have the elementary facts of morality been " seen as facts," yet with "a feeling of the whole "? On the contrary, much well-intentioned teaching, both of ethics and of religion, has become, at this point, self-defeating. Morality and faith have been often presented as fixed alternatives, subjects of statical sciences, cases where one must, so to speak, take all or none; when, in fact, morality is, according to the teaching of Jesus, not a fixed fact but a way of ascent, a growth from less to more, a movement toward religion.

One of the most curious of literary experiences is the sense of unreality which seems to pervade a considerable part of the literature of ethics. No subject, it would seem, could be more living than life, and ethics is the study of life; yet many a student of ethics will testify that its text-books have

Dynamic of Christianity," 1904, p. 142: " An intelligent man who should come to the reading of the Gospels for the first time and without theological predisposition would doubtless be impressed with Christ's sense of the partial nature of His own work in the flesh." p. 21: " Christianity is not a completed system . . . but an organism . . . with the power of an endless life."

appeared to him singularly desiccated and juiceless. "Never before," as has been said of these formal systems, "had human nature been so neatly dissected, so handily sorted or so ornamentally packed up. The virtues and vices, the appetites, emotions, affections, and sentiments, stored each in their appointed corner, and with their appropriate label, to wait in neat expectation for the season of the professional lecturer, and the literary world only delayed their acquiescence in a uniform creed of moral philosophy, till they should have arranged to their satisfaction whether the appetites should be secreted in the cupboard or paraded on the mantel-piece, or whether some of the less creditable packets . . . ought to be ticketed 'Poison.'" [1]

What is it which reduces the study of life to such lifelessness, and makes the language of life a dead language? It is the assumption that ethical distinctions are fixtures, when, in fact, the life of conduct grows, withers, and takes heart again, as the flowers of the field struggle for their existence among the weeds. The schools of ethical philosophy with their historic titles, Egoism, Prudentialism, Idealism, are not final choices, as though one must commit himself to a single and consistent view of life. One's moral experience must be, on the contrary, very meagre if it does not recognize in itself all three of these competing creeds, and incline in turn to differ-

[1] Cited by J. C. Shairp, "Studies in Poetry and Philosophy," 1872, "The Moral Motive-power," p. 272: "'Never before,' as one has smartly said." Who was it?

ent masters. At one moment one is a disciple of
Hobbes, and all that masks itself as duty seems to
show the mocking face of self-interest; again, one
joins himself to Mill or Bentham and computes the
consequences of pleasures and pains; still again,
in some high moment of joy or sorrow or love, one
goes up where selfishness and prudence shrink
into insignificance, as the details of a flat country
recede when one looks down on it from a height.
The great peaks of idealism come into view and
call one to their exploration and possession, and
one calls back to them, —

> "Wait there, wait and invite me while I climb,
> For see I come! but slow, but slow,
> Yet ever, as your chime
> Soft and sublime
> Lifts at my feet, they move, they go
> Up the great stair of time."[1]

Ethics, in other words, if it would describe life as
it is, must take account of its quality of surprise,
must welcome the broader horizon which unfolds
as one ascends, the influx of new power as one
breathes the higher air, the increasing sense of
reality and authority in the moral ideal. One may
be very selfish, but he is never safe from inroads
of generous desire; he may be habitually prudential, as one who sits on the shores of emotion and
does not trust himself to its depths; but in some un-
foreseen moment of self-forgetfulness a great wave
of emotion sweeps up upon him and snatches him
from his security into the ocean of self-sacrifice.

[1] David A. Wasson, "Poems," ed. Mrs. E. D. Cheney, 1888,
"Ideals."

" Just when we are safest, there's a sunset-touch,
A fancy from a flower-bell, some one's death,
A chorus-ending from Euripides, —
And that's enough for fifty hopes and fears
As old and new at once as nature's self,
To rap and knock and enter in our soul,
Take hands and dance there, a fantastic ring,
Round the ancient idol, on his base again." [1]

The same truth has an opposite and more solemn aspect. Idealism may ebb as it has risen; the vision splendid may fade into the light of common day; and instead of an ascent of ethics there may ensue the real fall of man, the shortening of the radius of duty, the narrowing of the circle of obligation. Capacity for moral growth means risk of moral decay. It is this appreciation of the remoter consequences of conduct which, in the teaching of Jesus, gives such significance to each lapse from integrity and each petty sin. Moral experience is seen, not as a series of disconnected incidents, but as a continuous process, in which each stumble retards the ascent and each blunder misses the way. "Every idle word that men shall speak," says Jesus, "they shall give account thereof in the day of judgment." [2] The reckless speech hangs round the climber's neck, and though he may still ascend, he must carry his burden to the top and give account of his delay. Ethics, in short, is not a piecing together of the fragments of life, but a description of the whole of life, the story of the

[1] Browning, " Bishop Blougram's Apology."
[2] Matt. xii. 36.

retarded yet persistent ascent of man, its gains and its pains, its advances and its pauses, its higher levels and its breathlessness, its detaining selfishness and its inviting ideals. It is all one life, beginning in the valley of commonplace duties and idle words, and proceeding to the vision of truth and the day of judgment. The will to do the will takes up the march, and the knowledge of the doctrine broadens as one climbs.

This sense of continuity is the first principle of a sound education in morals. Why is it that children so often find goodness uninteresting and repelling, and wrong-doing persuasive and exhilarating? Why does the routine of duty so often become, to grown people, monotonous or trivial? It is because goodness is looked at as a fixed condition, a dead weight, a pile of duties to carry one by one to their proper places, and then perhaps to carry back again. The woman in her household, the man with the hoe, the boy at his lessons, the worker at his work, — what are they but slaves and drudges, with the duty done to-day confronting them again with its inert mass to-morrow? What is their life but a treadmill, in which they seem to move; but in reality, like the horse in a treadmill, only move the wheels of the world from the pen in which they are tied fast? "Sir," said an employee in a vast government bureau as he looked up from his death-bed to a friend who spoke of death, "why talk of death? I have been dead and buried here for twenty years."

Nor is it alone the workers of the world who find duty on these terms a dehumanizing slavery. Many who seem most free from the burden of routine — the idlers, the pleasure-seekers, the increasing army of the prosperous unemployed — are not less oppressed by a sense of the insignificance, the triviality, the meaninglessness of life, and when they attach themselves to any philosophy of duty become docile converts to a creed of despair. Restlessness, despondency, *ennui*, are not so much products of work as of leisure; cynicism, pessimism, and self-contempt afflict the lives which seem most blessed. Why take this paltry human life, they ask, so seriously? What is it but a momentary bubble on the surface of an unknown deep? Why strive and sweat to build a straight highway of conduct with the stones of duty, when the wandering path of pleasure is unobstructed and fair? What is one's life but a descent into the dark, the flight of a bird, as the Saxon warrior said to the Venerable Bede, out of the darkness into the banquet hall, and out again into the night?

> " A moment's halt — a momentary taste
> Of *Being* from the well amid the waste —
> And lo ! — the phantom Caravan has reach'd
> The *Nothing* it set out from — oh, make haste ! " [1]

What is it which redeems life from this sense of flatness and impotence, and restores to duty its significance and scope? It is the truth of the

[1] Fitzgerald's " Omar Khayyam," 54.

S

ascent of ethics; the emergence of idealism; the translation of duty-doing into faith. To find in the routine of life, not a series of disconnected accidents, but the participation in an Infinite design; to follow the way of duty until it mounts to insight, composure, courage; to discover that the interpretation of life must be reached, not by going round one's duties, but by going through them; that to him only who is faithful in the least that which is much is revealed — this is what rescues life from fragmentariness and fixedness, and gives one, even among laborious and monotonous duties, a sense of unity, movement, and hope. "The sentiment of virtue," says Emerson, "is the essence of all religion. Whilst a man seeks good ends, he is strong by the whole strength of nature. . . . When he says, 'I ought'. . . then he can worship, and be enlarged by his worship. . . . In the sublimest flights of the soul, rectitude is never surmounted." [1]

This is the view of life which meets us both in the teaching and in the character of Jesus Christ. His ethics speak, not of stones to be moved, but of seeds to be planted. The routine of life is to Jesus the background on which he paints his picture of God's thought for man. The disciple of Jesus is like a soldier at the front, involved in much routine of marching and counter-marching; solitary, it may be, as he paces up and down a sentry's beat; but through all the monotony and solitude sustained by the sense that he is under

[1] "Miscellanies," 1868, Divinity School Address, pp. 66 ff.

orders, and that the Commander whose will has sent him is at his back. The follower of Jesus is a laborer, but he is a laborer together with God. He is the man with a hoe, but he has his part in the harvest whose reapers are the angels. He is a cog in the great machine of industry, but the whole great machine depends on the strength of each slightest cog, and each failure of the humblest part mars the fabric which issues from the whole. The Christian life trudges through the valleys, but its face is set to the hills. It moves, as a modern teacher has said, " from small moral matters up to large religious ones. The road up is man's natural path. It may see in the little the large, and may look through the finite limited duty into the friendly face of the eternal.

> ' Who sweeps a room as to Thy laws
> Makes that and the action fine.' " [1]

What is the effect of this view of life on the problems of practical conduct which perplex so many minds in the modern world? When one observes the way in which practical morality conducts itself under the conditions of the present age, its dealing with new duties, its experiments in philanthropy, its schemes for industrial or political justice, he is struck by the tentative, wavering, undetermined line which marks the movement of ethics. No directing principle or manifest end seems to give confidence to contemporary morals.

[1] Palmer, " Field of Ethics," 1901, 183 ff.

To many modern minds religion has become a remote, if not an unreal, support; and they must determine their duty by ephemeral, empirical, hand-to-mouth choices between the worse and the better. To many devoted lives, concerned with problems of philanthropy, no issue of their enterprise seems clear, and they are smitten with a sense of helplessness, a paralysis of enthusiasm, as those who have undertaken more than can be performed. To many who have pledged themselves to industrial or political reform, the signs of the times seem ominous, the prevailing philosophy of the working-classes seems blighted by materialism, and instead of national ethics we seem to be offered mere statistics of products or ships or guns.

What is it under such conditions which can restore to duty-doing its confidence, and to philanthropy its patience, and to industrial and political morals their idealism? It is the appreciation of the ascent of ethics, the discovery of the continuity of conduct, the recognition of the cumulative movement, which proceeds through the temporal toward the Eternal. How shall one act who finds duty real, but faith a receding vision? There is but one path to the rediscovery of faith, and it runs straight through the duty which is real. "It is an awful moment," said Frederick Robertson, "when the soul begins to find that the props on which it has blindly rested so long are, many of them, rotten, and begins to suspect them all. . . . In that fearful loneliness of spirit . . . I know but one way

in which a man may come forth from his agony
scatheless; it is by holding fast to those things
which are certain still — the grand, simple landmarks of morality. . . . If there be no God and no
future state, yet even then it is better to be generous than selfish, better to be chaste than licentious,
better to be true than false, better to be brave than
to be a coward. . . . Thrice blessed is he who —
when all is drear and cheerless — has obstinately
clung to moral good. Thrice blessed, because his
night shall pass into clear, bright day." [1] This, if
there be any way to a revival of religion, is the way
now open; — not by the assent to opinions, but by
the ascent of ethics. There are not two ways of
life running parallel through experience, — a way
of duty and a way of faith. The way to God is up
the steep path of duty, and the vision and peace of
God are for those who climb. This is the conviction which gives persistency and fidelity to duty-
doing. Life may not be all at once understood,
but the horizon of life broadens as the path of
duty ascends, and one may bear with many ob-
scurities and hindrances along the path if he
knows that he has not missed his way. To one
who sees what is right, and wants to find what is
true, the best rule is the simple maxim: "Turn to
the Right and keep straight on." [2]

The same discovery is made by modern phi-

[1] "Life and Letters," 1882, p. 86, from a Lecture to the
Workingmen of Brighton.

[2] "Both Catholics and Protestants have taught (*Spectator*,

lanthropy. How to maintain faith in one's own usefulness, how to be patient with its incompleteness and yet believe in its significance — this is the harassing sense of discouragement and scepticism which attacks many a servant of others' needs. There is but one way to the restoration of social courage. It is by the practical following of the path of social duty and the discovery that it is an ascending path, with constantly broader outlooks and clearer views. What seems a fragmentary and ineffective task is taken up into the total movement of social responsibility, and one is lifted and sustained by a faith which his works may not seem to justify, but to which none the less they point the way. The modern charity-worker, tempted by many failures to loss of hope and courage, takes heart again from the reviving words: —

> " Cleave ever to the sunnier side of doubt,
> And cling to Faith beyond the forms of Faith!
>
> . . . . . .
>
> She sees the Best that glimmers thro' the Worst,
> She feels the Sun is hid but for a night,
> She spies the summer thro' the winter bud,
>
> . . . . . .
>
> She finds the fountain where they wail'd 'Mirage!'" [1]

November 12, 1904, quoting *Daily Telegraph* of November 1 and J. F. de Bruno's " Catholic Belief,") that there is a ' Body of the Church ' and a ' Soul of the Church,' and that to the latter belong hundreds and thousands of men and women who could not, not anyhow at present, make explicitly even a short confession of faith. The Catholic teaching ' holds that these Christians belong to and are united to the Soul of the Catholic Church.' "

[1] Tennyson, " The Ancient Sage."

Many a helper of the poor is led by his patient service among them not only to freedom from himself, but also to the renewal of his faith in the moral order of the world. Seeking the Kingdom of God other things are added. To love one's neighbor as oneself has as its corollary a new appreciation of the Love which rules the world. The work of philanthropy turns out to be not a series of incidental skirmishes, but a great campaign of compassion; and courage returns when one becomes aware that he is not of "an ignorant army clashing in the dark," but that the ascent of duty discloses the plan of the campaign.

Finally, the affairs of modern industry and politics are to be redeemed by the same recognition of the ascent of ethics. Commercialism, materialism, and militarism have become so dominant and audacious that many lives are repelled from public affairs and many more are subdued to that they work in, like the dyer's hand. It seems a long way from industrial contentions and political ambitions to the Christian vision of a Kingdom of God, and ethical idealists are easily tempted to become social pessimists. Yet through precisely this region of life, where the keenest interests of the modern world are concentrated, through the treacherous ways of business where one must pick his steps or fall, through the mire of political corruption where many sink, goes the path of modern duty; and in this low ground, where the life of the time for the moment halts, the ascent of ethics must begin.   It is in vain to set the higher life of the time over against its lower life, as though they looked at each other across the way.   It is one world, with one way of progress, which begins in the malarial valleys and ascends to the purer heights.   " If any man among you seem to be religious," says the apostle, "and bridleth not his tongue, . . . this man's religion is vain." [1]   It is the same with any nation which thinketh itself to be religious, but finds some other starting-point for national religion than in industrial justice and political integrity. Here is the ground of confidence for those who in these muddy places of public life make firm the road which social morality must go.   They may not themselves accomplish the complete ascent of ethics, but they are at least preparing the way. The ladder of social progress may some day reach to heaven, but it must be none the less set up on earth ; and those who set it firmly on the ground make it safer for the angels to ascend.[2]

[1] James i. 26.

[2] Precisely the opposite course of argument is illustrated by M. Guyau in his two volumes : " Esquisse d'une Morale sans Obligation ni Sanction," 1903 ; and " L'Irréligion de l'Avenir," 1904.   " The Moralist," he warns us, " is tempted to invoke a law superior to life itself, a law intelligible, eternal, supernatural."   Ethics must be withheld from this vain idealism and reconstructed from the material of physical instincts and social hopes.   Instead of the sense of obligation disclosing opportunity, it is the sense of opportunity which creates obligations.   Duty will step more firmly if it ceases to look up.

CHAPTER VIII

THE DESCENT OF FAITH

THE ascent of ethics is a cardinal doctrine of the teaching of Jesus. The normal development of the Christian character, the straight path of Christian discipleship, leads from duty-doing to faith, from obligation to revelation, from fidelity in that which is least to possession of the true riches, from the plain of ethics to the heights of religion. It cannot escape notice, however, that this logic of discipleship, though it be explicitly taught by Jesus, does not seem to represent the logic of his own mind. As one surveys the Gospels he does not see Jesus pressing his way upward along the path of duty until the horizon of God's purpose expands before his thought. On the contrary, Jesus seems most at home when on the heights, and his habitual path leads rather downward, from the consciousness of God to the service of men, than upward, from human duties to Divine companionship. His view of life is a view from above. From the beginning of the record he is seen to be about his Father's business, as if in his Father's house. All things are delivered unto him of his Father.[1] One is his Father which is in heaven.[2]

[1] Matt. xi. 27.   [2] Matt. xxiii. 9.

The sources of spiritual strength and peace for Jesus are not in his human affections and associations, however precious these may be, but in his communion with the Father. He pauses in his busy life of teaching and healing, and seeks a solitude which is to him companionship, to return with a fresh accession of confidence and authority. He withdraws in a boat to a desert place apart;[1] he goes up into a mountain apart to pray, and when the even is come he is there alone;[2] he brings his chosen friends into a high mountain apart, and is transfigured before them.[3] "Come ye yourselves apart," he says to his friends, . . . "and rest a while, for there were many coming and going."[4] The horizon of his faith seems shut in by the pressure of work and care, and he goes up for his refreshing to some place of larger outlook where he may see life as it really is. He is like a man whose native air is in the mountains, and who brings the strength of the hills down to the weary world below. All this is but to say once more, that Jesus is primarily not an ethical, but a religious, Teacher. He finds his duty through his consciousness of God instead of finding God through his consciousness of duty. His doctrine of character is the corollary rather than the cause of his religious faith.

Does not this essentially religious quality in the ministry of Jesus appear to nullify all that has been said of the ascent of ethics? Is it true that he

---

[1] Matt. xiv. 13.
[2] Matt. xiv. 23.
[3] Matt. xvii. 1, 2.
[4] Mark vi. 31.

teaches the slow growth of character from duty to insight, or, if he does so teach, does not the testimony of his own experience contradict the teaching? Does he not, first of all, demand one supreme act of faith, and in that change of the heart's desire change all the motives of character? Is he not rather a Revealer than a Redeemer, Son of God rather than Son of Man? Should not his teaching read, " He that knoweth the doctrine will do the will," rather than, " He that doeth the will shall know of the doctrine " ?

This is the impression which has been made by the Gospels on many minds. The theological and dramatic element in the record, its disclosure of the purpose of God and the place of Jesus in that purpose, — what has been called the " self-assertion " of Jesus, — has appeared to be so dominating and significant, that it has seemed to be trifling, if not irreverent, to give serious consideration to Jesus as a teacher of character.[1] His ministry has appeared to move on quite another level, and to be primarily concerned not with conduct, but with faith. His teaching is of life with God rather

[1] This view is maintained with unusual power and candor by D. S. Cairns, *Contemporary Review,* November, 1903, January, 1904, " Christianity in the Modern World "; September, 1904, " The Self-Assertion of Jesus," p. 522 : " The Gospel is not simply a new interpretation of the standing facts and laws of the world, but a great cosmic event, the coming of God to his world after a new fashion "; p. 532 : " The great movement of Christological thought . . . is directly due to the deliberate and conscious action of the Founder of Christianity."

than of duties to men.   The ascent of ethics, with
its laborious advance, finds, according to such
minds, no confirmation in the confident and continuous faith of Jesus, which descends from the
heights of Divine communion to make God known
to men.   "No man knoweth the Father save the
Son, and he to whomsoever the Son will reveal
him." [1]

This sense of contradiction between the ethics
of Jesus and his religion fails, however, to take
account of the chronology of his experience.   The
Gospels, it must be remembered, do not undertake
to narrate the entire life of Jesus, but, with a few
fragmentary additions, only the story of its last
years.   We see the Teacher at the height of his
power, speaking with authority, saying to the
weary and heavy-laden: "Come unto me"; but
we do not see the path of spiritual education and
self-discipline by which he has reached this height.
Unless the life of Jesus be regarded as wholly
detached from human processes of development,
and therefore wholly valueless as a human example, it must have had its years of moral growth
and patient ripening of character before the fulness of its time was come.   The glimpses given
by the record of the childhood of Jesus indicate
this development of obedience, thoughtfulness, and
charm.   The boy goes down with his parents to
Nazareth and is "subject unto them"; he "grew
and waxed strong in spirit, filled with wisdom";

[1] Matt. xi. 27; Luke x. 22.

he "increased in wisdom and stature, and in favor with God and man." [1]   Between these glimpses of the boy and the work of the man lie unrecorded years of spiritual growth, from which Jesus is summoned by the preaching of the Baptist, and which have armed him to meet the triple temptation of conscious power.   It cannot, therefore, be inferred from the height of religious insight which Jesus has gained when his ministry begins that he has not reached that height by the path of duty. When he speaks of character as the way of faith, he is describing a way on which, indeed, he now looks down, but by which he himself has come. He too knows the ascent of duty, and through obedience and restraint has come at last to the spacious horizon which his religious consciousness surveys.

What is of more concern, however, than the chronology of experience in Jesus is the law of conduct which governs him when he has thus reached the heights.   The way by which he may have ascended is less important than the way by which he is now called to go.   His character, we may surmise, has "grown and waxed strong," like other characters ; and when he teaches that obedience is the path to knowledge, and that the pure in heart see God, he is but reporting that which he has learned through twenty silent years.   When, however, he has reached the height of the consciousness of God, it would seem as if the end of

[1] Luke ii. 40, 51, 52.

duty-doing were attained, and that he had but to point to the wide horizon which he sees. His mission would seem to culminate in some such testimony of high experience as is contained in the closing discourses of the fourth Gospel : " O righteous Father, the world hath not known thee : but I have known thee " ; "Glorify thy Son, that thy Son also may glorify thee." [1]

Such, however, is not the final expression of his religious faith. Having ascended to this intimate communion with the Father, there is set before Jesus a new compulsion, — the obligation to descend with these resources of power and peace to the world of duty which he had just left below. No sooner is the ascent of ethics accomplished than it is succeeded by the descent of faith; and the second law of conduct is, in imperativeness and persuasiveness, like the first. It is impressive to observe how often Jesus departs from human companionship to renew his strength in communion with God ; but more impressive than this departure is his quick return to the patient fulfilment of his human task. At evening he is on the mountain alone, but " in the fourth watch " of the same night he is helping his friends in their boat.[2] He departs " by ship into a desert place apart," [3] but is " moved with compassion " for the multitude and comes forth and heals their sick. He is in a high mountain apart transfigured, and his companions find it good to stay ;

[1] John xvii. 25, 1.   [2] Matt. xiv. 25; Mark vi. 48.
[3] Matt. xiv. 13; Mark vi. 32; Luke iv. 42.

but Jesus hears the cry of the epileptic at the mountain's foot and descends quickly from the company of the Prophets to heal the boy.[1] The religion of Jesus is thus at every point an applied religion. He teaches no ascent of ethics which leaves one on the Mount. His source of power is above, but his use of power is below. "He that descended," says the Epistle to the Ephesians, "is the same also that ascended."[2] Whatever effort it may have cost to find the upward path makes it easier for him to follow the same path downward. A slow ascent of duty to the horizon of God, a quick glance, a long breath, a far-away look, and then the descent of faith to the plains of human need — such is the picture of the life of Jesus.

Here, perhaps, is the secret of those contrasts of traits which have so often perplexed and divided the students of his character. He is, at one moment, on the height of conscious power and authority; and at another among the meek and lowly of heart; now claiming the high mission of the Messiah, now making himself the servant of all. Which, it is asked, is his real character? Is he Revealer or Consoler, Divinely commissioned or humanly compassionate, ascending in spirit until lost as example or descending in service until lost as Messiah? He is both of these; not because two competing characters are in him miraculously joined, but because the movement of his harmonious character feels the rhythm of the spirit. The

[1] Matt. xvii. 1–21; Mark ix. 1–30. [2] Eph. iv. 10.

tidal life of his nature, its ascent of duty and its descent of faith, are not opposing, divisive, alternative forces, but part of the total swing of character, which unites action and pause, inspiration and dedication, the consciousness of God and the service of man. "Now that he ascended, what is it but that he also descended . . . into the lower parts of the earth."[1]

At the conclusion of one of Bishop Berkeley's Dialogues, the two friends stand by a fountain, and Philonous says: "You see, Hylas, the water of yonder fountain, how it is forced upwards, . . . to a certain height; at which it breaks and falls back into the basin from whence it rose: its ascent as well as descent, proceeding from the same uniform law. . . . Just so, the same principles which at first view lead to scepticism, pursued to a certain point, bring men back to Common Sense."[2] The same picture may represent the movement of the Christian character. It has its impulse to rise and its attraction to descend; its ascent in beauty and its descent in service; and both ascent and descent proceed from the same general law. The teaching of Jesus, in other words, whether it be of ethics or of faith, is a teaching of the unity and continuity of experience. It recognizes no divided life, either of morality which does not ascend to God or of religion which does not descend to man. Duty-doing, following its own law, leads to the Eternal; but the sense of the Eternal with equal compulsion leads

[1] Eph. iv. 9.   [2] Works, 1837, I, 82.

back to duty. It is the river by its own nature seeking the sea, only to find the tide of the sea sweeping back into the river. Ethics remains tentative and preliminary until it fulfils itself in faith; religion remains empty and abstract until it dedicates itself to service. The test of religion is neither the height it gains nor the view it surveys, but the strength with which it descends. The Christian religion, like the Christian character, is not a detached, isolated, self-sufficient possession, but a form of power, an application of strength to weakness, of sight to blindness, of the soul that has found the heights to the soul of the world below. There is no Christian religion which is not an applied religion. The sanctified life is the serviceable life, and in that service finds its freedom. "For their sakes," says the fourth Gospel, "I sanctify myself." [1] The stream of the religious life rises in the quiet places of personal communion with God, but the law of attraction leads it down to the great places of the busy multitude and their unsanctified toil; and as it flows it sings to itself the Master's message: "I am come that these may have my life, and may have it abundantly."

> "Not always on the mount may we
> Rapt in the heavenly vision be;
> *   *   *   *   *   *
> The mount for vision, — but below
> The paths of daily duty go." [2]

[1] John xvii. 19.

[2] F. L. Hosmer, "The Thought of God," 1890, p. 45: "On the Mount."

T

Such is the law of the descent of faith, the utilization of power, the application of religion, the unity of the spiritual life. The same spirit which leads Jesus to God sends him back to man. "And Jesus was led by the Spirit into the wilderness, . . . and Jesus returned in the power of the Spirit into Galilee . . . and taught in their synagogues." [1] What is the record of Christian history and of contemporary religion concerning this application of faith to duty? Has there been a consistent acceptance of this test of pure religion? Has the ascent of ethics been supplemented by the descent of faith? Is religion doing the work it was meant to do, as though working with what the political economists call the maximum of production?

No one can survey the history of modern progress — its philanthropy, its reforms, its industrial responsibility, its political democracy — without recognizing that the chief accession of moral force which these movements have received has come from the Christian religion. On the other hand, however, it must be frankly admitted that no misinterpretation of the purpose of Jesus is so persistent as the belief that religion is an end in itself, a detached region of experience, to be explored and administered as a distinct province of life. When one has reached, by any path he may have followed, the knowledge of God, the life with Christ, the witness of the spirit, then, according to much religious

[1] Luke iv. 1, 14, 15.

teaching, the end of the soul's progress is attained,
and there is left only contemplation, obedience, delight, and peace.   It is as though one threw himself
down at the summit he had gained and surrendered
himself to the tranquil joy of the unclouded view.
What is the whole duty of man?   It is to glorify
God and enjoy Him forever.   What is the Christian Church?   It is the refuge of the saints.   What
is the Christian life?   It is a way of retreat from
the vicissitudes of life, —

> "From every stormy wind that blows,
>   From every swelling tide of woes,
>   There is a safe and sure retreat,
>   'Tis found beneath the Mercy-seat."

What is the evidence of Christian discipleship?
It is worship, praise, prayer, belief, conformity,
confession, a creed, a state of the heart, a submis-
sion of the will, a consent of the mind to Christian
truth.

Are not, then, these expressions and pledges
of faith of the essence of religion?   Undoubtedly they are the sublime heights toward which
the ascent of ethics leads.   The satisfactions
of religion are reached on the heights of faith
as a varied landscape unrolls itself when one
reaches the summit.   Yet neither one nor all of
these religious satisfactions represent, according
to the teaching of Jesus, the end of the journey
of the spirit, the abiding-place of Christian faith.
The whole duty of man is not to enjoy God forever, but to descend with the grace of God to the

help of man. The Christian Church is not a place
of refuge from the world, but a place of training
for the world. The Christian life is not a retreat
from stormy winds and tides of woe, but an advance
through them; not a hiding beneath the Mercy-seat,
but a rising from one's seat for the sake of mercy.
The evidence of Christian discipleship is not ecclesiastical or doctrinal, but ethical, social, political,
industrial, human. In short, the Christian religion
does not occupy a separated, even though it be
an elevated, plateau of life, but descends like a
fertilizing stream to the world below. " When he
ascended up on high," quotes again the Epistle
to the Ephesians from the 68th Psalm, " he led
captivity captive, and gave gifts unto men." [1] The
strength to release the captives, and the grace to
give unto men the gifts they need, are for those
who, having ascended up on high, are ready to
descend into the lower parts of the earth.

Are not many tendencies and movements of
the Christian Church brought to judgment by this
teaching of Jesus? They have concerned themselves with the defence of faith rather than with
the descent of faith; they have guarded religion on
its heights, while the world, which religion should
redeem, has trudged by, without looking up, along
its dusty way. They represent in religion what is
known in social affairs as provincialism. A person of wide experience finds himself some day in a
secluded village, and listens to the talk of its people,

[1] Eph. iv. 8; Ps. lxviii. 18.

as they discuss the weather and the crops, the price of hay and the gossip of the churches. What impresses this observer is the provincialism of this rustic life. These subjects of commanding interest are not fictitious or discreditable, but they are local, specialized, provincial. The great concerns of civilization — the wars of nations and of industries, the achievements of science and art — excite less real emotion in these villagers than the condition of the roads and the talk of the town-meeting; and it is not surprising that the alert and venturesome of the village youth escape from this provincial life and betake themselves to a world which is more diversified, comprehensive, and real.

Suppose, however, that it is not some modest village which is thus visited, but some dignified convocation of Christian believers; may one not still hear in its hot debates the same note of provincialism? It is a province of high altitude, indeed, which he has entered; yet these solemn deliberations seem not less detached from the interests of the real world. What is this organization, one asks himself, which is here administered? Is it a piece of machinery which is being wound up and repaired? Is it a court, assigning its penalties? Is it an army, with its officers and drills? These discussions which appear so absorbing to the participants seem to the looker-on, not indeed illegitimate, but simply uninteresting. They magnify the local until it shuts out the universal; they exaggerate the unimportant; they use a dead language ; their deliberations run on a side-track of thought which does not connect with the main line of the modern world ; they are provincial. In the preface to the sixth edition of Professor Paulsen's "Ethics" he cites Professor Sidgwick as applying to many controversies in philosophy a student's reply to an examiner's question concerning the occupations of the people of the Hebrides. "The people of the Hebrides," answered this youth, "obtain a meagre subsistence by washing one another's clothes." [1] A similar comment might occur to this observer as he watches the proceedings of some ecclesiastical convocations. The Christians, he might say, obtain a meagre subsistence by washing or soiling or criticising each other's clothes.

This separatism of religion, this provincialism of the saints, is not peculiar to contemporary Christianity or indeed characteristic of it. The same heresy has appeared in much more formidable shapes in earlier periods of Christian history. Gnosticism, with its interpretation of religion as an esoteric mystery; Mysticism, with its detachment of the believer from the ordinary channels of religious expression; even the familiar Prudentialism of self-interested religion, with its overwhelming concern for personal salvation ; — all have in them a quality of provincialism, as though the security of the single soul were separable from the fate of

[1] "System der Ethik," 1903, I, x: "Sidgwick macht Anwendung von der Geschichte auf die Metaphysiker. Sie scheint mir auch auf manche Moralphilosophen zu passen."

the world, like a single life which saves itself from a sinking ship. These forms which religion assumes are not so much misrepresentations of religion as fragments of religion. They miss the uniting bond and harmonizing principle of the descent of faith. They delay on the heights when they should be at work in the valleys. There is but one subject which is appropriate as the centre of debate in a Christian assembly. It is the question how to utilize the power of faith for the good of men. There is one Bible passage without which no convocation of Christians should end its deliberations. It is the last verses of the Sermon on the Mount: "Not every one that saith unto me, Lord, Lord, but he that doeth the will of my Father. . . . He that heareth my sayings and doeth them, builds upon a rock." The heresy in Gnosticism is not its conclusion that knowledge illuminates religion, but its assumption that illuminated knowledge may be a substitute for religion. The defect of Mysticism is not its emotional exaltation, but its emotional isolation. The inadequacy of Prudentialism is not its belief that to save one's own soul is of supreme concern, but its belief that one's soul can be saved alone. The life that escapes from the wreck may seem to be saved, but in deserting the wreck the soul may be lost. The problem of salvation is that of saving the ship; and a perfect statement of salvation was made of a life that seemed to be lost: "He saved others; himself he cannot save." [1]

[1] Matt. xxvii. 42 ; Mark xv. 31.

How is it, then, that the descent of faith may be accomplished under the special conditions of the modern world? Here, on the one hand, is a source of power; and here, on the other hand, is the world, waiting for a supply of power. What are the channels which are prepared by the circumstances of modern life for this movement of spiritual irrigation? What are the signs of the times which invite the descent of faith?

It is interesting to recall that this, which is the most pressing question of religion, has already met us in another form, as the question with which the civilized world is confronted as a new century begins.[1] The nineteenth century was a period of extraordinary development in the external, physical, mechanical arrangement of the world's work. It was the age of science, of invention, of machinery, of political consolidation, of industrial organization, — the period which made of human society in an unprecedented degree a fighting, producing, governing, administering machine. Religion also had its share in this movement toward mechanical perfection. It was the period of institutional churches, parish houses, denominational organizations, of conventions, conferences, delegations, committees. Never before did the machinery of the Christian Church work so well. It is the natural order of progress, — first that which is natural, afterward that which is spiritual. The development of natural science, the acceptance of natural

[1] Compare Ch. I, pp. 13 ff.

law, the interpretation of human society in terms
of biology, the conception of the social organism
with its many members — all these characteristics
of the nineteenth century had their inevitable influence on religious methods, as though they also
were physical, biological, material, with a mechanical and external work to do.

Such a period, however, though it be essential in
the history of religion, bears on its very face the
mark of preparatoriness, as though confessedly preliminary to a new movement of a new time. The
mechanism of nature, which has been so impres-
sively demonstrated during the nineteenth century,
is already seen to disclose within itself a spiritual
movement, of which natural law is the instrument
and expression; and the key of the modern philosophy of nature is found in the *dictum* of Lotze, —
that mechanism is everywhere essential, yet everywhere subordinate.[1] The vast organizations of
politics and industry which have been devised by
one generation now present to the next generation
a new problem of converting this gigantic machinery into forms of moral power. The conception
of society as a biological organism, which was confidently announced a generation ago, has proved insufficient, and social evolution turns to psychology
for its interpretation. These aspects of the world

---

[1] " Mikrokosmus," 2te Aufl., 1869, s. xv: "The life of science
consists . . . in proving how absolutely universal is the extent, and
at the same time how absolutely subordinate is the part, which
mechanism has to fulfil in the structure of the world."

and its affairs — a spiritual significance within the machinery of nature, a demand for the spiritualization of material life, a renaissance of ethical idealism — find unprecedented recognition as a new century begins. The nineteenth century had for its subject of inquiry the social body; the twentieth century has for its subject the social soul.

The same enlargement of its task is now offered to religion. If the churches remain primarily concerned with questions of their mechanism; if they continue to live in the era of organization while philosophy and sociology have advanced to the era of spiritualization; if religion is fenced in by separatism and provincialism, while the rest of the world is taking down its fences and discovering the unity of human life — then, even though religion concerns itself with the loftiest of themes and contemplates the broadest horizon of human thought, it must forfeit the right to primacy among the creative influences of the new world, and must become simply the refuge of the gnostic, the mystic, and the prudential.

In one of the most brilliant, though not perhaps most cautious, of modern treatises on early Christian history, Professor Wernle remarks that Jesus came "to save his followers from the theologians." [1] The statement has a certain historical justification in the attitude of Jesus toward the theologians of his own day; but it most imperfectly represents his

---

[1] "Anfänge unserer Religion," 1901, s. 60 : "Die Gabe dieser Gelehrten war Scharfsinn und gutes Gedächtniss, weiter nichts."

attitude toward theology. His purpose was not to save men from the theologians, but to save the theologians themselves. Theology must always remain the supreme interest of thoughtful minds, the height of loftiest contemplation and broadest horizon; but the theology of the separatist, the gnostic, the mystic, the priest, the Pharisee, has no more part in the Christian religion to-day than it had in the days of Jesus. The defence of faith must be made by the descent of faith. The theology appropriate to a religion of power is a theology which supplies power. The communion of the soul with God remains, as it has always been, the mount of vision to which theology may ascend; but the proof of religion which theology must give is to be found nowhere else than in the descent of theology to life, and the application to service of the heavenly vision. The modern world needs, indeed, new adjustments of its machinery to steady employment, to diminish the tragic waste of human life and the still more tragic idleness of the unapplied and inapplicable; but what the modern world much more needs is the power to set this halting machinery in steady and effective motion; and this spiritual power is from above, descending as by the law of gravitation from the sources of faith to move the wheels of work.

How is it, then, that the descent of faith may proceed? The first and most obvious application of religion to life was immediately made by the primitive Church in its extraordinary movement of compassion. The descent of Christian faith expressed itself from the beginning in Christian charity; the descent of pity was the corollary of the ascent of prayer. Even in this great movement of Christian charity, however, it has been by no means always recognized that the application of faith to service is an integral part of the religious process itself, as essential to Christian discipleship as worship or belief. Philanthropy has often appeared an accessory enterprise, which may be becoming for Christians to undertake, but which lies beyond the distinctive sphere and essential task of the Church. At a meeting in a Women's Settlement House — the most unimpeachable form of self-effacing service which modern philanthropy has devised — a minister of the Christian religion, looking about him for some technical expression of ecclesiastical loyalty, remarked: "This is very touching, but I wish there were more of Christ in it." How could there be more of Christ, one asked himself, than in such a work, just as it was, without technical confession or provincial limitation? Might not the Master, were he to walk those streets, pass with indifference many a temple built in his name, and laying his hands of blessing on these ministering women say: "Inasmuch as ye have done it unto these least, ye have done it unto me"?

Modern charity, in other words, is not an enterprise into which persons, being already religious, may venture, as into a foreign land of new customs and new languages, but lies within the natural boundaries of religion, a home-country whose language is the language of faith, and which needs no apology or symbol or flag to bring it within the Kingdom of God. " The poor," it was held in the early Church, as though charity were itself an act of worship, "shall be esteemed an altar unto God."[1] The workers in modern charity need, it is true, more knowledge of their science, better training, new schools of philanthropy; but if they should utter their deepest need, it would be a prayer for faith, the assurance that they were working with God, the grace to see their work from above and to descend to it with power. Religion is provincial if it does not annex this territory of pity. Undefiled religion is to be recognized not less by the wisdom with which one visits the widows and fatherless than by the grace to keep oneself unspotted from the world.

The same qualified appreciation must be expressed in a second instance where Christian faith has been applied to modern life. Nothing has of late so gravely impressed the Christian world as the significance to civilization of the institution of the family. The social peril of domestic instability which confronts modern life is a challenge to religion, and faith has descended into this scene of disruption and infelicity with its counsels and exhortations. Better laws, better comity between churches, more scrupulous obedience to ecclesias-

[1] "Apostolic Constitutions," Bk. IV, iii.

tical canons, are urged in the name of Christ. Through all this consciousness of social peril, however, there still persists in many minds the provincial impression that in this extension of responsibility religion is proceeding beyond its own special sphere, as into foreign territory, adjacent, but not its own. Is not the home, it is asked, a product of law and custom, which must be safe-guarded by the legislatures and courts, rather than a part of the field of religion, for which religious organizations have the chief responsibility?

The answer to this question must depend on one's conception of religion and its boundaries. Is the relation of religion to the home that of one institution patronizing another institution, or is the home itself a religious institution, historically created by moral sacrifices and restraints, and per-petuated by the ideals of faith and love? Behind all legislative questions which concern the family lies the religious question of recognizing in the family the social type selected by Jesus Christ to represent his religion. The stability of modern marriage is not to be attained by mechanical devices of law, but by a spiritual revival, which it is for religion to secure; a return from ostentation to simplicity, and from laxity to loyalty, which is for religion to preach; a restoration of faith in the home, not as a commercial venture, but as a spirit-ual opportunity and discipline. The problem of religion in the twentieth century begins in the descent of faith into the family, the recognition of the family as the type of God's Kingdom, the annexation of the province of the family as belonging to the Kingdom of God; and the order of procedure in this expansion of religion is to be, — not, first, the enactment of ritual and canons to be applied to the family, but first, the plain understanding that domestic integrity is an essential part of Christian discipleship.

It may be gladly admitted, however, that in these concerns of charity and of family integrity the descent of faith has been in large degree recognized as an essential part of a Christian civilization. It is otherwise with other great areas of the modern world, where the most commanding interests of the present age are to be found. Within a single generation new forms of industry and new movements of politics have created a practically new world, and the Christian Church still stands on the quiet shore of its secluded and specialized life and watches the life of the present age as it drifts among these tumultuous waves and conflicting currents, like a vessel driven toward the rocks. Something, the Church knows, ought to be done by religion, to save, not single lives alone, but the ship itself; yet how shall faith venture into so dangerous a sea? What means of help, what skill in salvage has it, what training to take command of so perilous a venture?

Precisely at this point, however, where the new risk is seen, is the new opportunity offered to religion to justify its claim to leadership, wisdom, and

power. Who shall rescue industry from mercilessness and rapacity, or politics from unscrupulousness
and sectionalism, if it be not those who have learned
that a man's life consisteth not in the abundance of
the things that he possesseth, and that righteousness
alone exalteth a people? A church is like a life-
saving station, set in a protected bay; but what
shall we say of life-savers who make no venture
toward a drifting vessel, but stand on the beach
and wave? What wonder is it that the industrial
movement of the present age believes itself beyond
the province of the Church, when the Church still
believes itself to be provincial? When Jesus
stood one day with his little company by the Lake
of Galilee, it was the meagre use of their great
opportunity which seems to have impressed his
mind, and he used the language of their vocation
as a parable of the work they had to do. "Launch
out," he bade them, "into the deep, and let down
your nets for a draught." [1] They had been fishing
along the shores of their opportunity, and he called
them to do business in great waters. They had
been as those who caught minnows, when he meant
that they should catch men. It is the call of the
present age to a timid Church: "Launch out
into the deep." The place of religion in the
modern world is not along its shores, but among
its waves and storms. The industrial agitations of
the time are a challenge to the courage of the
Church.

[1] Luke v. 4.

What is the fundamental provocation of our industrial discontent ?   It is the obvious fact that
neither party to the industrial conflict manifests
the slightest intention of applying the principles of
religion to the affairs of business.   The two prov-
inces of life are regarded as having distinct boundaries, as though in one continent of the spirit there
might be a state of war, while in another peace
and prosperity might endure.   There is, however,
no such division of Orient and Occident on the
map of religion.   Either the whole of life is ruled
by religion, or religion becomes formal, technical,
fictitious, and substitutes for religion must be found
which shall control the whole of life.   One of the
most instructive aspects of modern industry is
the passionate devotion which thousands of plain
people offer to the cause of industrial revolution.
What is there in the creed of socialism which gives
it this emotional quality ?   On its face it appears
to be a mere change of ownership, a new distribution of production, an economic proposition.   Why
is it that men sacrifice themselves so eagerly and
passionately for such a cause ?   It is because it is
the nearest substitute they have discovered for a
religion.   A religion of materialism it may be that
they have reached, a pathetic substitute for Christian faith; yet so long as the Christian Church
regards the world of industry as foreign territory,
so long those who are inextricably involved in the
industrial order will create a new religion for themselves.   The growth of socialism is an indictment

U

of the Christian religion.   It is the working-man's answer to religious provincialism.   The descent of religion into the problems of industrial life is the crucial problem of the Church in the twentieth century.

Finally, the same problem presents itself in the political conditions of the present time.   In the most unanticipated and dramatic manner the movement toward organization, concentration, and efficiency which has dominated industry has reappeared in national affairs.   The nations are confronted by questions of world-politics.   National expansion has become, not so much a policy to debate, as a condition from which it is impossible to retreat.   But what does political expansion indicate as the new task of religion?   It is often affirmed that it opens the way for religion to follow, as though, when other agencies had done their work, religion might reap the harvest.   What is this view of religion as a technical, specialized undertaking, which may follow on the track of politics, but sheer provincialism?   Religion cannot be exported to a foreign nation, like one more home-manufacture, after the politicians and the traders have opened the way.   It is in and through the spirit of conquest, in and through the conduct of commercial life, that religion must be conveyed.   Its missions will be regarded as mere hypocrisy and formalism unless its rulers, its soldiers, and its traders are themselves missionaries. It is not after the statesmen have finished that the

Church begins, but it is in that which the statesmen do that the religion they represent is weighed.
Politics is not extraneous to religion, a foreign
invasion to be followed by international peace; it
is itself a part of religion. The detachment of
political expediency from religious ideals is the
gravest indictment which can be made, not only
against the politics, but also against the religion of
a land.

In beginning the biography of Gladstone, Mr.
Morley calls attention to the essentially religious
character of that great political career. "Not
for two centuries," says his biographer, "had our
island produced a ruler in whom the religious
motive was paramount in the like degree. He
was not only a political force, but a moral force.
. . . Well was it said of him, 'You have so lived
and wrought that you have kept the soul alive in
England'"; and in another place Mr. Gladstone
himself makes his own confession of faith: "I
am desirous that the standard of our material
strength shall be highly estimated . . ., but I believe it of still more vital consequence that we
should stand high . . . as the lovers of truth, of
honor, and of openness in our proceedings. . . .
I value our insular position, but I dread the day
when we shall be reduced to a moral insularity." [1]
That is the descent of faith into the political world.
The Christian statesman keeps the soul of his nation

[1] "The Life of William Ewart Gladstone," 1903, I, 3, 5, and
II, 578.

alive and defends her from moral insularity. The Christian State, like the heavenly Jerusalem, is not built up from beneath, on material foundations, but descends, in the ideals of her statesmen, out of heaven from God.

Such, in imperfect illustrations, is the scope of the ethics of Jesus. In a heated political campaign, a distinguished American politician is said to have given as instructions to his adherents: "Claim everything." Such, with a different intention, is the message of Jesus to the Christian character. Nothing lies beyond its province. The chief peril of Christian conduct is in dealing with a great matter as though it were a small one; in mistaking a universal claim for a limited, fenced-in area, staked out like a miner's claim within which treasure must be found. "All things are yours," [1] says the Apostle Paul, reiterating the comprehensiveness of Jesus, — whether it be the divisions within the Church, of Paul or Apollos or Cephas; or the world outside the Church, with its philanthropy, its industry, its politics; or life, with its problems; or death, with its mystery; or the present, with its cares; or the future, with its hopes; — all is yours, if you are Christ's, as Christ is God's.

There are many subjects concerning which Jesus has little to teach the modern world. The circumstances of his life were primitive in their simplicity

[1] I Cor. iii. 21–23.

when compared with the storm and stress of the present time. He knew nothing of the industrial complexity which has brought with it such industrial perplexity; he heard but from afar the rumors of imperial politics; he was not concerned with the mechanics of theology or ecclesiasticism. One truth concerning human life, however, he taught, which is the secret, in any age or place, of peace in industry, of wisdom in politics, of tolerance in religion. It was the truth that life is not divisible, departmental, provincial; but organic, interdependent, one. He saw life in motion, as a process of growth, a sowing and harvest; a progress, not on a level, but through a land of hills and valleys, ascending to descend, obeying to know, and knowing to obey. There is, according to the teaching of Jesus, no duty-doing which does not lead one up its steep path toward religious faith; there is no religious faith which does not lead one down its slope to duty. These are not two ways of life but one, moving with the rhythm of the spirit, which is akin to the rhythm of nature, with its nights and days, its seasons and tides, its society and solitude, its activity and receptivity, its life and death and renewing life. One beat of the spiritual rhythm is character; another is religion. Ethics fulfils itself in its ascent; religion is perfected in its descent; and life keeps time to this rhythmic movement, from tasks to visions, and from visions back to tasks.

In the Book of Genesis it is written that a ladder was set up on earth and reached to heaven, and that the angels of God both ascended and descended on it; and in the fourth Gospel it is said of Jesus that the angels of God both ascended and descended upon the Son of Man.[1]   These two processions of celestial influences still attend the ascending life of duty and the descending life of faith.   The duty-doer as he goes up into the presence of the Most High joins the ascending angels; but even in that presence they do not pause with folded wings.   Downward they go once more, and he is their companion who leaves the vision to descend into the lower parts of the earth.   Up the ladder of life mounts duty, until the pure in heart see God, and down its stairs descends the wisdom from above to interpret the life below; and along both ascent and descent stand the angels of God to guard and cheer the sons of men.

[1] Gen. xxviii. 12; John i. 51.

INDEX

INDEX OF BIBLE PASSAGES

301

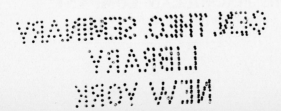

JESUS CHRIST AND THE SOCIAL QUESTION

An Examination of the Teaching of Jesus in its Relation to Some Problems of Modern Social Life

By FRANCIS GREENWOOD PEABODY

Author of " The Religion of an Educated Man," etc.

Cloth   12mo $1.50

" In this ' Examination of the Teaching of Jesus in its Relation to Some of the Problems of Modern Social Life,' Professor Peabody begins with *a careful discussion of the comprehensiveness of this teaching as at once perfectly apt and adequate* to every possible condition and need. He then considers the social principles of this teaching ; its relation to the family, to the rich, to the care of the poor, to the industrial order. The concluding chapter is especially good, setting forth ' the Correlation of the Social Questions.' It is shown how this fact should affect those who are actually interested in particular reforms." — *Times-Herald*, Chicago.

" It is vital, searching, comprehensive. The Christian reader will find it an illumination ; the non-Christian a revelation." — *The Epworth Herald*.

" The author is Professor of Christian Morals in Harvard University, and his book is a critical examination of the teaching of Jesus in its relation to some of the problems of modern social life. Professor Peabody discusses the various phases of Christian socialism in this country and in Europe." — *The Baltimore Sun*.

" Discussing in ' Jesus Christ and the Social Question ' the comprehensiveness of the Master's teaching, Francis Greenwood Peabody, Plummer Professor of Christian Morals in Harvard University, says that ' each new age or movement or personal desire seems to itself to receive with a peculiar fulness its special teaching.' The unexhausted gospel of Jesus touches each new problem and new need with its illuminating power."
— *St. Louis Globe-Democrat*.

" A thoughtful and reflective examination of the teachings of Jesus in relation to some of the problems of modern social life."
— *Louisville Courier-Journal*.

THE MACMILLAN COMPANY

64–66 Fifth Avenue, New York

has out

$L \times F$

JESUS CHRIST AND THE
CHRISTIAN CHARACTER